PRAISE FOR *SOLVED*

'A refreshing, cup-half-full approach to inspire each and all of us that we must and can do the hard work to make the world a better place.' —**Dana H. Born, Harvard Kennedy School of Government**

'In a world of endless outrage, armchair critics and keyboard warriors, *Solved* is that rarest of things: a book that actually offers solutions to the planet's problems instead of just listing them. It is only by listening to positive arguments such as these that we will ever stand a chance of fixing the world's problems.' —**Joe Hildebrand, co-host of Network 10's *Studio 10***

'Andrew Wear offers things valuable and rarely present in a practical book about politics: determined optimism, and real hope.' —**Van Badham, *Guardian* columnist and social commentator**

'At a time of mounting public dismay at the inability or unwillingness of our leaders to address the pressing issues of our time, Andrew Wear's book is a welcome dose of optimism that we can create change. With the positivity of a self-help guide, Wear takes us around the globe, showing us inspiring examples of progress and success across a number of challenging policy areas, from health to education to climate change. Buy it if you are over gloom and doom and ready for action!' —**Rebecca Huntley, author of *Still Lucky* and *Australia Fair***

'The times call for realistic and infectiously optimistic leadership – people are yearning for stories of hope. Andrew Wear's *Solved* inspires optimism, hope and a positive strategy to be the best we can be.' —**Victor Perton, founder of the Centre for Optimism**

'Optimistic, clear, compelling and realistic … A well-informed guide to the globe's most pressing problems. Andrew Wear has interviewed experts, considered the evidence and developed practical responses to pressing concerns such as global warming, schools performance and urban renewal. This uplifting and timely guide shows how policy – and citizens – can tackle even the largest challenges.' —**Glyn Davis, distinguished professor at Australian National University's Crawford School of Public Policy**

'Andrew Wear shows why in pessimistic times there are reasons to feel optimistic about our capacity to solve the big problems the world is facing. I know from my work at Apolitical how much appetite there is for vision-ary solutions broken down into practical steps – something for which Wear has a knack.' —**Robyn Scott, co-founder and CEO of Apolitical**

'In this evidence-based and immensely readable book, Andrew Wear takes us on a global journey of discovery to the places where our most chal-lenging public policy problems have been solved. Combining academic research with personal narrative, Wear offers powerful insights into the ability of municipalities, cities and countries to transform their economic, social and environmental outcomes. He also offers practical steps to help governments do likewise. Anyone interested in designing and imple-menting public policy that works should read this book.' —**Professor Helen Sullivan, director of Australian National University's Crawford School of Public Policy**

Solved.

How other countries cracked the world's biggest problems (and we can too)

ANDREW WEAR

ONEWORLD

First published in Great Britain and North America
by Oneworld Publications, 2020

Copyright © Andrew Wear 2020

Published by arrangement with Black Inc Books

ISBN 978-1-78607-901-5
eISBN 978-1-78607-900-8

Text design and typesetting by Akiko Chan
Printed and bound in Great Britain by Clays Ltd, Elcograf S.p.A.

Oneworld Publications
10 Bloomsbury Street, London WC1B 3SR, England

Stay up to date with the latest books,
special offers, and exclusive content from
Oneworld with our newsletter

Sign up on our website
oneworld-publications.com

MIX
Paper from
responsible sources
FSC   FSC® C018072
www.fsc.org

For Sophie, Genevieve, Charlotte and Alice

CONTENTS

INTRODUCTION

If Other Countries Can Do It, Why Can't We?

O
n a sunny Saturday, I was browsing my favourite bookshop when I was struck by a sense of gloom. The shelf in front of me was dominated by books that were depressing in their subject matter: our crisis in democracy, the rise of racism and global inequality, the decline of civilisation. I inhaled their sense of panic and malaise almost unconsciously; my previously sanguine mood skirted the aisle and disappeared out the back exit.

The politics section of this bookshop was a dismal place. The titles on display, although likely written with insight and wisdom, focused on the problems our world faces and conjured a bleak and desperate future. Yet just an aisle away, in the self-help and business sections, the books were affirming. They reassured the reader that with the right attitude and an appropriate strategy, change was possible and obstacles could be overcome.

The difference in approach between these categories sat uneasily with me. The world *was* facing serious challenges, but I knew from my work in public policy that there had been enormous progress in a number of areas, with some countries achieving remarkable results. I was fatigued by doom and gloom. I wondered if I could take the positive perspective of self-help and business books and apply it to the politics section. If I could shed some light on how countries around the world are working to crack the big problems, it might help to illuminate what sort of government and community action is required to make a difference. Readers might take heart from other countries' successes and be reassured that we *can* make real progress towards solving humanity's biggest challenges.

This book is the product of that ambition. I hope that the insights, stories and strategies in these pages inspire you. Because if other countries can do it, so can we.

For every depressing statistic you hear about, somewhere in the world there is also a story of incredible success. These stories show us that with sufficient will and the right approach, difficult problems can be solved.

For example, fifty years ago the average life expectancy in the United States was among the highest in the world. Americans could expect to live two and a half years longer than those in the rest of the developed world.[1] However, with rising obesity, a startling homicide rate and a lack of universal healthcare, life expectancy there is declining. A child born in the United States today will have a shorter life than one born in 2010.[2] Yet spin the globe to South Korea and the improvements in life expectancy are spectacular. In 1960, Koreans could expect to live just fifty-two years.[3] With universal healthcare, a healthy diet and a huge reduction in infant mortality, a South Korean child can now expect to live to eighty-three. Some experts even predict that by 2030, the average life expectancy for Korean women will exceed ninety years.[4]

In 1990, when climate change first began to be taken seriously, Australia's carbon emissions were among the highest in the industrialised world, trumped only by Luxembourg, Estonia and the United States. Subsequently, Australia has torn itself apart with rancorous, highly politicised debates about how to address climate change. The government introduced an emissions trading scheme only to abolish it soon afterwards. Thirty years later, each Australian emits 16 tonnes of greenhouse gas a year, the worst rate in the world, and an *increase* on 1990 figures.[5] But in Denmark, there is a national consensus on the scientific evidence and the moral obligation to respond. The Danes are moving steadily towards producing 100 per cent of their power from renewable sources. The country has managed to fast-track its economy while scuttling emissions: each Dane now contributes half the emissions they did twenty years ago, and Copenhagen is on track to become carbon neutral by 2025.[6]

Another example: in 2000, New Zealand school students were achieving some of the best results in the world. In reading, the country was third globally, behind only Finland and Canada. Yet the reading performance of New Zealand students has deteriorated. In 2018, fifteen-year-olds were reading at a level more than six months behind their predecessors of fifteen years earlier. By contrast, Singapore has built an education system from scratch, which is now delivering world-best results. Within a government-run system that values and invests in teachers, Singaporean students are reading at a level more than a year ahead of the average in many parts of the world, and achieving results in maths more than two years ahead of their counterparts in New Zealand.[7]

Our political leadership has been disappointing of late. Around the Western world, public trust in government is collapsing.[8] We could be forgiven for being pessimistic about governments' capacity to lead us through the tests that lie ahead. Yet several countries are doing well at tackling the challenges facing the world. Life expectancy at birth is eighty-five in Hong Kong. Sweden's annual per capita carbon emissions are only 3.8 tonnes. The reading performance of fifteen-year-olds in Singapore is almost four years ahead of their peers in Mexico.[9]

Historically, much economic policy was based on theory. Detailed mathematical models were built and hypothetical scenarios constructed. These usually involved many assumptions, including the rather heroic idea that people always behave perfectly rationally. These theories went hand-in-hand with ideologies: liberalism, conservatism, socialism. The ideologies drove the government policies that have shaped our world.

But theories don't always hold up in the real world. There are myriad complexities that confound the economists' models. For example, many economic models indicate that minimum wages lead to higher unemployment. But as Harvard economist Dani Rodrik writes, this is only the case 'if the labour market is really competitive and employers have no control over the wage they must pay to attract workers'. Many economists now argue that one of the underlying factors of the 2008 global financial crisis was a focus on abstract models that failed to consider the possibility of a systemic collapse in house prices.[10]

In recent years, the study of economics has begun to focus more on what works in practice. Using data, economists are now testing theories to see if they are supported by evidence. Economics has become less like philosophy and more like science, with economists conducting randomised control trials, lab tests and even field experiments.[11] For example, to assess how migrants gain economically from moving across borders, economists studied a group of migrants from the Pacific island of Tonga. The incomes of those who moved to New Zealand after being selected in a random ballot were compared with those not selected. In Australia, novel programs to address homelessness are evaluated by comparing participants to a control group.[12] At last, economics is interested in finding out which policy settings actually work.

The same impulse drives this book. Rather than starting from a theoretical or an ideological perspective, I'm interested in exploring real examples. Each chapter focuses on a different country. My starting point was to ask which country is achieving the best global outcome on a particular measure, such as education, crime or gender equity. Next was to gain an understanding of that country: the nation's history and the policy interventions that have led to its current success. Finally, I wanted to draw out the implications for the rest of us. What can we learn from our neighbours around the world to achieve a better outcome in our own societies?

The countries in this book come from a relatively narrow band. Of the ten, eight are in the Organisation for Economic Co-operation and Development (OECD), the body that represents the world's most industrialised democracies. The ten countries are home to a collective total of about 838 million people, which is only 11 per cent of the world's population. While you'll read about Indonesia – which has made a sustained and successful transition from dictatorship to democracy – you won't read much about China, India or countries in Africa, the Middle East or South America. That is because these places are not yet leading the world on the key global concerns. However, they are advancing rapidly, and it's possible that if a sequel to this book were to be written in twenty years, the countries featured would be quite different.

Solved was a journey of discovery for me, and I hope it will be for you too. Although public policy is what I do for a living, I am not an expert on every country in this book. So in writing each chapter, I sought out a range of experts from around the world, who offer their perspectives on the success of their nations. Some are academics, such as Professor Saravanan Gopinathan, an education thinker from Singapore; some are practitioners, such as Christine MacKay, who leads economic development for the City of Phoenix in the United States. And some are ordinary citizens, such as Icelandic parents Nicole and Sigurður, able to provide a valuable insight into everyday life in their country. They are all highly intelligent, passionate and knowledgeable about their societies, and were generous in sharing their experiences.

As I explored with them and through the data the issues that emerged, I wondered if it was possible to get a sense of the *types* of governments that are achieving the best outcomes. Where I live, in Australia, the low-tax, small-government model rules. The idea is that residents pay less tax and government plays a limited role in people's lives. It is assumed that the private sector is best equipped to meet the needs of citizens in relation to healthcare, employment, insurance and other services. Supporters and detractors of this model mount their arguments with fervour, but often the arguments are not backed by evidence. I wanted to know if the data supports the case for a low-taxing neoliberal government. Are such governments achieving results, or are other models – such as the high-taxing social democratic governments of the Nordic and Northern European countries, or the state-sponsored capitalism in the fast-growing countries of East Asia – outperforming them? The results surprised me, and tell a compelling story.

The final chapter outlines what we might do next to solve the world's most pressing problems. Drawing on insights from the featured countries, it suggests the types of policies governments might employ to achieve better outcomes for their nations, and what we can do as citizens to advance change, even if our governments aren't – yet – on board.

Without doubt, there is a lot to be positive about. Whatever the problem – climate change, loss of manufacturing jobs, violent crime – somewhere in the world there is a country making strides to address it. The nations in this book have booming economies, low inequality and populations that are becoming healthier each year. They have integrated migrants from around the world into their societies, dramatically increased students' abilities in literacy and maths, and are on the way to eliminating greenhouse gas emissions. If they can do it, why not us? Their stories show us what is possible. They give insight into what – with the right attitude and the right policies – we might just be able to achieve in our countries too.

1

GONE WITH THE WIND
How to Farewell Fossil Fuels

Although it's a rather agreeable place, there's nothing particularly exceptional about Samsø Island at first glance. Located off the coast of Denmark's Jutland Peninsula, this former Viking outpost is home to a traditional farming community, best known for producing the country's first potatoes each year. After arriving by ferry, as you travel around the largely flat island – perhaps by bicycle – you'll see cows and sheep grazing leisurely, weathered farmers driving tractors, and the occasional farm dog. The clink of ropes against masts resonates from the marina at the small village of Ballen; ducks dabble in the village pond at Nordby, overlooked by thatched houses.

This very ordinariness is what makes it so remarkable that, for the past twenty years, Samsø has been a world-leading green energy community. All of Samsø's electricity comes from massive community-owned wind turbines, while biomass boilers burning local straw meet 70 per cent of the island's heating needs. Each of Samsø's 3724 residents now emits an average of *negative* 3.7 tonnes of greenhouse gas per year.[1]

The Samsø Energy Academy serves as a sort of interpretative centre for those wishing to learn about the island. It hosts visiting scientists, schoolchildren and 'energy tourists' who come to hear more about Samsø's experience in transitioning to renewable energy. The academy provides advice to companies and homeowners and leads a busy program of tours, workshops and exhibitions about energy, climate change and sustainable development.

Søren Hermansen is the academy's director. When I interview him, he's struggling to make himself heard above the noise of dozens of students visiting the centre.

'We have lots of visitors,' he says. 'We have probably four, five thousand visitors every year from all over the world. It's not so much about the wind turbines or the solar panels but more like, "Hey, these guys did it. It's a little old-fashioned farming community, so if they can do it, we can do it."'

Hermansen's shock of grey hair suggests he is approaching middle age, but he gives the impression of a much younger man. He speaks passionately about Samsø, putting this very local initiative into the context of broader Danish energy policy and the global challenge of climate change. Occasionally a mischievous smile reveals itself, as though he is aware of the sheer audacity of what he has helped to achieve – leading a conservative rural farming community to the point that it's now demonstrating to the world the benefits of cooperatively-owned local energy production.

The success of Samsø Island is indicative of broader efforts in Denmark to address climate change. It ranks second in the world (behind Sweden) on the Climate Change Performance Index,[2] and it has succeeded in halving its per capita greenhouse gas emissions over a relatively short timeframe.[3] However, Denmark is determined to go much further. With a remarkable political consensus, it has committed to energy agreements that by 2030 will see 100 per cent of its electricity generated from renewable sources.

The experience of Samsø Island, and Denmark as a whole, shows that it's possible to almost eliminate carbon emissions using existing technology – we do not have to wait for some indeterminate future point in which new technology comes to market. It also shows that local communities, with the right leadership and supported by national policy, can drive real change.

Søren Hermansen grew up on Samsø Island. After finishing school in the late 1970s, he left in search of opportunities and adventure, like many of his peers. He spent time fishing in arctic Norway, farming in New Zealand and teaching in a democracy-building project in Lithuania. Hearing Hermansen recount these travels, it's clear that he has a passion for engaging with people from a range of backgrounds and philosophies.

When his parents separated and his father decided to 'realise himself and become an artist', Hermansen found himself suddenly inheriting the family farm. So he 'kind of by chance or coincidence' came back to Samsø in the mid-1980s. While running the farm, growing beets and parsley, he found himself in the midst of a major transition occurring on the island. 'I liked the work and philosophy of farming, but I didn't like the development it was going through,' Hermansen says. 'It was becoming more and more industrialised, with lower and lower prices for farm products, and if you wanted to survive you had to buy the neighbour's farm. This was quite depressing. It takes its toll on the local community because there's no people left.'

Perhaps partly in reaction to this increasingly competitive environment, another change was occurring. A number of local farmers were turning to growing organic produce, dairy products and grain. Hermansen studied organic farming. However, through getting involved in 'all kinds of local development and ideas', he discovered that communication was a greater strength than practical application, and he became a teacher in the field while continuing to farm.

The question that came to occupy Hermansen was: how can you strengthen the local community and plan for future development? 'That kind of became my passion.'

In 1997, Samsø was struggling. The abattoir – the largest private employer on the island – had just closed, taking with it 100 jobs. Like many rural communities around the world, the island's population was both ageing and declining. The Danish government, looking for a showcase opportunity to demonstrate that the 21 per cent emissions reduction target in the Kyoto Protocol was possible, launched a national competition to find a Danish Renewable Energy Island. It sought to identify the island or area with the most achievable plan for becoming 100 per cent self-sufficient in energy production. The Danish Energy Authority would provide funding to aid the transition.

The national government also wanted to see civic participation. Local businesses, the council and community organisations all had to support the plan. Although the focus was on using existing available technology, the government was interested in exploring new ways of organising, financing and owning the technology.

The winning location was expected to function as a demonstration of Danish renewable energy expertise that could be displayed to the rest of the world. Samsø's municipal government submitted an application, and in 1998 it won, beating three other islands and a peninsula.

The prize included funding for a coordinator to develop a ten-year plan. This role piqued Hermansen's interest. 'Because I had been around for a little while, and I made my voice heard every now and again at meetings, I was asked if I wanted to be the manager of the Energy Island. I accepted the position, just to give it a go, and had to keep on farming. But it very soon turned into a full-time job, so for the last twenty years I've been working in this field.'

The competition win was not like 'a golden ticket', Hermansen says. 'We didn't get a lot of money for it. We had to do it with the same conditions that any community in Denmark had at that time.'

Initially, the project met with some community resistance. 'People were like, "Thank you but no thank you. It sounds really expensive and complicated and we can't do this alone."' To engage the somewhat sceptical locals, Hermansen spent a lot of time talking with them. If a section of the island was holding a town meeting or an event, Hermansen would turn up, bringing sandwiches or beer. He'd go door to door, talking with people in their kitchens.

The plan was to quickly transition the island to wind power. By 2000 – just two years after winning the competition – eleven wind turbines were due to be installed, each with capacity to generate one megawatt of power.

The idea was not universally beloved. Residents had concerns about the potential noise and visual impact of the turbines. The challenge for Hermansen and his team was to bring around the local community. They undertook extensive public negotiations over the location of each turbine.

A crucial step in gaining community support was to invite locals to own the turbines. As Samsø Island's website notes: 'Windmills are much prettier when you are a co-owner, making money when the wind is blowing.'[4] A decentralised structure was created, with cooperatives being formed, or shares being sold in each turbine. Hermansen says that 'everybody who lives in the neighbourhood had a chance to invest their money in the turbines, giving a sense of local ownership that was strong enough to overcome the flip side of the turbines'. Locals signed on to this scheme enthusiastically, contributing enough through cooperatives to purchase two turbines, while individuals purchased the remaining nine. These eleven turbines generate enough power to make each of the island's twenty-two villages self-sufficient.

In 2002, to offset emissions from the island's cars, tractors and ferries, a further ten offshore turbines were installed, with a combined capacity of 23 megawatts of power. These turbines are located in relatively shallow water, with foundations fixed in the ocean floor. Sub-sea transmission cables connect the turbines to the electricity grid.

Offshore wind farms such as this are increasingly the norm in Denmark, as its ocean areas have strong and consistent wind patterns, and farms can be larger while generating less visual impact and noise for residents. Turbines are also often easier to install offshore, since ships can carry the massive components, which are difficult to transport on land.

Two of Samsø's offshore turbines are cooperatively owned. The municipality owns a further five turbines, which generate income that the local government can reinvest in sustainability measures. This includes smarter methods of heating and incentives for the purchase of electric cars.

Samsø is cold in the winter, with an average January maximum of 3 degrees Celsius (37 degrees Fahrenheit). To address the island's heating needs, three plants were installed between 2002 and 2005. These burn biomass, mostly local straw, and supply 70 per cent of the island's heating requirements. Many of those not on district heating have replaced old oil furnaces with solar collectors or biomass burners of their own.

Like much of the world, electricity use on Samsø has increased over the past two decades, as people use more appliances more often. However, because of the emphasis on retrofitting old houses with energy-efficient electric heat pumps, and thick insulation made from recycled materials, consumption has decreased more than 20 per cent since 1998.

Samsø also has the highest number of electric cars per capita in Denmark. The municipality changed its fleet to electric vehicles, powered by solar panels. When municipal employees need a car, they book these vehicles through a share scheme.

Samsø's efforts have strengthened the community and generated an enormous sense of pride. 'It's been such a successful marketing thing in Denmark,' Hermansen says. 'If you search "Samsø Energy Island" on the internet, it's all over the place. We've had headlines everywhere: CNN, BBC, *The Observer*, you name it.'

Samsø continues to make progress in reducing emissions and remains a shining example of a community-based response to climate change. But most compelling is that much of the technology underpinning Samsø's energy shift is common. There are now hundreds of thousands of wind turbines spinning around the world, producing about 6 per cent of the world's electricity demand.[5] The story of Samsø is not of new technology; it's about how a concerted effort and an engaged community can use existing technology to eliminate carbon emissions. This proved possible when people saw that addressing climate change aligned strongly with other community interests, such as economic development.

The Case for Renewables

The impacts of climate change are truly terrifying. Scientists estimate that in the absence of concerted efforts to reduce carbon emissions, global temperatures will rise by between 3.7 and 4.8 degrees Celsius above pre-industrial levels by 2100.[6] This would be catastrophic. The world's seas could rise by nearly 1 metre. On the way there, one in six species would become extinct; the Arctic Ocean would be nearly ice-free in summer by 2050; and within the next thirty years extreme weather events such as heatwaves and coastal flooding would become far more frequent.[7]

This assessment comes from the Intergovernmental Panel on Climate Change (IPCC), a collection of the world's leading scientists. The IPCC's latest report lists 800 lead authors from more than eighty countries. The conclusion these scientists draw about human involve-ment in climate change is unambiguous: 'The human influence on the climate system is clear.' Human-generated greenhouse gas emissions are at the highest point in history, and global average air temperatures have risen by almost 1 degree Celsius.[8]

We're already seeing the environmental effects of climate change. Coral reefs in Australia and beyond have experienced severe bleaching and decreased coral cover, causing habitat loss. Ecosystems in North America and elsewhere are being disturbed by an increase in the fre-quency and intensity of droughts, windstorms, fires and pest outbreaks.[9] The Belgium-based Centre for Research on the Epidemiology of Disas-ters estimates that in 2018, 5000 people died due to extreme weather, while 28.9 million more needed emergency assistance or humanitarian aid. In that year alone, there was a massive heatwave in the United King-dom, devastating floods in India, one of the worst hurricane seasons in US history and the largest-ever wildfire in California. Even if we could halt greenhouse gas emissions today, many of the impacts would con-tinue for centuries.[10]

In urban areas, climate change will increase the risk of heat stress, storm surges, flooding and sea-level rise. Rural regions will experience major challenges with water availability and supply, food security, infra-structure maintenance and the protection of agricultural incomes. And the poorest countries, which contribute the least to greenhouse gas emis-sions, are among the most vulnerable to the impacts of climate change. These nations depend on agriculture and fisheries, are often low-lying and subject to coastal inundation, and lack the financial and technolog-ical resources to cope.[11] There's a good chance that coral atolls in the Pacific Ocean will be uninhabitable by 2050, and small Pacific nations, such as Tuvalu and Kiribati, sitting just metres above sea level, are fearful for their continued existence.[12]

The single most important factor driving the change to our climate is the increase in greenhouse gas concentrations. A range of greenhouse gases are emitted due to human activity, including methane and nitrous oxide, but carbon dioxide is the main contributor to climate change. Our carbon emissions are largely due to the burning of fossil fuels.

The burning of oil, gas and coal accounts for two-thirds of the world's electricity generation. Australia generates 86 per cent of its electricity from these sources; India, 82 per cent; China, 73 per cent; and the United States, 67 per cent.[13] The impact of carbon dioxide is worse than that of other greenhouse gases because it remains in the atmosphere for so long: it has a lifetime of fifty to 200 years.

Carbon dioxide occurs naturally in our atmosphere at low concentrations. Two hundred years ago, when Napoleon was emperor of France and Jane Austen was writing *Pride and Prejudice*, atmospheric carbon dioxide was present at about 260 to 280 parts per million, the same as it had been for the previous 10,000 years. Since the start of the Industrial Revolution, the Earth's atmospheric carbon dioxide has risen steadily, and in May 2019 it reached 415 parts per million.[14] The IPCC estimates that if we are to keep warming to less than 2 degrees Celsius above pre-industrial levels, we need to limit the concentration of atmospheric carbon dioxide to, at most, 450 parts per million. To achieve this will likely require a complete transformation of our energy infrastructure.[15]

In 2015, 196 countries signed up to the Paris Agreement, which seeks to limit global warming to less than 2 degrees Celsius and to aim for a target of 1.5 degrees. Although there is no mechanism to force a country to set a specific target, each country is required to put forward their 'best efforts' through 'nationally determined contributions' and to strengthen these in years ahead.[16]

If humanity is to meet the objectives of the Paris Agreement, carbon emissions from the energy sector will need to decline to 90 per cent below 2010 levels in coming decades. By 2050, low-carbon sources of electricity such as renewables will need to supply at least 80 per cent of the world's electricity. To reach this level, annual investments in low-carbon electricity and energy efficiency will need to rise by several hundred billion dollars per year before 2030.

Far from being a cost to the economy, mitigating carbon emissions may actually contribute to economic growth. The 2017 OECD 'Investing in Climate, Investing in Growth' report notes that taking decisive action to transition to a low-carbon future would involve 'spending or tax measures that will foster productivity in the medium to longer term' such as 'raising spending on soft and hard infrastructure or education'. A key reason for the positive economic impact of this approach is the 'overall boost in investment, including in low-emission infrastructure'.[17]

The OECD argues that addressing climate change could 'add 1 per cent to average economic output' in wealthy countries by 2021 and lift 2050 output by up to 2.8 per cent.[18] This would mean material improvements to living standards across the wealthy countries of the OECD. If the predicted costs of extreme weather events, such as coastal flooding or storm damage, are subtracted, the net effect on economic output rises to 5 per cent.

Denmark has managed to reduce its climate impact while maintaining one of the highest standards of living and being the second-happiest nation in the world.[19] Since 1992, Denmark has reduced its per capita emissions by 46 per cent, performing better than any country in the OECD, except for tiny Luxembourg (see Figure 1 on page 17).

While Denmark has a unique set of attributes, including a reasonably high level of per capita wealth, a significant coastline and strong winds, it is technically and economically feasible for almost every country in the world to transition to 100 per cent renewable energy. For example, researchers from Stanford and Berkeley universities in the United States have developed roadmaps for 139 countries that involve 80 per cent conversion to wind, hydro or solar power by 2030, and 100 per cent by 2050.[20] While this shows that change is possible, Denmark is demonstrating how it can be done in practice.

I n 1973, the world experienced its first oil crisis, when a number of oil-producing Arab countries placed an embargo on oil exports to Israel-aligned countries during the Yom Kippur War. This caused an enormous shock to the global economy, with oil prices rising from US$3 per barrel to US$12 per barrel. Denmark was severely affected, as it had essentially only one source of energy. At that time, 90 per cent of its energy came from oil, almost all from Saudi Arabia.

In response to the crisis, the Danish government introduced a number of taxes aimed at reducing energy consumption, and hence reliance on foreign oil. The already high price of energy in Denmark became even higher. Yet when energy prices began to fall after the oil crisis, a broad consensus formed in Denmark that taxes should be kept high, with a view to reducing energy consumption long-term.

By contrast, US governments, in response to the same crisis, decided to reduce reliance on oil and gas imports by shifting the electricity sector to other fuels. As a result, a slew of new coal-fired power stations were constructed.[21] US president Jimmy Carter called for coal production to increase by 400 per cent each year, and outlined policies 'to ensure the greatest possible conversion of utilities and industrial installations to coal and other fuels'.[22]

In countries such as the United States, Australia and the United Kingdom, where political debate focuses on the need to keep energy prices as low as possible, the Danish consensus may seem somewhat unbelievable. However, according to Danish energy-policy expert Finn Mortensen, Danes 'have gotten accustomed to a very high level of taxation of all kinds of fossil fuels'. This is partly because the high taxation has been paired with financial incentives. Hefty subsidies have been made to business and industry, primarily to encourage renewables. Homeowners have been granted large tax rebates if they insulate their houses or put in new windows in order to lower energy consumption.

Mortensen heads up State of Green, a not-for-profit collaboration between government and industry. It was established in 2008, in the lead-up to the United Nations Climate Conference in Copenhagen, to secure 'maximum impact from a branding point of view' for Denmark's role as conference host. State of Green assists Danish companies, academic institutions and experts by promoting their knowledge and capabilities in clean energy and sustainability to countries all over the world. This leads to Danish-run projects and business opportunities. For example, Danish company BWSC built a biomass-powered electricity generator in Northern Ireland, and a Danish–Vietnamese partnership is improving water efficiency in Vietnam.[23] Initially home to five or six employees, State of Green has grown to a team of twelve, who work from its 400-metre-square showroom in downtown Copenhagen – host to more than 2500 visitors each year, all of whom come to learn about the Danish energy transition.

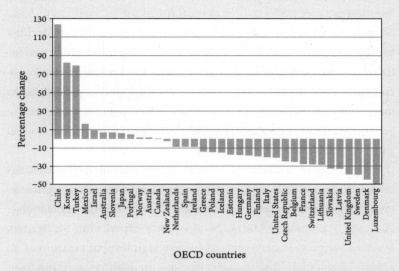

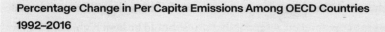

Percentage Change in Per Capita Emissions Among OECD Countries 1992–2016

Figure 1. Denmark and Luxembourg are leading the OECD in reducing per capita carbon emissions. Despite a few outlier nations, Europe is vastly outperforming the rest of the world.

A man who clearly loves his job, Mortensen is warm, enthusiastic and very familiar with his material. He came to the role after ten years working for the US embassy in Copenhagen, and then as a business writer and editor for major Danish newspapers. He believes the Danish government's decisions around energy policy in the 1970s laid the foundation for Denmark's current success in reducing emissions. It led to the creation of many companies focused on energy efficiency and renewable energy. Denmark is home to firms that are world leaders in areas such as water, thermostats (which maintain a set temperature by turning a device on or off) and wind. A prominent example is wind turbine company Vestas, which 'started out as one blacksmith making his own turbine'. It is now the world's largest wind turbine manufacturer and has installed more than 59,000 turbines across seventy countries.[24]

Following the oil crisis, Denmark introduced a subsidy scheme to promote wind power, and in 1979 the first commercial wind turbine was installed: a Vestas 30-kilowatt turbine, able to power about five homes. This scheme spurred a significant amount of investment, and 200 to 300 turbines were installed each year until it wound up. Forty years later, Denmark continues to support renewable energy, principally through a production subsidy for electricity generated through renewable sources. There are currently more than 6000 turbines installed in Denmark, distributed across the country.[25] 'This has been going on for forty years. We didn't do it overnight,' Mortensen says. 'It's been a very long process.'

Today, Denmark's largest turbine – the Vestas V164 – is 220 metres high, approximately as tall as a fifty-storey building. Able to generate nine and a half megawatts of power, one turbine is enough to run more than 8000 homes.[26] At peak capacity, about sixty of these turbines would generate as much power as a medium-sized coal-fired power station.[27] Turbines are now so efficient that it is likely the industry will no longer need subsidies to compete with fossil-fuel power generation. In 2017, Danish company Ørsted and German partner EnBW won a contract to supply renewable energy to Germany with their 'zero-subsidy' bids for planned offshore wind farms in Germany. This means the companies will receive only the wholesale price for electricity supplied from the turbines.[28] In a few years, 'nobody will talk about subsidies to the wind industry', Mortensen believes.

A key contributor to Denmark's success with wind power has been community engagement. 'You need to ensure the buy-in from the population,' Mortensen says. To address community concern about the impact of wind turbines, Denmark has encouraged local ownership of the turbines, as on Samsø Island. The country's first wind cooperatives date back to the 1970s. In 2009, the Danish government introduced legislation that imposes an obligation on wind-farm operators to offer at least 20 per cent ownership of turbines to local people through structures such as wind cooperatives.[29]

However, community ownership has become more challenging as the size of individual turbines has grown. Hermansen has experienced this on Samsø. 'The new turbines are four, five times more expensive than when we started,' he says. 'And then it's much more complicated to get a local group of people to be the investors and owners, because you need to expand the ownership group. And all of a sudden you get outside the boundaries of the local community. And then you lose this local feeling of commitment, where you can sit down in a meeting and look each other in the eyes and say, "Should we do this?"'

Nevertheless, Hermansen says it is not so much the size of the ownership share that is important, but the process of engagement. 'The interesting thing is how it's organised,' he says. 'The feeling of being involved. If you're left out it can produce so much resistance, and people can find all kinds of reasons for not liking the project.'

Denmark has also focused on improving energy efficiency, which has the triple benefit of reducing carbon emissions, improving productivity and saving energy users money. In 2006 the country introduced a unique program in which energy companies are required to contribute to nationwide energy savings. The Danish Energy Efficiency Obligation Scheme assigns a share of a national savings target to each energy sector (oil, electricity, natural gas and district heating), and the sector's trade associations allot a percentage of that share to individual companies. Companies are able to claim credit for energy savings to which they have contributed, either with technical advice or financial support.[30] Savings certificates can be bought, sold or shared when a company exceeds its annual target.

Energy companies have embraced this scheme enthusiastically, and the national target has been achieved every year since it began. The scheme is effectively cost-neutral for the companies, since the costs of energy efficiency investments are passed on to consumers in the form of network tariffs. It is also extremely flexible, with no specifications on how savings can be achieved. This has driven companies to find the most cost-effective means to achieve savings.

Also fundamental to Denmark's success has been a series of long-term energy agreements with cross-parliamentary support. Every government since the 1980s has made sure to include the opposition in the negotiation of the agreements. This provides for remarkable political certainty, giving the market the confidence for investment.

'If we have a change of government and the opposition comes in, these major agreements still stand,' says Mortensen. 'From an investor point of view, you want to be sure what will happen, or will not happen, in five, six years' time. You can rest assured that the agreements will stand, which is very important. I think this singles out Denmark from most other countries. This has also made it possible for us to have such a high degree of renewables in our system.'

In 2018, Denmark's centre-right government (political cousins to Australia's Liberal–National coalition, or to the Republican Party in the United States) secured the support of all sitting parties in the parliament for an ambitious new energy agreement. It outlines measures that will see 100 per cent of Denmark's electricity generated from renewable sources by 2030. This means that renewables will contribute 55 per cent of total energy consumption. Key measures in the agreement include three large new offshore wind farms and a complete phasing out of coal in the electricity sector by 2030. There will be fewer onshore wind turbines, as older turbines are upgraded to become more efficient and powerful, and greater emphasis is placed on offshore generation.

It's worth underscoring the significance of this. In a decade, with a credible plan to get there, Denmark's electricity will be generated entirely from renewable sources. By contrast, the European Union has a target of 32 per cent renewables by 2030, the Australian state of Victoria is planning for 50 per cent by 2030, and the US state of California has a target of 60 per cent renewables by 2030.[31]

Mortensen argues that what enables this long-term, bipartisan approach is trust. Trust in others is higher in Denmark than in any other country. Danes' confidence in national government is substantially above the OECD average too.[32] 'If the government comes up with a well-argued idea to do something, there will be some initial scepticism,' Mortensen says. 'But not the scepticism you would see in other countries, where you do not have the same degree of trust in your political system.'

This trust may be aided by the role of public broadcasting. All television stations in Denmark are government-owned, and citizens on both sides of the political divide obtain most of their national news from the same two channels: the Danish Broadcasting Corporation and TV 2 News.[33] The absence of a fragmented and polarised media is likely more conducive to political consensus. Without media-induced

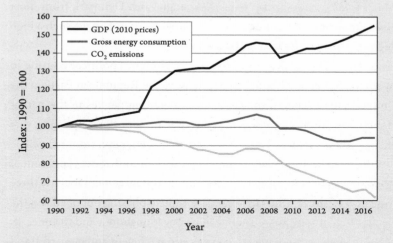

Denmark's GDP, Gross Energy Consumption and CO_2 Emissions 1990–2017

Figure 2. Denmark has seen strong economic growth in recent decades, accompanied by a decline in energy consumption and a huge reduction in carbon emissions.

political polarisation, there is scope for constructive debate that can lead to agreement over key national interests. This is a real strength over those countries that have recently seen political fragmentation, such as Australia, the United States and France. In these countries, bipartisan cooperation on policy has proved extremely challenging, and the overall result has tended towards political paralysis.[34]

Denmark's constructive policymaking appears to be working so far. The country is managing the transition to a low-carbon future better than any country in the world. Since 1990, Denmark's economy has grown by about 55 per cent in real terms (around the same as the European average), while over the same period gross energy consumption has decreased and total greenhouse gas emissions have shrunk by 38 per cent.[35] 'We have been able to decouple economic growth from the use of energy,' Mortensen says.

Building Renewables into the System

The speed at which Denmark is moving to reduce its dependence on fossil fuels is impressive. 'If we look at electricity, about 44 per cent is actually generated from wind today,' Mortensen says. 'It'll be 50 per cent by 2020.' The record figure he refers to – 43.6 per cent of electricity generation from wind in 2017 – is a rapid increase from just 19 per cent in 2009. On particularly windy days, Denmark regularly generates more than 100 per cent of its electricity requirements from wind. At times, wind has even produced up to 140 per cent of electricity demand.[36] When this happens, Denmark exports power to Norway, Germany and Sweden.

The arguments some countries have mounted against wind power do not hold sway in Denmark. According to the Danish Energy Agency, onshore wind is now the cheapest form of electricity generation – cheaper than coal, nuclear or natural gas. Electricity produced by the newest onshore wind plants costs about one US nickel (five cents) per kilowatt hour, far less than the cost of coal.[37] In Australia and the United States, some politicians and think tanks warn of wind's 'unreliability', arguing for coal- or gas-fired generation to 'firm up the system'.[38] But Danes scoff at suggestions that wind power might lead to grid instability and unplanned blackouts. Since 1990, Denmark has been able to maintain continuity of electricity supply 99.99 per cent of the time, ranking it equal first in Europe, along with Switzerland.[39] This equates to the average consumer being without electricity for just nineteen minutes every year. When there are interruptions to the power supply, they invariably arise from the distribution network. There has never been a blackout due to failure to produce enough electricity.[40]

The stability of Denmark's electricity supply is underpinned by a flexible grid of distributed energy resources, interconnected with the rest of Europe. Grid operator Energinet manages generation and supply for the whole country, and has been central to long-term capacity planning during this transition to renewables. Energinet incorporates weather forecasting into generation, dispatch and control to improve the predictability of natural sources. It also manages ancillary markets that see alternative means of power generation – such as combined heat and power plants, used for district heating – come online when production from renewables is insufficient to meet demand.[41] In many parts of the country, the energy generated from wind and other local sources exceeds demand, meaning local networks become power exporters. The system operates as a web of regional microgrids that can quickly connect or disconnect from the main grid, enabling renewables to be integrated while maintaining reliability of supply.

Denmark's electricity network is connected to Norway, Sweden and Germany by large interconnectors. These countries are part of Nord Pool, a group of nine northern European countries that share electric power. 'If we produce more electricity from wind than we can use – and that happens frequently, for weeks at a time – we can sell it to our neighbouring countries instantly,' Mortensen says. 'Luckily, it seems to be the case that when we are high on wind electricity, they are low on hydropower in Norway, and vice versa. Whenever we're low on wind, we can import electricity from a city in Norway, or from Sweden.'

Aside from providing energy security, Nord Pool also increases the economic value of wind, as it is sold at a predetermined market price. Wind energy has therefore become an important export product for Denmark. Further interconnectors are now planned, including Viking Link, a 770-kilometre submarine cable connecting wind-farm substations on the Jutland Peninsula to Lincolnshire in the United Kingdom. 'We try from a Danish government side to push for more integration in Europe,' Mortensen says. 'The more transmission lines to the rest of Europe and the more integration, the better.'

The Danish experience shows that it is feasible to abandon the concept of 'baseload power'. If intermittent distributed energy sources such as wind can be successfully integrated into a grid to provide a stable electricity supply, there is no longer a need to maintain a constant supply of electricity from non-renewable sources such as coal or uranium. With its remaining two coal-fired power stations due to close in the coming decade, Denmark will provide a test case for the transition from baseload to intermittent sources.

For many in industrialised countries, becoming self-sufficient by going 'off-grid' is an aspiration. This is typically driven by a desire to take personal responsibility for reducing carbon and water use or, as Nick

Rosen, editor of off-grid.net, argues in *The Guardian*, 'a weariness with consumerism, a desire to spend less and consequently a need to earn less'. Rosen estimates that in the United States alone, two million people are living off-grid.[42] Yet so effective is the Danish approach to electricity grid management that the idea of going 'off-grid' seems ludicrous. The Danish approach involves working together as a community. 'Going off-grid would be completely stupid and expensive,' Hermansen says. 'Instead of everybody having their own wall battery, which is really, really expensive, we should look at community batteries, look at how we can make an efficient source that serves many people who can get together.'

Denmark also leads the world in building sustainable cities. Its capital, Copenhagen, with an urban population of two million, has been recognised with a swag of awards, including being named the European Commission's Green Capital, Siemens' Green Index Greenest Major City in Europe and CNN's World's Healthiest City. It has a reputation as the cycling capital of the world, with 41 per cent of trips to work, school or university made by bicycle. Hundreds of millions of dollars have been invested into cycling infrastructure. Bicycle traffic has increased by 68 per cent over the past twenty years, and for every car in Copenhagen there are now 5.6 bikes. The average resident of Copenhagen rides three kilometres per day.[43] Indeed, only 34 per cent of all trips in Copenhagen are made by car; travelling by bike, foot or public transport is the norm.

Copenhagen is seeking to become carbon neutral by 2025. Heating is already 98 per cent energy-efficient district heating powered by municipal waste. Carbon emissions have so far fallen to 2.5 tonnes per capita, a reduction of 31 per cent over the past ten years. A new 600-megawatt combined heat and power plant powered by woodchips will open by 2020; it will reduce emissions by a further 1.2 million tonnes annually.[44] The city intends to purchase carbon offsets to achieve the balance of the savings.

There are criticisms of Denmark's transition to a low-carbon future. The Global Footprint Network claims that despite the country's efforts to tackle carbon emissions, it still has the world's twelfth-largest ecological footprint (worse than Australia, which is fourteenth).[45] It argues that if everyone lived like a Dane, we would require more than four Earth-like planets. A key contributor to Denmark's ecological footprint is meat production, which requires a lot of land outside Denmark to produce animal feed. Former politician and the secretary-general of the Danish World Wildlife Fund, Gitte Seeberg, says the distribution of Denmark's population contributes to its ecological footprint. 'Our country consists of roadways, cities and crop fields with hardly any nature,' she told a Danish newspaper in 2014.[46]

Critics also point to Denmark's household electricity prices, which are among the highest in Europe. The consumer electricity rate is about 50 per cent higher than the European average, and much higher than prices in the United States,[47] although electricity generation costs in Denmark are actually among the lowest in Europe. One analysis shows that 66 per cent of the average Dane's electricity bill goes to taxes and fees, while just 15 per cent pays for the electricity itself, and a further 18 per cent covers the cost of transmission and distribution.[48] But almost all of these taxes on electricity go into general revenue, which helps to fund services such as healthcare, education and aged care. It is not the cost of energy itself that keeps Denmark's electricity prices so high, but a government decision to ensure the nation has a strong social welfare system. Until fairly recently, consumers did also pay an 11 per cent Public Service Obligation, which provided funding for renewable energy such as wind and solar, but this tax has now been abolished. Renewables will instead be funded through general taxes rather than electricity consumption.

Denmark's efforts to reduce its carbon emissions function within the context of the European Union Emissions Trading Scheme. This is a cap-and-trade scheme whereby a maximum (a 'cap') is set on the total number of carbon emissions, and emission credits can be traded. The scheme has been operating – and evolving – since 2005. It has faced a number of challenges and has required modifications. For example, early on, an overly generous cap on emissions meant that no significant emissions reductions were achieved. Nevertheless, the scheme has since had some success. By 2020, the European Union expects to have cut emissions by 20 per cent from 1990 levels.[49] The cost of emissions reductions has been significantly lower than expected – just a fraction of 1 per cent of GDP – and with changes to the mechanism, the cost can potentially be eliminated entirely.

Denmark has not relied on the European emissions trading scheme alone. Government policy – to improve energy efficiency, offer subsidies for renewables and engage communities in turbine ownership – has played a central role in driving the Danish energy transition. 'The history of Denmark over the past forty-five years shows that you need to have a certain degree of government involvement,' Mortensen says. 'You cannot leave it up to the markets alone.' He believes that the European trading scheme is not yet functioning effectively. 'As long as you don't have an emissions trading scheme that is working properly, you simply need to have something else in place,' Mortensen says. 'It may be a pipe dream, but one day, when you have a carbon tax and an emissions trading scheme in place and working properly, you won't have the need for subsidies.'

While Denmark has made significant progress to reduce emissions from the electricity sector, other sectors have seen less improvement. 'The non-regulated emissions really are the toughest to deal with,' Mortensen says. 'You have buildings, you have agriculture and you have transportation.' Denmark has attempted to address transport emissions by exorbitantly taxing the purchase price of vehicles. 'In Denmark, when you buy a car, you pay for two and a half cars, simply because the taxes are so high.' For vehicles costing up to DKK185,000 (US$29,000), Danes pay a registration tax of 85 per cent. For those worth more than this, the tax is 150 per cent.[50] Although the rate is reduced slightly for fuel-efficient cars, it is still an enormous impost. By contrast, the tax on a vehicle in the United Kingdom is a flat rate of £55 (US$72).

The challenge with such a high rate of vehicle tax is that the government becomes reliant on the revenue it generates. So recently, when the headline rate of vehicle taxation was reduced – from 180 per cent to 150 per cent – the tax was also extended to electric vehicles, which had previously been exempt, in an effort to maintain revenue levels. But sales of electric vehicles plummeted in response, and the government decided to ease the tax for a couple of years.[51] It is grappling with this policy challenge, acutely aware of neighbouring Norway, with some of the world's most generous incentives for electric vehicles.[52] 'It's a really difficult nut for the Danish politicians to crack,' Mortensen says.

But Danish politicians have made great bounds forward. Through the 2018 energy agreement, all sitting political parties have united behind the goal of ensuring that by 2050, Denmark will have transitioned to 100 per cent renewable fuel sources for all its energy. This means that renewables will completely supply the electricity, heating and transport sectors. The ambition is immense. It means no more coal-fired electricity generation, no more oil boilers for heating, no more petrol-powered cars and no more diesel trucks or tractors. By 2050, Denmark will be independent of fossil fuels.

In 2019, the Danish government took this a step further, adopting a new climate law requiring the country to achieve complete carbon neutrality by 2050. This means zero emissions from the whole economy, including energy, transport, industrial processes, agriculture and waste. It includes a binding commitment to achieve a 70 per cent reduction in emissions by 2030.

What Denmark Can Teach the World

Denmark's experience in addressing carbon emissions provides some illuminating ideas about how we might go about tackling climate change on a global level.

Start Local

Many Danish initiatives have not been about addressing climate change specifically. The phenomenon of a warming globe is an abstract concept that can be difficult to connect with and can lead some to feel overwhelmed or disempowered. The moves to achieve energy independence on Samsø Island and improved liveability in Copenhagen – along with other Danish cities – have been about providing direct benefits to individuals and their communities. Denmark's success in achieving its targets shows that community development and grassroots approaches can foster an engaged local population, and minimise the social dissent that can result from 'top-down' government interventions.

But Samsø Island is one small community, with less than 4000 people. Copenhagen has a concentrated urban population. Is it realistic to
think we could replicate these models across the world? Søren Hermansen is optimistic it can be done, with just a little government assistance.
He believes that the success of Samsø Island is 'national policy in practice'. National government support is crucial, but change works best
when it is owned and driven by local communities. He says the solution
to our energy crisis lies in asking people 'what they are seeking for the
future and how they are prepared to help. Make them partners along
the way. Harness their ideas and energy.'

Invest in Long-Term Policy for Economic Growth

Denmark is a wealthy country, and over the past decades its economy
has grown just as fast as comparable countries. Yet Denmark has shown
us that economic growth does not have to rely on increased energy consumption – in fact, growth can be accompanied by huge reductions in
emissions. Denmark's experience suggests that it may just be possible to
be wealthy *and* save the planet.

Much of Denmark's success can be attributed to the policy certainty
that has provided companies with the confidence to invest in technologies to produce cleaner forms of energy and reduce carbon emissions.
Given the scale of investment required, and the long lifetimes of electricity generators and other infrastructure, companies are more likely to
invest when they have the confidence of long-term, bipartisan-supported
energy agreements.

Denmark has also been smart in its methods to raise revenue. It has
not relied solely on Europe's imperfect (but vastly improving) emissions
trading scheme to fund its success. Instead, Denmark has a long history
of taxing energy in order to reduce consumption. It has also been prepared to directly subsidise renewables and require energy companies to
invest in energy efficiency.

Serious responses to climate change require a major shift in global
investment patterns towards green infrastructure, such as renewable
energy, energy efficiency and sustainable transport. It's critical that adequate finance is available to enable this shift. In the long term, clear and

predictable policy frameworks will encourage private investment in low-carbon, climate-resilient options.[53] But unless and until the private sector is investing sufficiently, government needs to lead the way through scaled-up public funding and financial mechanisms. The Danish government partnered with pension funds and other institutional investors to establish the Danish Climate Investment Fund, which provides funding for renewable energy projects in developing countries. Another example is Australia's Clean Energy Finance Corporation, a government-owned 'green bank' that invests in clean-energy projects it deems commercially viable. It aims to deliver a positive return for taxpayers while investing in renewable energy technology.

Encourage More Sustainable Towns and Cities

Every year the world's population is continuing to urbanise. Most people across the globe now live in cities. Denmark has shown the power of municipal governments and councils working within effective national policy to develop attractive, liveable places that are also sustainable. With well-planned and effective transport systems, building regulations and urban planning, cities such as Copenhagen are exemplars of Denmark's success. Cities around the world are taking inspiration from Copenhagen. Melbourne is building 'Copenhagen-style' bicycle lanes on its road network, consultants from Copenhagen are helping to design a cycle network in Kazakhstan, and New York is developing new approaches to becoming more resilient to extreme weather, inspired by Copenhagen's 'climate adapted neighbourhoods'.[54]

Cities and towns are ideal environments for innovative sustainability measures that can make a difference to the entire population. Responses to climate change are often more effective when they are considered along with related issues – such as economic development, employment, and access to clean water, sanitation and healthcare – and policy is formulated to address multiple systemic challenges together.[55]

Leadership Matters

The experience of Samsø Island is instructive. This small rural community has shown that with leadership and commitment, climate change is a challenge that we can take on. It has inspired community efforts across the world, such as Hepburn Wind, a community-owned wind farm in Australia, and Sust`ainable Molokai, a community-based sustainable energy group in Hawaii.

Part of the success of the Samsø model is due to Søren Hermansen's passion and charisma. He helped to negotiate community resolutions to the issues with wind farms. Today, he promotes the island widely on the international stage. He spends almost a third of each year travelling and speaking with groups all over the world about Samsø's shift to renewable energy. He also has big plans to take the Samsø model global. It is testament to the impact that one committed individual can have on not just their own community but the world. 'I think you can find people like me everywhere, who just need a little help to do a lot of work,' he says.

Hermansen's roots will remain on Samsø Island, though. He wants to be there to help the island to achieve its next goal: complete independence from fossil fuels by 2030, twenty years ahead of the rest of Denmark. 'We plan to get rid of oil completely by 2030,' Hermansen says. 'This is very ambitious too, because we still have tractors.'

As a step towards this goal, the Samsø municipality recently bought a large new ferry, capable of transporting 600 passengers and 140 cars. In a first for Denmark, it has a dual-fuel engine, which makes it possible to run on liquefied natural gas rather than heavy fuel oil, reducing carbon emissions significantly. However, it can also run on locally produced biogas.[56] It's quite possible that if you visit Samsø in future, you'll arrive on a ferry powered by methane produced from household waste or pig manure. And you may even run into Søren Hermansen, with his mischievous smile.

FIVE THINGS
WE CAN DO NOW

1. **Put a price on carbon.** This is the most powerful way to reduce greenhouse gas emissions while keeping costs low. A price on carbon means that responsibility for the damage wrought by carbon emissions rests with those responsible for them. Polluters can then decide whether to act to reduce emissions or continue to pollute and pay for the privilege. Because it is a market-based mechanism, it drives technological innovation and changes behaviour. There are differing views on the best way to price carbon: a *carbon tax* sets a defined tax rate on carbon emissions, whereas an *emissions trading scheme* (sometimes known as a cap-and-trade scheme) caps the total emissions allowed in an economy, and creates a market for permits to emit greenhouse gases.

2. **Promote energy efficiency.** Greater energy efficiency reduces emissions, improves economic productivity and saves consumers money. Even with a price on carbon, people don't always respond to price signals. This could be due to imperfect information (e.g. not knowing how much energy an appliance will use when it is purchased) or principal-agent problems (e.g. a landlord having no incentive to insulate a rental property). Energy efficiency policies – such as mandatory labelling or minimum green standards in residential properties – can achieve reductions in emissions at an extremely low cost and are complementary to a carbon price.

3. **Stop subsidising fossil fuels.** Governments around the world – including wealthy countries in the OECD – spend hundreds of billions of dollars each year subsidising the production and consumption of fossil fuels such as petroleum and natural gas. This directs investment towards carbon-intensive sectors, wasting public funds that could be put to better use. If we're serious about addressing climate change, these subsidies need to stop.

4. **Provide incentives for renewable energy.** Renewable energy incentives such as feed-in tariffs or national targets are important to bring down technology costs and hence the long-term cost of decarbonisation. Some economists argue that when there is a price on carbon, renewable energy incentives distort the market. However, emissions trading schemes in most jurisdictions are far from perfect, and most experts believe that renewable energy incentives are needed even when carbon is priced.

5. **Encourage low-impact methods of transport.** City and local governments are critical in driving change through transport systems, building regulations and urban planning. Cycling has become synonymous with Copenhagen, which has overtaken the Netherlands' Amsterdam and Utrecht as the world's top cycling city. Any community, especially those with a flat topography, can encourage cycling through investment in infrastructure such as dedicated bicycle lanes. Investing in better planned, high-functioning rail, train and bus services will also help to reduce a city's carbon footprint.

2

EDUCATION NATION

How to Better Educate Our Youth

Just fifty years ago, Singapore was an impoverished tropical island with no natural resources, little fresh water and rapid population growth. Its GDP per capita was lower than that of South American countries Chile and Ecuador. Licking its wounds after Japanese occupation during World War II and an ill-fated period as part of Malaysia, Singapore had no compulsory education and only a small number of high-school graduates.[1] With few skilled workers, Singapore faced significant unemployment and a severe housing shortage.

However, in these inauspicious beginnings were the foundations that Singapore built on to achieve the best educational outcomes in the world.

Professor Saravanan Gopinathan's life parallels the story of modern Singapore. Born to migrant parents during the Japanese occupation, Gopinathan went on to become a dominant figure in Singapore's education system, serving for long periods as dean of the School of Education and dean of Initial Teacher Training, and employing new research to revolutionise the way education is delivered. Now an adjunct professor at the Lee Kuan Yew School of Public Policy, he has advised governments around the world. Despite his high profile, when I approach him for an interview he accepts my request enthusiastically, and sends materials for me to read before we meet. In our phone conversation, he is full of spark, keen to help me understand the journey Singapore has been on.

'The question for post-colonial Singapore was: how could it be viable and credible?' Gopinathan says. 'What could it do to become a nation-state, given that it was small, had no natural resources and had a Chinese population which was viewed with suspicion?'

In the mid-1960s, Singapore, no longer part of Malaysia and with only a small domestic market, sought to shift its economic development strategy away from its role as a trading post and towards the development of an export-oriented manufacturing sector. But to achieve this, the country needed a workforce that was literate and trained.[2]

'This explains the emphasis on education, human capital development, making sure that every child has an opportunity to go to school,' Gopinathan says. 'Because otherwise, we would have nothing.'

Gopinathan was fortunate to study at an English-language school, and he attributes this to much of his subsequent success. 'The social mobility that was available to my family was in part due to an English-speaking education.'

Singapore is a multi-ethnic nation. Today, ethnic Chinese make up about 76 per cent of the population; Malays, 15 per cent; and ethnic Indians, 7.5 per cent.[3] As a consequence, the major languages spoken in Singapore include English, Mandarin, other Chinese dialects, Malay and Tamil.[4] To accommodate this diversity, the government decided several decades ago that English would be the language of instruction, with students also required to study their mother tongue. Over time, this decision has revealed itself to be fortuitous, allowing Singapore to serve as a global business hub in the heart of Asia.

Singapore's ethnic diversity has had other impacts, too. It has led to an intense focus on meritocracy – the belief that people should obtain success or power due to their abilities, not their money or social position.

'Meritocracy is important as a concept because Singapore left Malaysia in 1965 in part because of ethnic affirmative action,' Gopinathan says. The constitution of Malaysia provides ethnic Malays a 'special position' safeguarded with quotas.[5] 'The Singaporean government said no, we can't go down the route of affirmative action. We can't privilege somebody because they say, "I'm poor because I'm Malay" or "I'm poor because I'm Chinese."'

This decision in the formative stages of modern Singapore's history laid the foundation for an incredible success story. Over just fifty years, Singapore managed to transition from a tiny, third-world island to a wealthy, business-friendly city-state with a high degree of urbanisation and a strong focus on education. Singaporean students now achieve some of the best results in the world, supported by the nation's almost entirely government-run school system. Singapore is near the top of the international education rankings on just about every metric, including reading, science, mathematics and collaborative problem-solving. The average fifteen-year-old reads at a standard a year and a half ahead of their Australian counterparts, and has a skill level in maths three years ahead of students in the United States.[6]

How has Singapore done it?

A gleaming, modern city, Singapore is home to five and a half million people. That's a slightly larger population than Finland or Norway, but squeezed into an area half the size of Greater London, or two-thirds the size of New York City. A South-East Asian finance and trading hub, it is now one of the richest countries in the world, with a GDP per capita higher than Australia or the United States. The World Economic Forum ranks Singapore the most competitive country in the world, with policy settings that are likely to lead to continued high economic growth.[7] According to US-based think tank The Heritage Foundation, it provides among the most economic freedoms in the world (second only to Hong Kong), with labour, capital and goods able to move freely without government intervention. Transparency International rates Singapore as the third-least-corrupt nation in the world, behind Denmark and New Zealand, and the World Bank ranks Singapore second, after New Zealand, for ease of doing business.[8]

Tax revenue accounts for just 14.1 per cent of GDP, which is about half the rate of countries such as the United States (24.3 per cent), Australia (28.5 per cent) and the United Kingdom (33.5 per cent). Yet when other non-tax revenue is also factored in, such as profits from government-owned enterprises, the difference is not as stark, with the Singaporean government generating revenue equivalent to 23.3 per cent of GDP.[9] Tax rates might be low, but given Singapore's significant wealth, the government actually generates more revenue per person than Australia.[10]

While Singapore is a low-taxing free market country, government plays a huge role. The public sector is used as both an investor and a catalyst for economic development and innovation. 'Government-linked corporations' are found in sectors such as shipbuilding, air transport and development banking; companies such as Singapore Airlines and Singtel owe their success to the role of government funding. Temasek, the state-owned investment fund, had revenue equal to US$75 billion in 2016, or more than 18 per cent of Singapore's GDP that year.[11] Over 80 per cent of Singaporeans live in public housing,[12] and the government more or less runs all of Singapore's schools. (Government involvement does not mean a strong democracy, though. With a political system dominated by one party since 1959, the Economist Intelligence Unit Democracy Index considers Singapore a 'flawed democracy': it scores highly for government functioning but poorly on 'electoral process and pluralism'.[13]

Education in Singapore is well funded, with US$109,060 spent on the education of each child between the ages of six and fifteen. Although less than countries such as Austria, Norway and the United States, Singapore's education expenditure on students of this age is 2 per cent more than Australia, 11 per cent more than Germany and 13 per cent more than Canada.[14]

At the age of seven, Singaporean students begin six years of primary school. There are formal exams from the second grade. After the fourth-grade examinations, students are streamed according to ability into 'subject-based bands', where they take subjects at different levels based on their scores. At the end of primary school, at the age of eleven or twelve, students undertake the high-stakes Primary School Leaving Examination (PSLE), a national test administered by the education ministry. The results determine which of three high-school streams a student will participate in: the 'express' stream, the 'normal' stream or the 'technical' stream. This influences the chances of a student going on to university or to an institute of technical education. As all high schools are effectively selective, the best schools choose the students with the highest PSLE results. There is no right to attend the local high school.

Honorary professor David Hogan brings a uniquely informed outsider's perspective to Singapore's education system. An Australian based at the University of Queensland's School of Education, Hogan was invited to Singapore back in 2004 to review a research proposal. After that, 'they kept on asking me to go back and do more work'. He ultimately spent six years in Singapore at the National Institute of Education, including time as dean of the Office of Education Research. He tells me that what stands out most about Singapore is the importance placed on education. This view is shared by pretty much everyone – students, teachers and policy-makers. He observes, 'Parents are deeply committed to a kind of highly motivated system of exams and assessments and getting ahead that way. And the system rewards people. They do get ahead.'

To parents in some countries, the focus on stressful, high-stakes examinations may sound unnecessarily cruel. Yet in some respects it is not dissimilar to the systems found in other countries. In Germany, students are streamed into one of three different types of high school based on primary-school academic performance and student attributes. In Australia, tens of thousands of primary-school students each year sit examinations for entry into selective high schools or accelerated learning programs.[15]

And such examinations and streams are only part of the reason for Singapore's success. Globally, recent evidence seems to suggest that streaming has only a small positive impact for higher-achieving students, while it has a small negative impact for low- and mid-range-achieving learners.[16] In fact, as will be explored later in this chapter, Singapore has recently begun to move in a different direction. The long-term structural factors underlying Singapore's results are a deep cultural commitment to education, investment in quality teaching, and a systematic and rigorous approach to the administration of the education system.

No one can argue that what Singapore is doing isn't working. Every three years, the OECD's Program for International Student Assessment (PISA) measures the ability of fifteen-year-olds to apply their knowledge in real-life situations. It's a complex test that requires creative and critical thinking. Singapore has consistently topped the rankings in reading, mathematics and science, although in 2018 it was surpassed by the collective results of the Chinese cities of Beijing, Shanghai, Jiangsu and Zhejiang. In maths, Singapore scores 569, while Anglo countries such as Australia (491), the United Kingdom (502) and the United States (478)

PISA Scores, Maths and Literacy, 2018

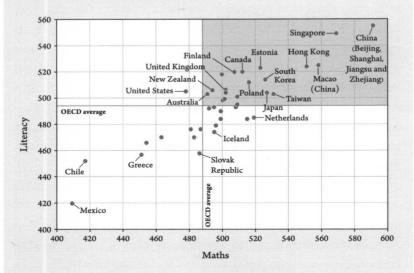

Figure 3. Singapore streaks ahead in student performance, with their students years ahead of those in countries such as Australia, the United Kingdom and the United States.

are far down the list. The average Singaporean teenager is roughly three years ahead of their American peers in maths. In reading, Singapore scores 549, well ahead of Estonia (523), the highest-performing country in the OECD. The average Singaporean student is about two years ahead of their peers in the OECD when it comes to literacy.[17]

More than 49 per cent of Singaporean students are among the top performers globally in reading, mathematics or science. No other country comes close. For comparison, the rate in Finland is 21 per cent, Canada is 24.1 per cent and Australia is 18.9 per cent.[18] Sixty per cent of young adults (aged twenty-six to thirty-five) in Singapore have achieved a better level of education than their parents. This rate is higher than any country in the OECD, and the highest of any country surveyed.[19]

And if you think that education in Singapore might be all about rote learning, note that Singaporean students also perform higher than students in any other country in 'collaborative problem solving', which is

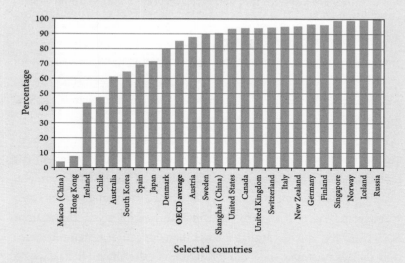

Percentage of Students in Government Schools

Figure 4. Singapore is a good-news story for government schools. A strong, well-funded public education sector can lead to remarkable results.

measured by students' ability to work with two or more people to try to solve a problem.[20] Singapore's education system places great emphasis on collaboration, both in and out of the classroom. It incorporates co-curricular activities such as spelling bees, school plays, writing competitions and chess clubs, as well as group project work and applied learning programs, where students put the knowledge they have learnt in the classroom to use in practical situations. As the OECD's director for education and skills, Andreas Schleicher, notes, Singapore demonstrates that 'strong academic performance does not have to come at the expense of weaker social skills'.[21]

Singapore's performance in education is a central pillar of its national development agenda. 'One of the reasons Singapore does so well economically is that it's able to signal to investors that it's got a really high-quality labour force,' Hogan says. 'Singapore doesn't have natural resources, it can't farm, it can't dig gold out of the ground, so it invests heavily in human capital. The government emphasises it, the community supports it, and they want a system that will give everyone a shot at doing well.'

A Government School System

Singapore's success is fundamentally a story of its government school system. As Figure 4 shows, 98.5 per cent of Singaporean students are enrolled in public schools.[22] The small number of private schools in Singapore generally admit expatriate students rather than locals.

By contrast, only 61 per cent of Australians are enrolled in government schools, with large numbers attending Catholic or independent private schools, which charge annual fees of up to US$28,000 per student.

Singapore's system of exams can be brutal, stratifying students into winners and losers at an early age. Yet at its heart is a genuine attempt at meritocracy, and it is arguably fairer than education systems in countries such as Australia, the United Kingdom or the United States, which effectively stratify students into different types of schools, colleges or universities based on their family's ability to pay. The Singaporean notion is that whether you are rich or poor, or whether you are ethnic Chinese, Malay or Indian, the state will support you, and you have a chance to 'make it'.

'The government will commit itself to providing the basic social infrastructure that you need to get ahead in Singapore,' Saravanan Gopinathan says. 'But the rest is up to you. So you have got to be able to put in the effort. The family has got to be able to put in the effort, and the examinations will show who has managed to meet the requirements of the system.'

Singapore's lack of investment in private schools is sensible, and consistent with the evidence of student performance from across the globe. After analysing results from countries that take part in the PISA assessment, the OECD concluded that 'there is no evidence to suggest that private schools help to raise the level of performance of the school system as a whole' and that 'countries with a larger share of private schools do not perform better in PISA'.[23]

Similarly, many parents are told that smaller class sizes better facilitate learning, but class sizes in Singapore are among the largest in the world. The average class size in lower secondary school is 35.5 students. This compares with an average of 17.8 students in Finland, 23.9 students in England, 24.7 students in Australia and 27 in the United States.[24]

'In Singapore they do have much larger classes,' David Hogan says. 'However, teachers have a lighter teaching load than Australian teachers. Australian teachers have smaller classes but more classes.'

Although Singaporean teachers are some of the hardest-working in the world, with an average of forty-eight hours per week, they spend just seventeen hours in the classroom. By contrast, Australian teachers spend 18.6 hours, English teachers are in front of the blackboard (or whiteboard) for 19.6 hours, and American teachers spend a whopping 26.8 hours in the classroom, more than in any other country.[25]

The evidence on optimal class size is mixed, and leads to a nuanced debate. In a review of the evidence, the Melbourne Graduate School of Education concluded that a reduction in class size in isolation 'has little effect on student academic performance'. There is some evidence that students – particularly in 'the early primary years, and those who have unsatisfactory results, language background other than English, or low socioeconomic backgrounds' – learn better in smaller classes. But in order to increase student performance across the board in smaller classes, different teaching methods are needed. There is little research on how to instruct teachers to adapt their teaching practice for smaller class settings.[26]

Rather than invest large sums of money to reduce class sizes – which would yield an uncertain outcome – Singapore has instead opted to focus its investment on teaching. 'Good teachers are a much more important factor,' one Singaporean education expert tells me. 'If we have a very good teacher, that will be much more helpful to all the students in the class than reducing the class size by, say, one or two students.' Or even, potentially, ten or more.

Investment in Teachers

Singapore's educational success has been achieved by investing in a quality teaching force, and by raising the prestige and status of teaching to attract the best graduates.

Associate Professor Ng Pak Tee is the author of the book *Learning from Singapore*. Speaking to me via Skype from his office at Nanyang Technological University, Ng explains that Singapore is recruiting from the top one-third of its secondary-school graduates: 'We are hiring very, very good people into our system, and it seems to be working.'

Ng initially started his career as a teacher. As a young man he obtained a scholarship to the University of Cambridge to study mathematics, and 'returned as a maths teacher'. He went on to become an official in the Ministry of Education, and for the last nineteen or so years he's been at the National Institute of Education.

'One of my main jobs is the training and development of school leaders,' Ng says. To date, he has trained more than half of Singapore's school principals. By the time he retires, it's possible he will have trained every principal in Singapore.

On average, only one out of every eight students who applies is accepted into the teaching program, after passing through a gruelling assessment process.[27] 'When we choose people, we are not choosing based on qualifications,' Ng says. 'There's a certain baseline, but once we have a small pool of people that we're looking at, we no longer look at qualifications. We are looking for people who genuinely have a love for teaching, have a love for young people, and an aptitude for the profession.'

In most countries, students apply for a teaching position after graduating, and only then enter employment. However, in Singapore, teachers are employed as civil servants from the moment they commence their training. During their study, they receive a salary and all the benefits accorded to civil servants, including paid annual leave, and medical and insurance cover. Following their training, they are guaranteed a job.[28] These advantages lead to a higher standard of applicants and a higher rate of retention.

Singaporean primary and secondary teachers with ten to twenty years of experience are paid about US$55,000. This is not the highest rate in the world, but it is above the median Singaporean salary,[29] and above the OECD average for teachers.

Once in the workforce, teachers are also supported with ample professional development. Almost all participate in team-based learning, classroom observation and feedback exercises, as well as receiving mentoring from more-experienced 'master teachers'.[30] Each individual teacher is entitled to up to 100 hours of professional development per year. This can involve undertaking courses at the National Institute of Education, school-based development or even going overseas to examine aspects of education systems and pedagogy in other countries.[31] 'They've really improved the nature and the quality of professional development,' David Hogan says. 'The system really wants to reward merit and not promote people out of pathways where they are exceptionally good. So, it's really smart about keeping good teachers in the system.'

Performance is appraised each year, with outstanding teachers receiving bonuses. After three years, teachers are assessed to determine whether they have potential to pursue a career as a master teacher, school leader or specialist, each of which comes with an increase in salary. Master teachers mentor new teachers for several years and focus on classroom skills. Teachers with leadership potential are moved to middle management and assessed for their potential to become an assistant principal or, later, a principal. The specialist track supports teachers to develop deep knowledge and skills in a specific discipline. These teachers may develop curriculum, set course lists or potentially write examinations for the Ministry of Education.[32]

Announcing this career structure in 2001, the then Minister for Education, Teo Chee Hean, emphasised the 'need to ensure teaching remains an attractive career choice'. The system would provide teachers with a 'challenging and enriching career with paths that cater to the different talents, abilities and aspirations'.[33] It appears to be working.

One unique feature of Singapore's education system, which this focus on career pathways shows, is an extremely close alignment between the key leaders of the education ministry, the National Institute of Education and individual schools, who share responsibility and accountability for teacher training and student performance. This is made possible by the fact that almost all students go to schools in the one government system. Hogan says that no education policy is announced 'without a plan for building the capacity to meet it'. This contrasts with other countries, where reform priorities are not supported by teacher training, or are not consistently applied in schools.[34]

'One of the big reasons for Singapore's success is the very high quality of the leadership by the senior managers in the system and all the way down through the middle ranks of the bureaucracy,' Hogan comments. 'They have a very clear view about what's important, and they have a very good understanding about what they need to do. And the curriculum, the pedagogy, the teaching, the staff development, are all well aligned.'

Many education systems struggle to find the balance between centralised direction and autonomy for schools. Ng says that Singapore is 'both highly centralised and highly decentralised at the same time'.

The Ministry of Education summarises this approach with the slogan 'tight-loose-tight'. The first 'tight' is a reference to 'the key, non-negotiable objectives of the education system, the reason why education is funded and is so important,' Saravanan Gopinathan explains. The last 'tight' relates to outcomes. 'That has largely been the examinations that we have had, because they become the indicators of both system performance and individual student performance.' And in between there is the 'loose', which means that schools can have a degree of autonomy in developing their curriculums and teaching methods. 'They can run enrichment classes; they can run remedial classes. They can work the timetable according to cohort characteristics. So, it is at the individual school level that the autonomy part comes into play.'

To make this work effectively, there's an intriguing cultural aspect to school leadership. 'A principal in Singapore has two identities,' Ng says. 'One, you are indeed the leader of a local school, so you work with all of your teachers, parents and students. Two, you are also a national leader. That is to say you are, together with other principals, a fraternity of leaders for our system.' Clusters of ten to fourteen schools are led by a superintendent. Every month, principals in each cluster gather together, providing an opportunity to discuss challenges, brainstorm solutions and collaborate.[35] As Singapore has 'one united system', Ng says that 'what one does in one school actually has an effect on other schools. Teachers, educators, school leaders, we are all nation-builders.'

Learning from Around the World

As a young, small, business-oriented nation in one of the world's most strategic locations, Singapore is inherently international in its outlook. The Malaysian city of Johor Bahru is just 1 kilometre away from Singapore's shores, across the Straits of Johor; the country has no domestic flights, so every flight to and from Changi Airport is international; and 45 per cent of the population was born overseas.[36] In Singapore, it is almost impossible *not* to engage internationally.

That is a perspective it brings to its education system, too. 'Singapore basically says, "We will learn from the world,"' Saravanan Gopinathan says. 'But we are confident that we will need to learn how to adapt things for our needs. So it's not copying, it's not borrowing. It's a process of internalising, learning, adapting.' In recent years, Singapore has drawn from the experiences of Australia, the United Kingdom, Hong Kong and the United States to inform the development of its early childhood education and care system.[37]

David Hogan says that in Singapore, 'anyone who is a manager or above will travel overseas at least two or three times a year, and at a senior level, four to five times a year, to go and see what's going on' in education around the world. This is usually not just a quick visit, but several days or weeks spent exploring initiatives in classrooms. 'So they are really focused on learning and adapting initiatives that would work in the Singapore context.' School principals who have served for at least six years are eligible to take one-year sabbaticals on full pay. This allows them to make international study visits, conduct research, write books or undertake further training. The Building Educational Bridges program, which is run by the National Institute of Education together with counterparts in the United Kingdom and Denmark, also offers school leaders the opportunity to spend two weeks exploring 'key leadership issues in national and international contexts'.[38]

Evidence-based policymaking underpins Singapore's approach to education, and substantial national investment is made in educational research. Reforms are tested and outcomes are carefully monitored. The Office of Education Research – which Hogan previously led – has a significant pool of grant funds for researchers in the Ministry of Education, the National Institute of Education and universities. Hogan says that when he was there, the research budget was 'about $150 million' (US$110 million). This approach to evidence-based policy was partially a function of 'outstanding leadership and management from the minister on down'. 'They are really informed,' Hogan says. 'They are willing to learn, they are highly strategic, they invest money – lots of money – in research and in strategic learning and adaptation.'

Singapore's educational research covers an enormous field – from teacher training to better support students on the autism spectrum through to engaging students via social media. A recent study undertaken in collaboration with schools looked at how to encourage a reading culture within individual school communities. This led to incremental changes, such as the way books are displayed in school libraries, and new methods to encourage students and teachers to recommend books to other students. Another research project tested the potential of software that allows students to work collaboratively to create 3D models from sketches. By allowing students to immerse themselves in a game-based virtual world, they learn 'by exploring, collaborating, being, building, championing and expressing'.[39]

There have been enormous improvements in educational outcomes across the world in the last few decades. The World Bank reports that the global youth literacy rate has increased from 77.6 per cent in 1976 to 91.4 per cent in 2016. Over the same period, the adult literacy rate has increased from 68.9 per cent to 86.2 per cent.[40]

But challenges remain. Across the world, there are still 750 million children and adults who cannot read and write. This effectively excludes them from full participation in their communities and societies. Even in the wealthy countries of the OECD, more than 20 per cent of fifteen-year-olds do not obtain the baseline level of proficiency in reading, maths and science to equip them to participate in modern life.[41]

Education is important for so many reasons. It reduces poverty. It increases productivity. It leads to improved health outcomes. The United Nations considers there to be a clear link between education and child and maternal health. Girls who have a basic education (primary and lower

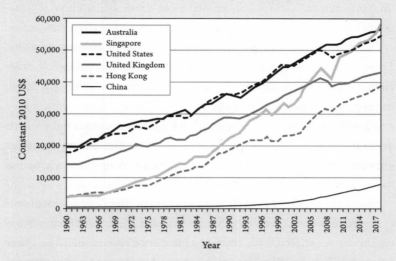

GDP Per Capita in Selected OECD Countries

Figure 5. Singapore's GDP per capita has skyrocketed to overtake the GDP of Australia and the United States.

secondary school) or higher are more likely to have smaller families, to provide better care for their children and to send them to school. Studies show that a one-year increase in a mother's education is associated with a 7 to 9 per cent decrease in mortality for children under five.[42]

Education is central to the economic development of nations, too. Because knowledge has become key to economic competitiveness, the wealth of a nation is vested in its people.

In Figure 5, you can see that in 1965, GDP per capita in Australia and the United States was *five times* greater than that of Singapore. Twenty years later, in 1985, Singapore's GDP per capita was only half that of those two countries. Today, Singapore's GDP per capita has overtaken both, and is among the highest in the world.

Hong Kong's growth has followed a similar, although not quite as spectacular, trajectory. China's growth may have started from further behind, but China today is more than thirteen times richer than it was in 1985. Education has been central to the economic development strategies of these East Asian countries, and by simple extrapolation, it's not hard to imagine a future in which billions of people in Asia enjoy a level of prosperity that far exceeds that of their counterparts in the Anglo countries.

To maximise the productive potential of a nation, it is important for governments to support the education of all citizens. This applies especially to low-income earners, who may under-invest in their education, meaning the country does not benefit from the productive efforts they might otherwise have contributed. The OECD argues that there is 'evidence for human capital as a channel through which inequality may affect growth'. Therefore, it is vital 'to promote equality of opportunity in access to and quality of education'.[43]

Conversely, one of the best ways to improve overall educational outcomes is to reduce inequality. Across the OECD, income inequality is negatively associated with average educational attainment.[44] In other words, where there is less inequality, the average student has more years of schooling. Whether to improve health or to generate wealth, countries that wish to prosper in the remaining years of the twenty-first century will need to focus on education.

While Singapore is achieving the best education outcomes in the world, it continues to grapple with some issues.

The focus on meritocracy has created a high-pressure environment for students. Subject to regular exams, with the outcomes shaping long-term opportunities and even life trajectories, Singaporean students report significant levels of stress. An alarming 76.3 per cent report feeling very anxious even if well prepared for a test, and 59.9 per cent report getting 'very tense' when they study. Such reported anxiety levels are far higher than any country in the OECD.[45]

David Hogan recalls meeting with a group of teachers who lamented, 'We've robbed our children of their childhood. They don't have a childhood. They just work, they go to school, they come home, they have after-class school with tutors at different times, and they just prep for exams.'

Not everyone feels the same on this. A former colleague of mine in the Victorian Public Service, Chirag Agarwal, grew up in Singapore and completed his schooling there before migrating to Australia. Over coffee, he reflects that while the system has its drawbacks, he believes it provides students with the motivation to succeed. 'If you do well, you can get into a good school, you can get in the express stream, you can get to a good junior college and pick subjects you want to study, you can get to a university and pursue a degree in line with your career aspirations,' he says. 'There's always some carrot that you're able to strive for and achieve by sheer hard work, regardless of your background.'

Yet Argarwal – who finished school in 2005 – admits that the system does shape the way students interact with one another, and there is not always enough value placed on non-academic achievements. 'There was a certain way we viewed people who did not do well in exams, were not in the express stream or did not go to university,' he says. 'When we heard someone was going to a polytechnic (rather than to junior college), we would just imagine that this person didn't do well in their O Level examination and was not interested in studying. There is an unfair judgement and an unnecessary stigma attached to going down an alternative education pathway.'

The focus on exams impacts on teachers, too. Hogan tells me that 'teachers have to basically make a decision between whether they are going to be a responsible teacher – which is to prepare the kids for the system that exists in Singapore and encourage their students to do well in that system – or do the kind of teaching that they think is the most beneficial for the students in a broader sense, across a broader range of learning outcomes.'

Saravanan Gopinathan agrees, confessing that 'the flip side of meritocracy is that the system becomes very much a preparation for testing'. Teachers know that they will be highly regarded in the school community if their students perform well in the national examinations. So they teach for the test.

Singapore's dedication to meritocracy makes life particularly difficult for children with special needs. While those who require intensive learning assistance typically attend a special education school, as in other OECD countries, students with mild special learning needs attend mainstream schools. Those who designed the education system have introduced measures to try to ensure such students are not disadvantaged. Students with special needs can receive support through tailored programs, and have access to specifically trained teachers. Schools run dyslexia remediation programs to help with literacy and numeracy. When sitting exams, students can also apply for special access arrangements such as extra time.[46]

Singapore is acutely aware that the strong focus on meritocracy can mean some students get left behind, Ng Pak Tee says. It has opened 'many other educational pathways so that children can always find success in their own ways, based on their own different aptitudes' and has provided additional resources to support them. For example, over the past decade Singapore has opened specialised schools, such as the School of Arts and the School of Science and Technology. Rather than university, high-school graduates can choose to attend an institute of technical education to develop technical skills and knowledge relevant to industry, or a polytechnic to learn specific skills for the workplace.[47]

Because of the focus on exams, many parents enrol their children in tutoring and enrichment classes out of school hours. 'There's a lot of what you might call shadow education, private tuition, in order to prep,' Gopinathan says. This often begins early. Primary-school students attend, on average, more than three hours of private tuition per week, with 80 per cent receiving some form of tuition. Even in preschool, 40 per cent of Singaporean children receive private tuition, attending an average of two hours of tuition per week.[48]

All this means that Singaporean parents spend large sums of money on tuition. Half of Singaporean families with children enrolled in private tuition spend more than US$370 per month, and 17 per cent spend more than US$730 per month.[49] Considering that the bottom fifth of households earn about US$1470 per month,[50] and might have more than one child, it's easy to understand how this might exacerbate inequality. Only 20 per cent of families in the lowest income bracket have children enrolled in private tuition.

Compared with most countries, few children fall through the cracks in Singapore. Just 11.1 per cent of fifteen-year-olds fail to achieve the baseline level of proficiency in reading. This is as good as – or better than – the result achieved in Nordic countries such as Finland (11 per cent) and Norway (15 per cent). Anglo countries such as the United Kingdom (17.1 per cent), Australia (18 per cent) and the United States (18.9 per cent) do far worse.[51]

While hard work and talent ensure students get ahead in Singapore, those from disadvantaged backgrounds don't get ahead to the same extent. The OECD rates the Singaporean system as below average on equity, and the socioeconomic status of a student in Singapore is more likely to influence their educational outcomes that it is in many other countries. For example, a Singaporean student from a disadvantaged background is over four times less likely to obtain the baseline level of proficiency in science than someone who is not disadvantaged.[52] But while equity is clearly a challenge for Singapore, it needs to be discussed with nuance, because even the most disadvantaged students are achieving impressive results. More than 40 per cent of Singaporean students from a disadvantaged background finish in the top quarter of students globally. The most disadvantaged Singaporean teenagers are now achieving results in maths, reading and science on par with the *average* Australian student. And students attending a school in a low socioeconomic neighbourhood in Singapore achieve results in science similar to students attending the average school in the United States.[53]

The literature shows that early childhood education and care is perhaps the most important social policy intervention that governments can make. High-quality childcare predicts higher academic achievement at age fifteen, and has particular benefits for children who have a poor early-years home-learning environment.[54] Quality early childhood education and care environments have appropriate staff-to-child ratios, with carers qualified in early childhood education. This care is overseen by appropriate governance and regulation.[55] Long-term randomised control trials involving thousands of children have shown that all things being equal, students who participate in quality early childhood education go on to have lower criminality, reduced welfare participation and teen pregnancy, and higher incomes.[56]

Despite this evidence, Singapore has not invested heavily in early childhood education, and the programs it has are not integrated with the school system. 'I would argue we dropped the ball on that,' Gopinathan says. 'Public schooling starts from elementary. Even though every child in Singapore has a guaranteed place in a decent school, well-resourced by the ministry, they are not necessarily ready for the demanding curriculum in Grades One and Two.'

In 2017, Singapore's prime minister, Lee Hsien Loong, announced that spending on early childhood education and care would double over the following five years. In a relatively short period, Singapore is on track to double the number of early childhood places, mainly for children up to four years old. Centres will receive subsidies to deliver new early childhood education places, particularly in public housing developments. New government-run kindergartens are also being built across the island, with a third of the places reserved for children from lower-income households.[57]

'We are putting in a lot more resources to help build the early childhood sector,' Ng says. 'Now it's early childhood that we are paying attention to.'

What Singapore Can Teach the World

The culture and context in which Singapore has developed the world's best education system may not always translate directly to Anglo and European countries. However, there are a number of lessons that other countries could learn from Singapore's experience.

Value Teachers and the Work They Do

Teachers and teaching are at the heart of the Singaporean education system. According to Saravanan Gopinathan, the Singaporean government has the attitude, 'We want the best people to come into teaching, and we want to be able to keep them. We need to pay them well. We need to attend to their concerns and their issues in the system.'

While Singapore recruits teachers from among its top-performing students and provides intensive support during training, the system also shows the importance of supporting the ongoing development of teachers. Mentoring, team-based learning, classroom observation and feedback all play a critical role. With 100 hours of professional development available to each teacher every year, there is opportunity to participate in research, learn new approaches to delivering the curriculum and running the classroom, or even travel and learn from best practice overseas. A more informed, engaged and productive teaching force leads to better educational outcomes for students.

Government Schools Are Great

With almost all students attending government schools, Singapore shows that a well-resourced and well-led public school system can achieve the best results in the world.

Across the OECD, only about 11 per cent of primary students, 14 per cent of lower-secondary students and 19 per cent of upper-secondary students are enrolled in private schools. Most of these students are supported with some degree of government funding. In fact, 90 per cent of funding for schools in the OECD comes from government. In many Nordic and Northern European countries, this figure is close to 100 per cent, while in countries such as Turkey, Australia, Mexico and New Zealand, it is a little lower, with up to 20 per cent of funding for schooling coming from private sources.[58]

Within the OECD, students who attend private schools do tend to achieve better educational outcomes, but this is likely almost entirely due to these students coming from higher socioeconomic backgrounds. Students in public schools with a similar socioeconomic status to those in private schools do equally well. Overall, countries with more private schools do not achieve better educational outcomes.[59]

It often seems that, no matter the country, education budgets are subject to slashes in straightened economic times, or fall on the chopping block when there is a need to find government savings. With more funding for school education than almost any other country in the world, one of the most valuable lessons Singapore offers is that the education budget is not the place to look for savings. Educational outcomes might seem intangible, but high-quality education ultimately leads to a stronger workforce, economy and society.

Use Assessment Meaningfully

Singapore's focus on exams ensures a strong alignment between government policy, schools and student outcomes. 'One of the things that I learnt in Singapore was that the assessment system does drive improvements in learning and achievement,' David Hogan says.

Many countries already collect data from student assessments. Australia, for example, requires students to sit formal exams every two years for the National Assessment Program – Literacy and Numeracy (NAPLAN). In most places, the problem is not the availability of data. As Australian educational expert Professor John Hattie has written, what is needed is better handling of the data – the ability to use it to make evaluative judgements. Frequent assessments of student progress through exams and tests can help teachers to understand learning needs and enable them to adjust their classroom methods appropriately. Research suggests that this practice, known as 'formative assessment', is an extremely effective means of raising student achievement. And helping teachers to adapt their teaching to diverse student needs is also an effective way of improving equity in education.[60]

Change Policy Sparingly

Educators in Singapore have the advantage of being able to assess their teaching, schools and curriculum in the context of a relatively stable policy environment. Education policy takes time to have an effect, and frequent policy shifts can be harmful. 'Because we have had fifty years, effectively, of the same government, we can afford to take a long-term view,' says Gopinathan. 'If you think about it, you start at Grade One, you're going to see the results of some policy shift in six years, at the Primary School Leaving Examinations, and ten years later at all the levels. But if you have two changes of leadership in that period, with different ideas, then teachers are basically going to be saying, "Well, you know, we'll wait for the next guy to come along because it may be something different again."'

The consistency of education policy in Singapore stands in stark contrast to the policy shifts in countries such as the United Kingdom. Over decades, such shifts have been the cause of periodic 'education crises', including problems in the delivery of national exams for primary-school students, changes to A Levels (subject-based qualifications required for entry into university) and issues with school funding that led to teachers being made redundant.[61]

Culture Matters

Singaporean culture values education enormously. 'The parents usually want their children to do very well in education,' Ng Pak Tee says. 'And education is seen as the pathway to a much better life.'

The OECD's Andreas Schleicher says that 'leaders in high-performing school systems have convinced their citizens to make choices that value education more than other things'. This begins outside the school environment. The challenge – definitely a long-term proposition for some countries – is to convince parents and grandparents to 'invest their time, energy and money into the education of their children, their future'.

Parental involvement in learning is a crucial reason for Singapore's success. The OECD tells us that greater parental involvement is 'strongly associated with children's socioemotional development, later reading proficiency and academic success, student engagement and enjoyment of reading, high school completion, as well as adaptation in society'. Involvement can mean participating in learning activities with children at home (including reading and supervising homework), being active in the school community and holding schools to account for their children's learning.[62]

Parental involvement can be supported by policy. For example, early childhood programs can encourage parents to read books to their children, and schools can take extra steps to engage parents from migrant or disadvantaged backgrounds who may otherwise be less likely to get involved in the school community due to social barriers.[63]

David Hogan says that in Singapore, 'there is a very broad cultural commitment to educational achievement across all population groups'. It is difficult to identify just how much of Singapore's success is due to the education system and how much is culture. Interestingly, Professor John Jerrim at University College London analysed the PISA data and found that children in Australia born to East Asian parents do as well as their counterparts in East Asia. They score second only to kids in Shanghai in the PISA rankings – outperforming their peers with Australian-born parents by about 100 test points. Why? Jerrim concluded that 'a combination of school selection, a high value placed upon education, substantial out-of-school tuition, hard work ethics, a belief that anyone can succeed with effort and high aspirations for the future all play an important, inter-linked role'.[64]

It's possible that in Western countries, changes to the education system alone may not be enough to catch up to the top-performing nations in East Asia. Jerrim suggests that 'this goal may only be achieved with widespread cultural change, where a hard work ethic and a strong belief in the value of education is displayed by all families and instilled in every child'. This is what Anglo and European countries should be working towards if they aim to become knowledge nations.

Keep Improving

In recent years, Singapore's education system has been going through a quiet revolution. With the confidence that comes from impressive outcomes, it has been gradually loosening some of its education policy settings.

Not rashly, though. In a very Singaporean way, the changes are considered, evidence-based and implemented thoughtfully, with a long-term perspective. 'Singapore doesn't do big-bang reform, really,' Saravanan Gopinathan says. 'Singapore does reform in an incremental sort of way. Singapore basically says, we've got something good, we tweak it, we monitor it, we change.'

Amendments announced recently will see far fewer exams in primary school, and school reports will no longer directly compare students with their peers. Bursaries are now being awarded to students with positive attitudes towards learning, not just those with the highest marks.[65]

And after forty years, Singapore is preparing to change one of the hallmarks of its system. From 2024, students will no longer be sorted into 'express', 'normal' or 'technical' streams at high school. Gopinathan explains that there has 'been a major educational shift' from streaming to 'subject-based banding'. This will see students take subjects at more advanced or lower levels, depending on their ability. These changes are being introduced partly in recognition that students learn at different paces in different subjects, and partly to reduce the stigma or self-limiting beliefs associated with studying in one of the lower streams. Subjects such as mathematics and science will be taught at three different levels.

After four years of secondary education, students will graduate with a common secondary-school certificate that lists the subjects taken and the band of each subject.[66]

The content of Singapore's curriculum is also changing, to focus on twenty-first-century competencies such as 'self-awareness' and 'responsible decision-making'. Exam questions have been reframed to become more open-ended, to encourage critical thinking. By 2023, all schools will have applied learning programs in subjects such as robotics, computing and electronics, but also in subjects such as drama and sport. The intent is that students develop practical, real-world skills, aligned closely with the emerging needs of industry.[67]

Singapore may now be dominating the education rankings, but it is not complacent. Policymakers are constantly asking whether things could be improved. 'This is a system that, even though it does well on a number of indicators, is still asking itself: how do we ensure balance between rigour and creativity, or autonomy and accountability?' Gopinathan says. 'How do we prepare for the future?'

FIVE THINGS WE CAN DO NOW

1. **Invest in early childhood education.** Quality early childhood education leads to better learning outcomes, particularly for children from disadvantaged backgrounds. Funding for universal kindergarten attendance is one of the most important social policy interventions governments can make. For countries such as the United States, Switzerland and Poland, which have not yet achieved this, the year before school is a good place to start on education reform. Other countries, such as Australia, Ireland and Austria, should focus on expanding the number of kindergarten places for three-year-olds.

2. **Encourage teacher learning and development.** Improving teaching is the best way to raise student performance. Evidence shows that a student with a great teacher can achieve in six months what a student with a poor teacher can achieve in a year. Schools can focus on improving the quality – not the quantity – of time teachers spend in the classroom. They can support teachers to learn and develop, including through mentoring, coaching and professional collaboration.

3. **Reward good teachers.** Given how important quality teaching is, we can support the best teachers to stay in the classroom (rather than making them feel that a move to school leadership or administration is the only option). We can create new categories of highly paid teachers whose role it is to coach others, build school expertise or develop deep knowledge in a specific discipline.

4. **Track student performance in nuanced ways.** Data drives performance and helps ensure there is alignment between government policy, teacher training and schools. It's important to look beyond headline literacy and numeracy figures to consider a range of nuanced data incorporating skills in collaborative problem-solving, levels of equity and student wellbeing.

5. **Learn from the best.** Support education department officials, principals and teachers to learn from the world's highest-performing education systems. Education departments could make funding available to enable leading teachers to travel to countries such as Singapore, Finland, Hong Kong and Canada, or to attend an international conference or short course.

3

PARTNERS IN CRIME

How to Prevent Harm from Violence

n the early 1980s, Jonathan Shepherd was a young doctor working in the Accident and Emergency Ward at Pinderfields Hospital in the former coal-mining heartlands of Yorkshire in north-east England. He was training to be an oral and maxillofacial surgeon – someone who operates on the mouth, jaw and face. This is the sort of surgeon you typically need if you've been a victim of violence.

Shepherd was seeing a steady stream of patients through Emergency, and the numbers only seemed to be increasing. He wondered what was going on. 'Oh, we always see more assault patients when there's a miner's strike,' an experienced colleague said casually. Seeking to prevent the closure of mines, local workers had begun to take industrial action. This would eventually lead to what was arguably the 'most bitter industrial dispute in British history',[1] involving 142,000 miners at its peak.

The passing observation piqued Shepherd's curiosity, and he began to pay greater attention to patients' stories. It seemed that a lot of the injuries were linked to just a few Yorkshire pubs and licensed premises.

Shepherd went on to complete a PhD investigating violence. He discovered that only a quarter of violent incidents that put people in emergency departments were reported to the police. So, he concluded that data from emergency departments was a source of 'unique intelligence about where violence is happening, times and days, weapons use and assailants'.

When I talk with Shepherd, he's just returned from his son's wedding in Scotland and is relaxed. He says that people don't report violent incidents because 'they are afraid of reprisals, they don't want their own conduct scrutinised by the police or they just think, "Well, what can the police do?"'

The emeritus professor has been studying violence prevention for thirty years, but his enthusiasm remains palpable. Now based at Cardiff University in Wales, he has published about 350 academic articles and has won the Stockholm Prize in Criminology – the equivalent of a Nobel Prize in his field.[2] His PhD findings have influenced approaches to crime prevention across the United Kingdom and around the world.

In 1996 Shepherd, by then a professor of oral and maxillofacial surgery, moved to Cardiff. There he called together police, local government officials, health agencies and national charity Victim Support, and offered a radical strategy: 'Look, it's clear that the police don't know about a whole lot of violence. Why don't we pool data from the emergency departments and from the police, and see if we can prevent, between us, more violence than is possible just using police data?'

That first meeting led to the establishment of the Cardiff Violence Prevention Board, which Shepherd went on to chair for 153 meetings over twenty years. Its work has led to changes in police patrol routes ('because cities are dynamic and hot spots of violence move as new clubs and pubs are opened'), the shutting down and limiting of hours for notorious licenced venues and the deployment of closed-circuit television cameras in places where violence is common. The data collected from hospital admissions indicates that a high proportion of assaults happen in the home, so it is also used by health and community services agencies to better support women who are experiencing domestic violence.

This approach – now known around the world as the Cardiff Model – quickly led to significant reductions in violence across the city. Monthly hospital admissions due to assaults fell from seven per 100,000 to five per 100,000, at the same time as similar UK cities – such as Birmingham, Leeds and Edinburgh – were experiencing increases.[3] The homicide rate in Cardiff fell from 1.8 per 100,000 to 1.2 per 100,000 in just four years.[4]

Another of Shepherd's PhD findings was that a remarkable 10 per cent of those who presented at hospital with injuries caused by violence were wounded by glass. Shepherd discovered that one type of glass – the 'nonik' pint glass, which has a bulge near the top – did most of the damage. After testing the breaking point of many different glasses in the lab at the Bristol Dental School, Shepherd and his team discovered that toughened glass was much more difficult to break. 'We then did a randomised trial,' he says, 'comparing toughened with non-toughened glass in fifty-seven pubs in the West Midlands and South Wales, and basically found that the chances of glass breakage and injury were 60 per cent less if the glass was toughened.'

Working with the Welsh Development Agency, Shepherd put together the 'face of Wales' campaign – the name a reference to the facial injuries caused by assaults with glass. After 'a lot of campaigning and advocacy, and talking to the trade', Shepherd was able to convince the hospitality industry that every pub in the UK should switch to toughened glass. An assessment conducted by the nation's Home Office later estimated that in the year following the switch, there were 40,000 fewer injuries.[5]

Shepherd's efforts have contributed to the UK's extraordinarily low crime rate. By one measure, the UK has the lowest homicide rate in the OECD. Violent crime has decreased dramatically and is now less than one-third of what it was twenty years ago. Most police don't carry guns, and there are almost no police shootings. With an approach to violent crime that has more in common with public health strategies than traditional heavy-handed policing, the UK is arguably now the safest of all industrialised countries. How has it achieved this remarkable feat?

The United Kingdom of Great Britain and Northern Ireland is known to the rest of the world as a cultural powerhouse. Its capital, London, exerts a global influence on everything from finance to fashion. The UK has a total population of about 67 million, making it slightly more populous than continental neighbour France. For now, it is the fifth-largest economy in the world – but it is soon likely to be overtaken by fast-growing India.[6] The UK has struggled to remain united, with Catholic Republicans in Northern Ireland opposing British rule for decades and Scotland almost voting for independence in 2014. There are now separate legislatures and governments in Scotland, Wales and Northern Ireland, which have considerable powers to make their own decisions.

It is probably not the first place that comes to mind when thinking about the safest spots on the planet, not least because of the brutal violence of the Troubles. For thirty years, from 1968 to 1998, the world became familiar with footage of street fights, bombings and sniper attacks as conflict raged between Loyalists and Republicans, with the military patrolling the streets of Northern Ireland. A civil war in all but name, about 3600 people were killed and 30,000 more wounded before a peaceful settlement could be reached.

In other countries, the UK is also portrayed as a nation of binge drinkers, prone to engaging in drunken brawls. Think of the pub scene in the movie *Trainspotting*, where a man is attacked with a broken pint glass. This perception is not too far from the reality. According to the Global Drug Survey, people in the UK get drunk more often than those in any other country surveyed – 51.1 times per year, or about once per week. This is only marginally more than in other English-speaking countries, such as the United States (50.3), Canada (47.9) and Australia (47.4), yet significantly more than those in European countries such as Germany (21.5), Switzerland (28.1) and Norway (29.0).[7]

The nation has also experienced periodic waves of rioting, particularly during the years of Margaret Thatcher's government in the 1980s.[8] In 2011, a series of riots involved thousands in cities and towns across England. By their conclusion, five people had died and more than 3000 had been arrested.

Yet this history belies what is, for most, the quiet reality of everyday life in the UK. Not only is it arguably the safest of all the countries of the OECD, it is getting safer. As Figure 6 on the next page shows, the UK has the lowest homicide rate in the OECD (0.2 per 100,000 population). The homicide rate in Australia is about five times worse (1 per 100,000); in the United States, 30 times worse (6 per 100,000); and in Mexico, more

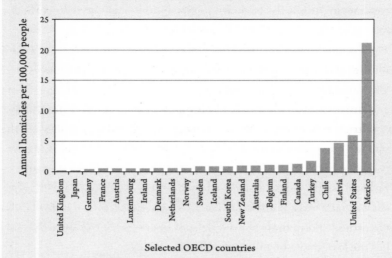

Figure 6. Medically certified 'cause of death' data collated by the World Health Organization shows that the United Kingdom is leading the OECD with its low homicide rate.

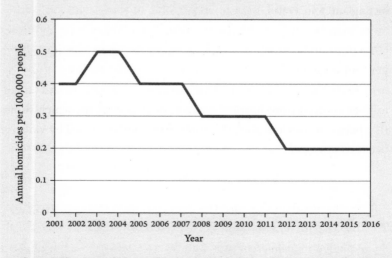

Figure 7. The same data set reveals a halving of the UK homicide rate between 2001 and 2016.

than 100 times worse (21.3 per 100,000).[9] Figure 7 shows that the homicide rate in the UK has been declining steadily. In fact, over a decade the rate halved, from 0.4 in 2007 to 0.2 in 2016.

Homicide, the unlawful killing of a person (which includes both murder and manslaughter), is just one form of crime. Why focus on it? Crime data is notoriously confusing and difficult to compare across time and jurisdictions. The legal definition of various crimes differs across countries. Police data is subject to changes in recording practices and the public's propensity to report crimes.[10] Studies show that homicide data is closely correlated with the incidence of other violent crimes such as physical assault, sexual assault and robbery. Homicide rates are therefore the best and most consistent way to compare the level of crime across countries.[11] From these figures, we can conclude that the UK very likely has the lowest rate of violent crime in the OECD.

This is reinforced by data from within the UK. The Crime Survey of England and Wales – an annual face-to-face survey that asks people about their experiences in the previous twelve months – shows a dramatic decline in incidents since the mid-1990s. It estimates that in 1995, there were 19.79 million crimes (excluding fraud and computer misuse) in England and Wales. By 2019, the number of crimes had declined by more than two-thirds, to 6.43 million. This includes very significant reductions in the number of violent crimes, which had declined by 70 per cent since 1995.

This trend is broadly consistent with the data Shepherd and his colleagues collated from hospital emergency departments, which shows that between 2010 and 2018, the number of injuries caused by violence declined by 41 per cent.[12]

Around the world, criminal activity causes considerably more deaths than war and terrorism combined. In 2017, there were 464,000 victims of homicide – a number that far exceeds the 89,000 killed in armed conflicts and the 26,000 who died in terrorist attacks.[13]

Yet the globe has seen enormous reductions in violent crime over time, and there is now less violence committed by individuals than at

Violent Crime in England and Wales 1981–2018

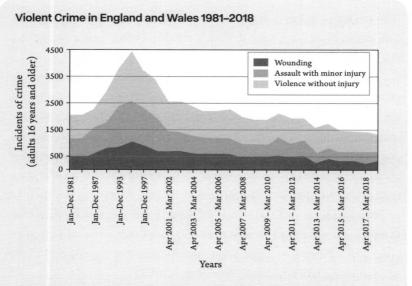

Figure 8. The Crime Survey of England and Wales shows that violent crime has declined by more than 70 per cent since the mid-1990s.

any point in human history. Cambridge University criminologist Professor Manuel Eisner has collated available data sources to estimate that in Europe, the average annual homicide rate in the thirteenth and fourteenth centuries was thirty-two per 100,000 people, and in the bloody fifteenth century it was forty-one. From there, it has declined steadily, from nineteen in the sixteenth century to eleven in the seventeenth century, 3.2 in the eighteenth century, 2.9 in the nineteenth, and 1.4 in the twentieth.[14] Steven Pinker argues in *The Better Angels of Our Nature* that this enormous reduction can be seen across violence in the family, within neighbourhoods and between countries. He writes that it 'may be the most important thing that has ever happened in human history'.[15]

Still, criminal violence remains an enormous problem. In some countries, it is the leading cause of death among those aged fifteen to twenty-nine; millions of years of life are lost unnecessarily. North and South America experience particularly high rates of homicide, where the drivers are often gangs and organised crime, and guns are the most common cause of death. The homicide rate for men aged twenty-five to twenty-nine in the Americas is sixty-four per 100,000 – far higher than in other world regions. Violence places enormous strain on public health services and additional burden on the criminal justice system. Mental health problems are more common where violence is prevalent, with psychological stress caused to those affected by crime, such as victims and their friends and relatives. Violence has a negative impact on school attendance and educational achievement, and in the home it affects women disproportionately. It has an economic consequence too, driving down property values, undermining business growth and exacerbating poverty. The direct and indirect costs of violence slow economic growth.[16]

There is huge variance in rates of violence across countries. We've already seen the difference in homicide rates across the developed countries of the OECD. The variance across the world is even more stark. According to the United Nations (which, it should be noted, uses a different methodology to the OECD), the intentional homicide rate ranges from 0.2 deaths per 100,000 people every year in countries such as Japan and Singapore, through to sixty-two deaths per 100,000 in El Salvador.[17]

What explains the differences? The United Nations argues that around two-thirds of the variation in the homicide rate is due to six factors: the percentage of young people in the total population; GDP per capita; the number of people living in urban areas; the level of income inequality; the level of gender inequality; and the female labour force participation rate.[18]

Demographic factors play a large part in influencing the rate of violent crime. Young people are disproportionately the victims and the perpetrators of violence, so where there is a higher proportion of young people in a country, there tends to be a higher homicide rate. Conversely, while cities generally have a slightly higher homicide rate than rural areas, the crime rate is decreasing faster in cities than it is elsewhere. The United Nations investigated the homicide rate between 2005 and 2016 in a sample of sixty-eight cities and found that the rate in cities decreased by 34 per cent, compared to just 16 per cent in the countries where those cities were located. The differences between the city homicide and the overall homicide rate is particularly pronounced in the Americas, where it seems the increase in murders has mostly affected rural areas.[19]

Economic development also plays a part in influencing the homicide rate, particularly in Europe and Asia. Low-growth or declining economies increase the risk that people will turn to violent crime as a way out of difficult circumstances. A shrinking economy can also lead to reductions in law-enforcement spending, contributing to an environment in which people are more vulnerable to violent crime. Countries with more acute income inequality are also more likely to have a higher homicide rate. Likewise, gender inequality is associated with higher levels of violence, particularly against women. The United Nations argues that the relationship between inequality and violent crime 'is so strong that it accounts for almost 40 per cent of the variation in homicide rates across countries'.[20]

The UK performs well on any of these metrics, but there's nothing to suggest that it should be leading the world. It has an ageing population, with a median age of over forty, but so do many countries.[21] It is wealthy, with an impressive GDP per capita, but there are seventeen OECD countries that outperform it on this measure.[22] Four out of every five UK residents live in cities, but many countries are more urbanised.[23] The UK does reasonably well on gender inequality, but income inequality is quite high.[24] If you were to plug these results into the United Nations' formula, you'd expect a crime rate about average for Europe.

This shows us that data only takes us so far. We'll have to dig deeper to examine the reasons for the UK's impressive success in reducing crime.

Force Versus Prevention

On the morning of 13 March 1996, Thomas Hamilton scraped the ice off his van and drove 8 kilometres from his home in Scotland to the village of Dunblane. After severing the telegraph pole cables, he walked into Dunblane Primary School armed with four legally owned handguns. In the space of three to four minutes, Hamilton shot thirty-two people, killing sixteen children and one teacher, before turning a gun on himself. It remains the worst mass shooting in British history.

After the massacre, the UK (excluding Northern Ireland) introduced gun restrictions banning private ownership of handguns. An amnesty period was introduced and compensation offered to those who surrendered their weapons.

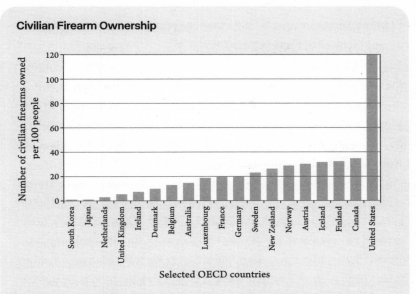

Civilian Firearm Ownership

Selected OECD countries

Figure 9. The 2017 Small Arms Survey shows that gun ownership in the UK is among the lowest in the OECD.

Gun ownership in the UK is now among the lowest in the OECD. Only the Netherlands and the countries of East Asia have fewer guns. There are just 4.9 civilian guns for every 100 people in the UK. In Australia there are three times as many (14.5 per 100) and in Canada there are seven times as many (34.7). In the United States there are more guns than people, and civilian guns are *twenty-five times* more prevalent than in the UK.

Dr Peter Neyroud was a police officer for thirty years, ultimately serving as the chief constable of the Thames Valley Police in Oxford and the chief executive officer of the National Policing Improvement Agency. He is now a lecturer in evidence-based policing at Cambridge University, where he is involved in randomised trials and field experiments testing the efficacy of different policing strategies. Unusually for a law-enforcement officer, he started out studying history at Oxford University, and when I speak with him his explanations are framed within a broader global and historical context.

Neyroud tells me the reasons for low rates of gun ownership 'go back a long, long way in English history'. He says it is due to the UK not having a culture of private armies 'and therefore private citizens being allowed to arm themselves for protection'.

Only 8 per cent of homicides in the UK involve a firearm. And since the restrictions on handguns have been introduced, there are almost no murders committed with a handgun.[25] This is known as 'situational crime prevention': ensuring that the weapons to inflict violent harm, such as guns – or broken pint glasses – are not readily available. It is something that the UK has been particularly good at.

Removing guns from the community is proven to reduce violent crime. Researchers at Harvard University's School of Public Health have reviewed the academic literature and concluded that there is 'a broad array of evidence that gun availability is a risk factor for homicide'. In the United States, in homes, cities, states and regions where there are more guns, 'both men and women are at a higher risk for homicide, particularly firearm homicide'. Even when US data is excluded, 'across developed countries, where guns are more available, there are more homicides'. Widespread gun ownership presents a risk to police: in high-gun states in the United States, 'law-enforcement officers are three times more likely to be murdered than law-enforcement officers working in low-gun states'.[26] It also has an impact on suicide figures. Each year in the UK, there are just 0.16 suicides per 100,000 people committed with a gun. In Australia, where guns are roughly three times as prevalent, there are 0.8 gun suicides per 100,000 people. The gun suicide rate in the United States is 7.32 per 100,000 people – nearly fifty times more than the UK.[27]

The United Nations notes that 'civilian possession of firearms is positively correlated with the homicide rate, even though it may become secondary to other factors of a socioeconomic nature, most notably income inequality'. In other words, all things being equal, where there are more guns, there are more homicides. The UN advocates 'stricter regulation of firearm ownership, along with efforts to reduce the number of illicitly held firearms' to help lower the rate of firearm-related homicide.[28] The evidence is clear.

Less than 5 per cent of UK police carry guns.[29] 'There's absolutely no universal issue of guns,' says Neyroud. 'About 30 to 40 per cent carry a taser, but there's no handguns.' Tasers are non-lethal weapons that inflict an electric shock, disrupting voluntary control of muscles. Each individual police service makes the decision to provide tasers to certain officers who have undertaken the necessary training.[30]

Not arming police with guns is a conscious strategy aimed at reducing violent crime in the community. 'There's a strong sense that it's more important to remove that particular barrier between the police officer and the citizen than it is to have the guns,' Neyroud says. Giving guns to police sends the wrong message. 'If you've got a police service that's so clearly geared to trying to protect itself using violence, that seems to me to go with the wider narrative about violence.'

Officers do have access to firepower. Neyroud says there is a system of 'twenty-four-hour gunships, with a fifteen- to twenty-minute time of arrival, in every force, which gets backed up with a specialist firearms team when required. It's a balance of risk.' Even so, guns are rarely called to use. For example, in the year to March 2016, across all of England and Wales just seven shots were fired by police (excluding accidental shots, shooting out of tyres or the killing of dangerous or injured animals).[31]

There are financial arguments in favour of this model. Not routinely issuing guns to officers 'has a very, very significant financial benefit to the police service', says Neyroud. 'If you're in virtually every other country, you spend a significant proportion of your time training your officers to use and to re-qualify with a firearm. We don't.'

There are also moral arguments. Given that most police do not carry guns, it's not surprising that there are hardly any police shootings. Between 2006 and 2016, a total of twenty-three people were killed by police shootings across England and Wales – that's about two per year. Neyroud says in recent years, those shot, 'broadly speaking, have been terrorists, intent on homicide'. By contrast, in the United States there were 957 deaths caused by police shootings in 2016 alone. On a per capita basis, the annual rate of police shootings in the UK is 0.06 per 1,000,000 people, whereas the US experiences 3.01 shootings per 1,000,000, about fifty times the rate.[32] In Australia, where all police carry guns but private gun ownership is low, there are about five police shootings per year, or roughly 0.2 shootings per 1,000,000.[33] This is about three times the rate of the UK.

When he was the chief constable of Thames Valley Police, Neyroud oversaw the introduction to the UK of less lethal weapons, such as tasers and plastic bullets. 'I worked out that what was missing was something in the gap between hitting people with a baton, trying to get them to release their weapon – particularly a knife, because they're mostly knives in the UK – and a fatal shot.' He says that after the introduction of tasers, average police shootings went down from about eight per year to zero.

Neyroud argues that police shootings create an environment that legitimises the use of force by the public. 'If you're in a country where you shoot a lot of citizens, that creates far greater legitimacy for the citizen to shoot than it does in a country like the UK, where we shoot so few citizens,' he says. This has played out in the United States, where there is a concern that police shootings disproportionately affect black and Hispanic communities. A lack of confidence in the police is the result. Professor David Kennedy of John Jay College of Criminal Justice in New York writes that

> when communities don't trust the police and are afraid of the police, then they will not and cannot work with police and within the law around issues in their own community. And then those issues within the community become issues the community needs to deal with on their own – and that leads to violence.[34]

One study by sociologists from Harvard, Yale and Oxford found that in the year after a young black man, Frank Jude Jr, was beaten severely and threatened with a gun by off-duty police officers in Milwaukee, Wisconsin, 17 per cent fewer calls were made to police. More than half of this decline was due to fewer calls from black neighbourhoods. The effect persisted even after the offending officers were sentenced. Yet while calls to police dropped, crime did not: the homicide rate in the period following the incident increased by 32 per cent. The researchers surmise that because people couldn't trust the police, they took their own – sometimes violent – means to protect themselves.[35]

A typical British police officer wears a stab vest and carries on their duty belt a baton, a radio, a spray similar to pepper spray, a torch and handcuffs. Some also carry a taser. Male officers in England and Wales wear the custodian helmet synonymous with the 'bobby on the beat'. Officers routinely patrol the community on foot or on bicycle.

The presence of non-threatening police officers in the community is a deliberate strategy to evoke respect and legitimacy for the force. It sees the police invested with authority due to public consent, not by state force. 'It's a civilian police service,' says Neyroud. 'It's not military, and it's determined not to be.' This idea reaches back to the establishment of the first professional police force. 'The police service in the UK wore blue because the military wore red. We have a tradition of being determinedly non-military.' As constables are officers under the Crown, they aren't given orders. 'They're expected to make their own mind up, and they are expected to exercise discretion, within policy and constraints. Individual constables have a great deal of discretion. That's very important, because the result of that of course is if you're a constable and you're face to face with a citizen, it introduces a level of humanity into the dialogue that I think is critical.'

At the heart of the British approach to policing is a set of principles often attributed to Sir Robert Peel, the British Home Secretary who in 1829 established the first professional full-time police force. These principles focus on the prevention of crime and disorder, not its repression by force and legal sanction. The absence of crime, not the visible evidence of police action, is the test of effective policing.[36]

'The object of the exercise is to prevent something happening, not to catch people doing it,' confirms Neyroud. 'That ethos of trying to prevent rather than catch is still important.' He says the British police system has been reasonably good at balancing multiple demands: 'You have to prevent enough crime and detect enough of it that the public feel that you're making a reasonable attempt to try and reduce it. You have to be approachable enough. Your police stations have to be open enough for you to be accessible. You have to have enough humility to admit when you've got things wrong. And the officers that you're drawing on need to come from a broad range of backgrounds. That's probably the one the British police services struggle with quite a bit, but has got a lot better at in recent years. It should be ordinary people joining the police service, not some specialist corps. The more you gravitate towards a paramilitary force, armed to the teeth, with a distance between you and the public, the more you're in trouble. When the British police service does things at its best, it has that level of proximity to the citizen.'

This focus on crime prevention and community involvement seems to be serving police in the UK well. Only 7 per cent of those in England and Wales believe that the police would not treat them fairly if they needed to contact them.[37]

Clever Approaches to Stopping Crime

Expert in combatting violence Jonathan Shepherd thinks that community partnerships – along with an improvement in data – have been a major cause of the UK's dramatic decline in crime. Such partnerships, which are similar to the model he pioneered in Cardiff, mean 'it's not just the police responsible for prevention, but it's police, city governments and health together'.

Shepherd's work and advocacy has led to the creation of more than 300 Community Safety Partnerships across England and Wales. These legislated programs are aimed at addressing crime in a particular community and consist of police officers, fire and rescue authorities, probation services, local government representatives and health services. Unlike the Cardiff Violence Prevention Board, which is concerned only with violence, Community Safety Partnerships are responsible for tackling 'all kinds of crime, including antisocial behaviour, car theft, robbery and burglary'. Yet addressing violence is a major focus. For example, in south-east England's Thames Valley, a number of people were treated at the accident and emergency ward after being pushed off their bikes. This data was depersonalised, analysed and mapped before being brought to the monthly Community Safety Partnership meeting for discussion. A senior nurse from the hospital raised her concern that this appeared to be a pattern of mugging, but none of the cases had been reported to police. Made aware of this cluster of incidents, police allocated resources to that area and the pattern of this type of injury stopped.

In another example from the Thames Valley, patients were presenting at hospital with injuries caused by wood, bricks and concrete, claiming they had been involved in fights. The violence was linked to one particular location and discussed at the Community Safety Partnership meeting, where the local council agreed to clear away the building debris. Upon inspection of the site, it was revealed that an open rubbish skip in use for a home renovation was situated next to a nightclub. The council made changes to the licence arrangements to ensure only closed skips could be used within a certain radius of nightclubs. This prevented similar problems from occurring in future.[38]

Accident and emergency departments across the country are supported to collect and share information with Community Safety Partnerships. Funding and training for data collection are provided through contracts with the National Health Service.[39] Shepherd says the UK has been able to 'increase the quality of data from the police and from the emergency departments and have that analysed and used professionally'. However, it's not just the data that is powerful. 'It's that if professionals from police, from local government and from health are meeting together, they become accountable to each other for violence prevention in a way that they would never do if they were working in silos, independently. That helps to inculcate an evidence-based approach.'

It is little surprise that in the UK, where getting drunk is a regular pattern of behaviour, there is a strong link between alcohol and violence. Shepherd says that intoxication increases the risk of injury through violence. This is because drunk people 'can't run away, they don't make the right decisions and they tend to wander home alone through risky urban environments late at night'. Furthermore, they aren't very good at identifying assailants to police.

The incidence of domestic violence also increases with alcohol consumption, and victims' injuries are more severe.[40] Large spikes in domestic violence are associated with major sporting events, which involve excessive drinking and heightened emotions.[41] When England plays in the football World Cup, there is an average 26 per cent rise in domestic assaults if they win and a 38 per cent rise if they lose.[42] Other cultural celebrations involving significant alcohol consumption, such as Christmas Day, are also associated with spikes in domestic violence.[43]

Local authorities in the UK have considerable powers over licensing of premises where alcohol can be sold. Informed by data, including from emergency departments, police can close down any premises for up to twenty-four hours. Police and other authorities can also seek to review a problem venue's licence, which may ultimately lead to reduced operating hours or permanent closure.[44] Neyroud says that this system of penalties has been successful in encouraging 'the landlords or the licensee to police themselves' and in involving 'the local authorities to try and crack down on premises'.

A wealth of evidence suggests that crime is not evenly distributed throughout a city, or even a neighbourhood. Instead, it tends to cluster around specific sites, such as shopping centres, apartment buildings, street corners or train stations. These 'hot spots' generate about half of all criminal events in most industrialised countries around the world.[45]

Improving the quality of crime data has enabled police in the UK to target resources and efforts to these hot spots. 'Go back thirty, forty years – with very minimal computer power, the ability to do effective hot-spot patrolling and to target your resources was not great,' says Neyroud. But with powerful algorithms, police are now able to identify crime hot spots with accuracy. A number of police services in the UK are even using artificial intelligence to predict when and where crime is most likely to occur. For example, Kent Police uses PredPol, a predictive policing software that can generate a series of locations on a map, showing where crime is most likely to occur at any given time. These maps inform where officers patrol at which times of day.[46]

There is robust evidence that hot-spot policing is effective in reducing violent crime. 'Hot-spot policing in particular for late-night violence is extremely effective,' says Neyroud. 'You should be expecting to see 25 to 30 per cent reductions if you can consistently sustain the approach.' And rather than simply displacing crime to nearby locations, the benefits of this type of policing actually spill over into adjacent areas. This is because of the way offenders' minds work: studies show that they are made wary by the increased police presence in the neighbourhood and a perceived increased risk of being apprehended.[47]

Hot-spot policing is widely used around the world. For example, nine in every ten police forces in the United States report using it.[48] However, while targeted patrols and additional enforcement in problem areas makes a difference, hot-spot policing is most effective when used with a 'problem-oriented' approach – when specific crime problems are identified and analysed, along the lines of the Cardiff Model.[49] Police in the UK have been adopting stop-and-search powers in target hot spots to address knife crime. While ordinarily police can only search someone if they have 'reasonable grounds', officers have been routinely putting in place a 'zone of search' around a hot spot, which enables them to legally stop and search anyone in that location. Neyroud says this practice is integral to the success of hot-spot policing. 'It's all very well to say you can put police officers in hot spots,' he says, 'but the question then comes, "Well, what are they doing?" The obvious thing they should be doing if you were targeting violence, and in particular knife violence, is using stop-and-search powers.'

As we might imagine, this has been controversial. Young black or Asian men have been subject to a disproportionate number of searches.[50] Neyroud says 'the highest level of crime commission is between the ages of fourteen and seventeen, so logically that's the group you should be stopping'. But he concedes that stop-and-search powers do pose issues. 'You are creating a problem in the relationship between young men and the police,' he says, and the practice leads to 'a high level of entry into the criminal justice system'. Consequently, he says stop-and-search powers need to be deployed with precision and not as a general strategy. He also warns that 'you have to track what your officers are up to'. Over the past decade, many police services have introduced body-worn cameras, and in these cases 'there are now virtually no complaints about stop-and-search'.

I t hasn't all been good news in the UK. In recent years, there has been a substantial rise in knife crime. According to England's National Health Service, over a six-year period there has been a 30 per cent increase in the number of hospital admissions for injuries caused by assault with a knife or a sharp object. The upsurge in the number of teenagers admitted to hospital has been particularly dramatic.[51] Neyroud points to 'the availability of knives through the internet' and 'gang culture in some of the bigger cities', along with 'changes in the distribution structure for cocaine and heroin'.

This increase is concerning, but it also needs to be kept in perspective. In 2017–2018, the rate of knife deaths in the UK was about the same as in the United States.[52] The difference, of course, is that unlike in the United States, there are very few gun deaths, meaning the overall homicide rate is much, much lower.

A decade of austerity following the 2008 global financial crisis is also a potential factor driving the increase in knife crime, Neyroud says, as it has led to cuts in funding for youth services. The number of youth centres receiving government support has reduced by half since 2011, and youth-services staff have dropped by more than 40 per cent. Javed Khan, chief executive of children's charity Barnardo's, says that removing youth workers and safe spaces is creating a 'poverty of hope' where children are unable to see a positive future.[53]

This austerity has also led to a substantial reduction in police numbers. In England and Wales, there are about 22,000 fewer police than there were a decade ago, a decrease of about 15 per cent.[54] The number of police per capita in these countries is now the lowest in Europe.[55] Neyroud says this has been catastrophic, with the lack of police capacity meaning many crimes are going unsolved and perpetrators remaining unpunished. He says the UK is experiencing 'the lowest rate of detection in recorded statistical history for all offences, and that includes serious offences'. In 2018, only 9 per cent of crimes in England and Wales ended up with someone being charged or summonsed, down substantially from 2015, when it was 15 per cent.[56]

In a typical criminal case, evidence 'used to be primarily physical and forensic', Neyroud says. Now it is 'hugely informational and digital'. Due to funding cuts, police 'haven't got the people and the capability to analyse the material in a way that will satisfy the court. They're just drowning in digital information.'

While violent crime overall has reduced dramatically, Neyroud says efforts to reduce sexual assault and domestic violence have been less successful. 'It has been really, really difficult to get the number of homicides down.' In 2018, the number of people killed as a result of domestic violence – the vast majority women – reached a five-year high.[57] According to Neyroud, the perpetrators of about 50 per cent of intimate-partner homicides are not known to police. 'And of the other half, not all of those are predictable. So, it's a fairly tricky one to predict and prevent. Getting an effective risk assessment tool has been a serious problem, so domestic violence is still a major, major challenge.'

In 2019, the UK government proposed legislation to impose a legal duty on councils to provide housing for people fleeing violence, along with their children. The legislation would also establish a legal definition of domestic abuse extending beyond physical violence to include economic abuse and controlling behaviour.[58]

What the United Kingdom Can Teach the World

Given its success in reducing violent crime, other countries could have much to learn from the UK approach.

Focus on Prevention

Rather than putting greater resources into responding to crimes and pursuing perpetrators through the justice system, UK authorities fund measures aimed at preventing crime from occurring. This focus on prevention is at the heart of policing in the UK, with a culture and tradition that dates back to the establishment of formal policing almost 200 years ago. This has been enhanced over recent decades by the use of evidence-based approaches.

The UK has had success in introducing programs and legislation to ensure that the weapons involved in violent crime – such as guns and easily broken pint glasses – are not available to perpetrators. The rate of gun ownership in most countries far exceeds that of the United Kingdom, and so do their rates of homicide. There is much scope for such countries to explore improvements in gun control, drawing from the UK model. Even incremental reductions in gun ownership are likely to make a difference to overall crime rates.

Like the United Kingdom, some countries have already made determined efforts to reduce the number of guns. After a mass shooting in 1996 that left thirty-five people dead, Australia introduced tight controls on semi-automatic weapons. Voluntary surrenders and gun buybacks removed more than one million firearms – possibly up to a third of Australia's national stock – from circulation. These changes have contributed to a significant decrease in firearm homicides and gun suicides.[59] Following a shooting at a mosque in 2019 that killed fifty-one people, New Zealand also banned most semi-automatic and military-style weapons and instituted a buyback scheme.[60] It will be interesting to see whether this leads to a reduction in New Zealand's already low homicide rate.

Build Community Trust

Police can only intervene to respond to crime – and prevent its future occurrence – when it is reported to them. UK police services are acutely aware that their efficacy rests on their ability to secure the trust and respect of the communities in which they work. UK police consciously try to remove anything that might create a barrier between them and the community. For this reason, officers are not armed with guns. Sending unarmed officers out into local neighbourhoods normalises police presence and encourages greater community trust. The emphasis on police patrols on foot and by bicycle and the significant discretion given to constables also speaks to the importance placed on relationships with the community.

UK police face similar challenges to police around the world, and must respond assertively to threats such as violent crime and terrorism. But the culture of policing in the UK is unlikely to lead police to default to heavy-handed or militaristic responses. Among police leadership there is always debate about the need to balance strong responses with maintenance of the trust in and reputation of the police service. For example, police leadership is aware that while implementing stop-and-search policies in hot spots is effective in reducing violent crime, they need to ensure it does not undermine the relationship between young men and the police, thereby creating a longer-term problem.

By contrast, US police forces have increasingly adopted the equipment, tactics and mindset of the military. Since the 1990s, the Department of Defense has provided military-grade equipment to police, including machine guns, armoured vehicles, grenade launchers and aircraft. There has also been an increase in the use of military tactics such as SWAT teams and no-knock raids.[61] Yet, according to a study of 9000 police agencies in the United States, militarisation neither reduces the rate of violent crime nor improves police officer safety.[62]

Use Data Meaningfully

The UK's success in reducing violent crime demonstrates the importance of high-quality data to inform policing. The Cardiff Model and Community Safety Partnerships to combat violent crime are both underpinned by the sharing of information and data. Key to the quality of this data is the range of sources from which it is drawn, including police reports, hospital emergency admission forms and community surveys. As crime is caused by a complex set of factors, it's clear that any single agency working alone is not as effective as multiple agencies sharing data.

This data-centred approach can easily be replicated elsewhere. Drawing on Shepherd's work, the US Centers for Disease Control and Prevention has developed a simple toolkit and checklist to assist cities wanting to adopt the Cardiff Model. At its most basic, it involves building relationships, collecting and sharing data and forming a community culture of responding together to issues the data reveals.[63]

The Cardiff Model is currently being trialled in the Australian cities of Melbourne, Sydney and Canberra.[64] Shepherd says there have been 'scores' of other examples, with 'requests for advice from the chief medical officer in Halifax, Canada, and from the attorney-general in the Colombia government', who has decided to implement it across the country.

In addition, the World Health Organization has adopted a form of the partnerships approach Shepherd pioneered. Given the startling results, it is no surprise that the model is being adopted in a host of countries and by health organisations around the world.

Engage Young People

Jonathan Shepherd might be retired from clinical practice, but he has not slowed in his efforts to prevent violent crime. Through his appointment to a recently established body called the Youth Endowment Fund, he is taking on the next frontier in crime prevention. This government fund has £200 million (US$240 million) to support 'interventions and the evaluation of interventions designed to prevent youth from going on into a life of crime'. Shepherd says that 'early intervention, preschool education, early family support – those sorts of things have really important effects'. Promising initiatives include family support services, such as parenting programs and maternal and child healthcare services, as well as measures to keep at-risk children in school. But Shepherd says that we don't yet know 'enough about when and how those things work, not just on crime but on truancy and educational attainment'.

Inherent in the UK approach to crime is a conviction that violence is a public health concern, and that with appropriate interventions it can be prevented. We don't reflexively think of violence as a public health issue in the same way as we do smoking or sunburn. Yet 'violence causes physical injuries and also significant mental health issues', Shepherd says, 'so thinking of violence prevention as a public health goal is very rational and a natural extension of that'.

FIVE THINGS WE CAN DO NOW

1. **Better regulate firearms.** Fewer guns in the community means fewer homicides and suicides. In countries such as the United States, banning semi-automatic weapons and those with high-capacity magazines would be a good start, as these weapons are common to almost all mass shootings. Young people are far more likely to commit homicides, so introducing minimum age and safe storage requirements will keep guns out of young hands. It also makes sense to mandate universal background checks for everyone purchasing a gun, so that people who shouldn't have weapons – such as those with a history of family violence or violent criminal records, and those with certain mental-health conditions – are prevented from buying them.

2. **Improve data collection.** Accurate and detailed data on violence informs the development of effective responses. Data can be drawn from multiple sources, including police reports, emergency admissions and community surveys, and shared between authorities to gain the best picture of crime patterns. As most violent crime is not reported to police, legislation requiring hospitals to share non-confidential information with police and liquor-licensing authorities will help to identify when, where and how violent crime is occurring. Protocols for data collection and sharing could be developed, and hospital staff supported with training.

3. **Develop collaborative approaches to combat violence.**
   No single agency can address violence effectively.
   Establishing partnerships that bring together police,
   local government, licensing authorities and health services
   will enable sophisticated approaches to violence prevention.
   With leadership and goodwill, this model can be transformative.
   It can be adopted in a single town or city – as in Cardiff – or rolled
   out more systematically across a country.

4. **Increase hot-spot policing.** Given that half of all crime takes
   place in and around particular buildings, streets, clubs or train
   stations, targeting police efforts and resources in these areas
   is an effective way to reduce crime. This can involve more
   frequent patrols in hot spots through to measures to deal with
   the underlying problems causing crime in that location, such as a
   lack of streetlights or the opening hours of nightclubs.

5. **Tighten venue licensing.** Licensed venues – particularly those
   frequented by young men – are major contributors to alcohol-
   fuelled violence. Ensuring that there are sufficient powers to
   close down or restrict the trading hours of problem venues will
   address the conditions that enable violent altercations and
   street brawls.

4

FIRST AMONG EQUALS

How to Reduce Gender Inequality

'Tʜis is probably the most important time to bond with a kid. Why not take the chance to be with your child when they're just becoming an individual?'

Sigurður Bragason is outlining his approach to parenting. Sigurður, who is Icelandic, and his Swiss wife, Dr Nicole Keller, have two young children: Felix, six, and Miriam, three. They are speaking to me via Skype from their kitchen with their kids on – and off – their knees.

Nicole explains that she came to Iceland eight years ago. 'I'm a geologist and I had been specialising in volcanoes and geothermal areas. I got a postdoc in Iceland and I was just going to be here for two years. That was eight years ago.' The couple met at a local club that holds twice-weekly Argentinian tango classes. 'I met Siggi the third day after I moved to Iceland,' Nicole says. 'And six months later, it turned out to be a little bit more than just dancing tango.'

When each of their children was born, both parents took extended parental leave. Nicole returned to work six months after the birth of Felix and eleven months after the birth of Miriam, and each time Sigurður took six months. Both now work – Sigurður full-time as a graphic designer and Nicole four days per week at the Environment Agency. Sigurður explains how things work in their family. 'We divide the parenting quite equally. It's not like one of us is taking care of everything.'

In Iceland, it is normal for fathers to take extended parental leave, although six months is less typical. 'Most men I know have taken three months,' says Nicole. As a consequence of this early time with their children, fathers tend to be extremely involved in parenting. 'In general, when you go out, shopping or something, I find that fathers seem to have a larger role in taking care of children than in Switzerland,' says Nicole.

The Icelandic government provides each parent with three months of non-transferrable leave at 80 per cent of their salary (up to a ceiling). This leave must be taken within eighteen months of the child's birth. Parents also have a joint right to an additional three months that can be used by one parent or divided between them.[1] So Icelandic parents face a 'use it or lose it' situation. While the flexible component of parental leave is mostly used by mothers, about 80 per cent of fathers take at least three months of paternity leave to care for their children as infants.[2]

Paid paternity leave is just one of a host of measures that have helped Iceland to address historical gender-based inequalities in the areas of education, health, employment and political representation. With the world's smallest gender gap, Iceland has topped the World Economic Forum's Global Gender Gap Index for eleven years running, and *The Economist* ranks Iceland as the best place in the world to be a working woman.[3] Iceland's experience shows us that with organised and persistent community campaigning and a government prepared to legislate protest demands into practice, we can move much closer to a world in which the gender gap is eliminated. But how did Iceland get to this point?

An underpopulated island on the edge of the Arctic Circle, Iceland is best known for the volcanic forces that shape it: geysers, geothermal pools and ice-covered volcanoes. Nearly two-thirds of its population live in the world's northernmost capital city, Reykjavík. Not that this urban centre is big – the population of Greater Reykjavík is just over 200,000 people, making it smaller than the Australian city of Hobart, the English town of Reading or Brownsville, Texas, in the United States.

Iceland has a long history as a seafaring nation, which meant the men were often at sea for extended periods. Women were farmers, hunters or builders and managed the household finances. Like many maritime nations, Iceland's ability to prosper was underpinned by its women.

In the mid-1800s, Icelandic leaders passed legislation to give women the vote. However, Iceland was part of the kingdom of Denmark, and the legislation was rejected by the more-conservative Danish Crown. But in 1850, Iceland became the first country in the world to grant equal inheritance rights to men and women.[4] The Icelandic Women's Association was established in 1894, and the struggle for women's suffrage grew to become a powerful movement. In 1915, women finally received the right to vote. Initially the vote was granted only to women aged over forty, but by 1920 the voting age was lowered to twenty-five, equal with men.[5]

Yet by the 1970s, Iceland was no longer leading the way on equality. Women earned at least 40 per cent less than men,[6] and there were just three female members of parliament, 5 per cent of total parliamentarians. The Red Stockings, a radical women's movement, proposed action. Their plan to strike felt too confrontational for some citizens, but when the protest was renamed the Women's Day Off, it achieved near-universal support, including backing from influential unions.[7]

On 24 October 1975, 90 per cent of Iceland's female population went on strike, refusing to work, cook or look after children for the day, demonstrating the 'indispensable work' women did for the nation's economy.[8] Schools, childcare centres and businesses were closed for the day. No newspapers were printed, as most typesetters were female. Flights were cancelled as flight attendants did not come to work.[9]

One-fifth of the country's female population took to the streets, protesting against gender wage discrepancy and discriminatory employment practices.[10] Businesswoman-turned-artist Rut Ríkey Tryggvadóttir – who dances tango with Sigurður and Nicole – lights up when she talks with me about the protest. Someone who would stand out in a crowd, Rut's hair and lipstick are bright, candy red, set against the thick black frames of her glasses. 'I was there. I was seventeen years old and I remember everything. It was fantastic. It was like all women in Iceland had gathered together – it was magnificent. I was so optimistic, and at that moment I thought yes, we will get equal rights.'

The air that evening was thick with the smell of burnt meat as the men cooked.[11]

The Women's Day Off had a major impact on politics and industrial relations in Iceland. A year after the strike, Iceland formed the Gender Equality Council and parliament passed the *Gender Equality Act*, which prohibited discrimination on the basis of gender in workplaces and schools. In 1980, Iceland elected a female president, Vigdís Finnboga-dóttir, who went on to hold office for four terms.

More than forty years later, Icelandic women are still taking to the streets to agitate for equality. They have gone on strike five times since 1975: in 1985, 2005, 2010, 2016 and 2018.[12] At the 2018 Women's Day Off, women walked out at 2.55 p.m., in protest over the fact that Icelandic women earn 74 per cent of men's income on average and have therefore 'earned their wages after only 5 hours and 55 minutes'.[13]

One of the organisers of the 2018 Women's Day Off is Fríða Rós Valdi-marsdóttir, chair of the Icelandic Women's Rights Association. When I speak with her, she is buzzing after another successful event. 'It's like an ocean of women fighting for our rights, and we agree that we do not want unequal pay and we do not want the harassment that exists in too many workplaces. So this was about both: equal pay and harassment in the workplace or violence in our lives. This year it was freezing cold, but the women did not leave the protest. It was a magical day.'

Fríða is also a gender violence specialist at the Centre for Gender Equality. A long-time women's rights activist now in her early forties, she first formed a feminist collective in her twenties. Her words are restrained, but her passion shines through the longer we talk. Fríða tells me that the power of the women's movement has been constant in Iceland. 'And somehow more than in other countries, the women's movement here has been listened to,' she says. 'I think that's the difference.'

Partly due to its history of feminist activism, Iceland now tops the world on measures of political empowerment. In the Global Gender Gap Index, no other country comes close. Iceland has closed 70 per cent of the gap between men and women, while the second-ranked country, Norway, has closed only 60 per cent. The United Kingdom (40 per cent), Australia (23 per cent) and the United States (16 per cent) are a long way down the list.[14]

In 2016, women accounted for 48 per cent of elected representatives in the Icelandic parliament, although this has since dropped to 38 per cent.[15] Forty per cent of ministers are women.[16] While far from equal representation, progress is better than in most countries. In the United States, just 24 per cent of the House of Representatives are women. In Australia, the figure is 30 per cent; in the United Kingdom, 34 per cent of members of the House of Commons are women.[17]

Fríða says that Iceland has had 'very strong role models that show us that women can lead the country'. She names Vigdís Finnbogadóttir, the world's first democratically and directly elected female president. Iceland has had a female president or prime minister for twenty-two of the past thirty-nine years. 'These role models, they count. To have these strong women that can do it, other women perhaps draw influence from that.'

The Global Gender Gap Report collates economic, educational, health and political data to measure the overall gender gap. After Iceland, Norway, Sweden and Finland fill out the top four positions, as Figure 10 on the next page shows. According to the 2020 report, all of these countries have closed at least 82 per cent of the gender gap. By contrast, the United Kingdom and Canada rank nineteenth and twenty-first, with 77 per cent of the gender gap closed, and Australia ranks forty-fourth (73 per cent). The United States is a lowly fifty-third (72 per cent) – behind countries such as Bangladesh, Zimbabwe and Zambia. It scores particularly poorly on political representation: it has never had a female president, and at the time of the report just 22 per cent of ministerial positions were occupied by women.[18]

There have been significant advances in the empowerment of women in recent decades. Globally, the gap in educational attainment between women and men is now just 3.9 per cent. Thirty-five countries have achieved full parity here, and another fifty countries have closed 99 per cent of the divide. Among developing countries, the remaining gulf is closing quickly. Similarly, the difference between men and women in health and survival (incorporating the ratio of girls born to boys, as well as life expectancy) is quite small – just 4 per cent on average. All 153 countries surveyed in the Global Gender Gap Report have closed at least 92 per cent of this divide.[19]

But according to the World Economic Forum, at the current rate of progress it will take another 257 years to close the global economic gender gap.[20] Across the wealthy countries of the OECD, women work-ing full-time still earn 14 per cent less than men, and this has not changed materially in more than a decade.[21] As at 2020, only 21 per cent of minis-ters and 25 per cent of parliamentarians globally were women. Forty-five countries have parliaments with less than 20 per cent women.[22]

Improving the status of women is a critical global challenge, and not just because there is a moral imperative to do so. The empower-ment of women has been one of the most important drivers of social change over the past century and is central to addressing almost all the key challenges facing humanity – including economic development, poverty rates and overpopulation. Gender inequality also impacts on women's ability to cope with and respond to environmental challenges such as climate change. This is particularly the case in the developing world, where women have insecure land rights, limited participation

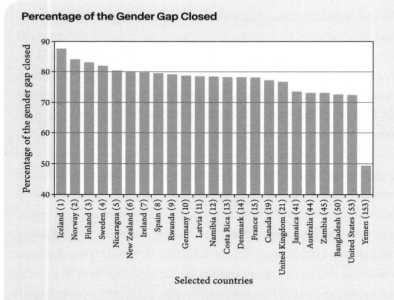

Figure 10. 2020 World Economic Forum data shows that the Nordic countries lead the world on gender equality, with Iceland in first place.

in decision-making and lack of access to markets, capital, training and technology.[23]

The economic arguments in favour of increasing female workforce participation are overwhelming. For example, greater female participation in the US workforce since 1970 accounts for at least *a quarter* of current GDP.[24] In other words, if women went to work at the same rate as they did in 1970, the US economy would be three-quarters of the size it is today. Countries have invested hugely over decades to educate girls and women; however, without gender equality we are not maximising women's economic potential and not fully reaping the economic rewards of this investment.[25]

The United Nations identifies three key barriers preventing women from participating in the workforce at the same rate as men. First, women spend far more time on childcare and looking after ageing parents. Globally, women undertake three times more unpaid work than men. This is true in highly industrialised countries as well as in developing countries. Second, in many parts of the world it is not safe for women to travel to work or education, with sexual harassment and violence far too prevalent. Third, cultural expectations often confine women to the home and create a stigma around working women. Even in industrialised countries, some employers are reluctant to hire women who may have children.[26]

US consulting firm McKinsey argues that if these barriers could be overcome and participation rates for women were to reach those of men, it would contribute an additional US$28 trillion, or 26 per cent, to global annual GDP by 2025. GDP is a rough proxy for standard of living, so that would be more or less like everyone *in the entire world* becoming 26 per cent better off. If countries merely matched the current 'best in region' rate of progress towards gender parity in workforce participation (for example, if all countries in Asia closed the gender gap at Singapore's annual rate of 1.1 percentage points), US$12 trillion would still be added – equivalent to the current GDP of Japan, Germany and the United Kingdom combined.[27]

There is also strong evidence that reducing the gender pay gap may have public health benefits. For example, one influential study found that increased pay parity leads to a reduction in family violence.[28] Plus,

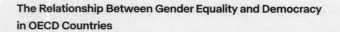

The Relationship Between Gender Equality and Democracy in OECD Countries

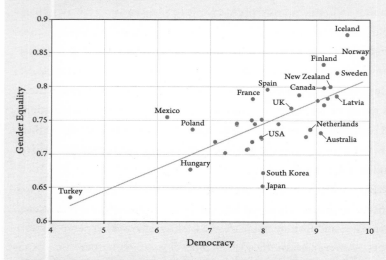

Figure 11. More-democratic countries tend to have a smaller gender gap, and those countries with less gender equality tend to be less democratic.

democracy and gender equality go hand in hand. There are few democratic countries that do not also have a relatively good gender gap score. Japan and Korea are the exceptions – while they are reasonably democratic, they have a relatively large gender gap.

Equal Pay for Unequal Work

Working women around the world earn about 22 per cent less than men each month.[29] A large part of this is because they do more unpaid work in the home. Hours spent here mean there is less time for paid work, and as a consequence, women are more likely to work part-time and are less likely to advance to management.

Yet women's hourly wages are also less than men's. This is partly because women often work in different jobs to men. Globally, women continue to be poorly represented in the lucrative science, engineering, technology and mathematics (STEM) fields and are less likely to be entrepreneurs than men.[30]

Data on the gender pay gap is quite complicated, and there are a number of ways to measure it. The average wages of Icelandic women are about 26 per cent less than men's. But because women work in paid employment for fewer weekly hours than men, when earnings are considered on an hourly basis the gap is about 16 per cent. The data set most commonly used internationally compares median full-time earnings, and on this measure Icelandic women earn about 9.9 per cent less than men. This gap is better than Australia (14.3 per cent), the United Kingdom (16.8 per cent) and the United States (18.2 per cent), and is far better than the worst performer in the OECD, South Korea (34.6 per cent). However, there are twelve countries in the OECD that perform better than Iceland. The gap in Belgium is just 3.7 per cent.[31]

Some of the pay gap in Iceland can be attributed to structural issues, such as men and women being more likely to choose careers in different sectors. However, an analysis by Statistics Iceland shows that there is an 'unexplained' gender pay gap of 4.5 per cent. This discrepancy can't be accounted for by factors such as volume of work, education level, age, amount of responsibility or length of career.[32]

To address this, Iceland made headlines all around the world when, in 2018, it became the first country to enact legislation requiring companies and government agencies that employ at least twenty-five people to prove their pay is fair, or face fines. This requires them to undergo audits and receive certification to show that they are an equal-pay provider. Companies need to demonstrate that their pay system complies with national equal pay standards. The standards were developed by employers and unions between 2008 and 2012 and were originally designed as voluntary. The compliance process is complex, and involves assessing the worth of different jobs, classifying and ranking occupations, analysing salary structures and ensuring consistency with labour agreements.[33] The government has a goal of completely eliminating the gap by 2022.

Fríða says that the changes have been widely supported. 'When we were talking about the change, fighting for change, companies stopped talking negatively about it, and that shows us that we are making feminist discourse mainstream.'

A poll of Icelanders conducted at the time the law was enacted showed majority public support. Sixty per cent were in favour of the law and only 21 per cent opposed, with the remaining 19 per cent neutral.[34]

The laws seem to have the support of employers too. Interviewed by Australian television station SBS, Svavar Halldórsson, general manager of Icelandic Lamb (which markets Iceland's sheep products to the world) says the legislation was 'the thing to do': 'This is how we try to run our company. I think that overall, at least among younger executives, that is a very common opinion. People were happy about it.'[35]

Fríða believes the laws were necessary to bring about a level of change that would not have occurred organically. 'I think that we really have to make standards or use any kind of tools to monitor and to bind in law that you cannot pay unequally, because we've had it in law since the 1960s or 1970s in most Western countries [including Iceland], yet we have all these unequal payments, gendered payment. So we must be doing something wrong.'

Improving Workforce Participation

The laws won't affect the structural issues that contribute to the gender pay gap, including women's disproportionate share of unpaid caring and domestic work, and time spent out of the workforce for parenting, impacting on career progression. Fríða says these factors need to be addressed over the longer term 'with a shorter working week, with childcare, by tackling gendered violence, and with respect – more respect for human rights especially'. Iceland has been working hard to deal with issues such as these and has led the world with a number of reforms.

Since 2008, Iceland has required at least 40 per cent female representation on national and local government committees, councils and boards. Since 2013, companies in Iceland with more than fifty employees have also been required to achieve a quota of at least 40 per cent of women on their boards, although there are not strong penalties for non-compliance. By 2017, women made up 44 per cent of boards of publicly traded companies and 32.6 per cent of boards of companies with more than fifty employees, the latter up from 9.5 per cent in 1999.[36] Iceland now has one of the highest rates of female board participation in the world.

By contrast, in Australia, where there are no quotas, women represent just 28 per cent of board seats on the ASX200 (the 200 biggest companies), and in the United States, women hold just 22 per cent of board seats on the S&P 500 (the 500 biggest companies).[37]

'It has worked,' says Fríða. 'It's not perfect, but it has had an impact.'

The business case for diversity is increasingly clear. For example, McKinsey found that companies in the top quartile of gender diversity 'were 15 per cent more likely to have financial returns that were above their national industry median.'[38] This trend has been replicated in other studies.

In 2000, Iceland's parental leave legislation came into effect, giving parents a total of nine months of leave, including three months for each parent. Both parents are entitled to this leave regardless of gender, custody arrangements, or size or shape of family. The full nine months can be allocated to one parent in special circumstances, such as serious illness or when one parent is serving a prison sentence.[39]

Since the law's introduction, about 80 per cent of fathers have taken paternity leave to care for their children as infants. In 2013, fathers took an average of eighty-seven days of leave after the birth of their child.[40]

Take a moment to reflect on what this means. Almost every male truck driver, lawyer or construction worker spends months out of the workplace to care for their child while their partner returns to work. Picture these men *en masse*, pushing prams at the playground or changing nappies at home. Think about what this means for how their families function.

Fathers' participation in caregiving is essential to ensure that mothers can remain and advance in the workforce. Research into Icelandic paternity leave arrangements has shown that it has led to greater involvement of fathers in child-rearing and women returning to work faster – and returning to their pre-childbirth hours faster too.[41] Furthermore, parenting behaviour established at childbirth tends to persist as children age.[42] This in turn shapes children's experience of gender. Fríða says, 'Those measures are so important. You can see changes in the society.'

Although most Icelandic men are taking their three months of 'use it or lose it' leave, women overwhelmingly take up the transferrable component of parental leave. Only 19.7 per cent of men use any of the transferrable leave.[43] Fríða says that with the nation's relatively low payment ceiling, and men still generally the main income earners, 'parents see that they don't have a choice'. As Nicole explains: 'For most people, it's the mother who takes six months and then the father takes three months after that. The regulations are that you take leave at 80 per cent of your salary. It's often still the man that earns more money than the woman. And so, the dads are not taking more paternity leave because that would be a greater pay cut.'

Discussion in Iceland has been focused on extending paid parental leave still further. In 2019, the Icelandic parliament enacted legislation to extend paid parental leave to an impressive twelve months. From 2020, each parent will be given five months of leave, with the remaining two months to share between them.[44]

Returning to work after having children is made easier in Iceland by a workplace culture that supports flexible approaches to parenting. 'Our work supports parenting,' Sigurður says. 'If I tell people I need to take care of a sick child, or I need to go to the kindergarten because there's a festival there, they're super supportive. They just say, "Yes, go for it."'

Government in Iceland plays a critical role in supporting parents through heavily subsidised childcare. In Reykjavík, a married couple would typically pay about US$215 per month for eight hours of childcare a day (that includes food), while a single parent would only pay US$145.[45] By contrast, typical childcare costs in Australia can be US$250 per week, even after a government subsidy is applied.

Access to affordable childcare is fundamental to achieving gender equality as it helps parents return to work when children are young. In a survey of twenty-three OECD countries, more-accessible childcare was the most commonly cited way of removing barriers to female workforce participation.[46]

Perhaps due to these measures, Icelandic women participate in the workforce at almost the same rate as men. The workforce participation rate is 86 per cent for women and 92 per cent for men. This rate for women is among the highest in the world, far higher than countries such as Australia (72 per cent), Canada (74 per cent), the United Kingdom (72 per cent) or the United States (66 per cent). Iceland has also managed to smash the stereotype of women in STEM careers. While women are underrepresented in STEM careers globally, in Iceland men are now a minority in these disciplines – some 56 per cent of 'professional and technical workers' are now women, the highest rate in the world.[47]

celand is not without its areas for improvement. For one, subsidised childcare does not usually commence until a child is two years old. As Fríða points out, 'There is no security in childcare until the kid is two years old, so we have this magnificent system, but still women are not free to go to work after their parental leave.' Parents have a period of fifteen months during which they must improvise childcare arrangements through a combination of means, such as unpaid leave or informal caring arrangements. Parents can also pay for home-based childcare by a *dagsmamma* ('day mother'), who typically looks after five children each, though this is costly and there are no subsidies.

Rut Ríkey Tryggvadóttir, who raised a disabled son, also points to limited social support for people with disabilities and those caring for them. 'I've had to cope with the system and authorities in Iceland,' she says. 'There was not much social support. It was difficult. This has changed. But there are cases still today that are difficult, and families with kids who have severe disabilities can experience costly challenges.' This is backed by a survey that found parents of children with an intellectual disability experienced support services as 'fragmented and uncompromising' and that some services were 'consistently regarded as hard to reach and not in accordance with the needs of the family'.[48]

Icelandic women have realised that improving political representation or reducing the pay gap does not eliminate gender violence. Over the course of their lifetime, 22 per cent of Icelandic women will experience domestic violence. Other Nordic countries – including Norway, Sweden, Finland and Denmark – have even higher rates, despite being among the best in the world for gender equality. This is the 'Nordic paradox', a surprisingly under-researched phenomenon.[49]

'Maybe because kids are involved, but this is the issue that's getting some attention,' Fríða says. She points to an initiative she's working on with the police forces aimed at early intervention in domestic violence to prevent its escalation. The program is called Keep the Window Open, named because there is traditionally a small window after an assault during which a victim is more likely to accept help. Along with police powers to issue restraining orders and remove the perpetrator from the family home, under this program women are provided with a suite of services and support.[50] If the police are called to a domestic violence incident, they now arrive with a team: a social worker, a doctor, a child protection worker and a lawyer. Each of these service providers follow up again with the woman a week later. This approach has led to a dramatic increase in the number of family violence cases reported to Reykjavík police, indicating that victims are aware of the available services and confident their complaints will be taken seriously.[51]

The next step for achieving greater equality between men and women is shorter working hours, as this takes the pressure off families and enables a more equal division of labour – both paid and unpaid. The OECD argues that 'greater gender equality in working hours is not just about more women in full-time employment. It is also about more men reducing their long hours in paid work.'[52] In countries where unpaid work is more equally shared, there tends to be smaller gender-specific differences in hours spent in the workplace.[53]

A reduction in working hours was a focus of the collective bargaining agreement between Icelandic employers and unions in 2019. The Federation of Special and General Workers argued for a reduction in full-time working hours from forty to thirty-two per week.[54] The deal that was eventually agreed paves the way for a reduction in the working week by up to four hours, but does not specify how this will be implemented. That is left to individual workplaces to determine.[55]

What Iceland Can Teach the World

Iceland's experience offers insights that can inform other countries' efforts to reduce the gender gap.

Legislation Makes a Difference

The clear lesson that emerges from Iceland's experience is that equality won't come about by itself. There are too many economic and cultural factors that lead to a preservation of the status quo. If things are to move forward, existing arrangements need to be disrupted through a determined effort at systemic change. Iceland demonstrates that legislative measures are an important way of achieving this. 'Legislative and policy change is the main agenda now,' Fríða Rós Valdimarsdóttir says. 'We are getting lots of new legislation. We have been preaching for such a long time, we have had a lot of governments, but we are heading in the right direction.'

Rósa Erlingsdóttir, head of the equality unit at Iceland's welfare ministry, agrees on the benefits of legislation, arguing that it sometimes needs to happen without a national consensus. 'People accept that. We saw it with mandatory quotas for women on company boards. If politicians want to wait until no one opposes it, it will never happen.'[56]

Solidarity Is Key

Iceland's success in reducing the gender gap would not have been possible without a massive community campaign, sustained over many years. This campaign has involved a huge portion of the country's population. Iceland is unique in some respects, says Fríða. 'We are a very small nation. That helps. Gender equality became a big issue.'

Rósa Erlingsdóttir and her colleague, Magnea Marinósdóttir, argue that gender equality requires women's rights defenders to challenge and protest the status quo. It needs women elected to positions of power (such as the presidency), creating alternatives to traditional male-dominated models of power and 'making the invisible realities of women visible'. And finally, it involves more men supporting gender equality, as women and men learn to share power.[57]

Hrafnhildur Hafsteinsdóttir, managing director of the Association of Women Business Leaders in Iceland, points to the country's unique geography and history as one of the reasons that mobilisation around gender inequality has borne results. 'Icelanders live in an environment that is ever-changing,' she says. 'We have had to adapt from the Viking times to an environment of fire and ice that's given us many challenges. We have had to rely on one another and use the strength of everyone. We work best together by using our diversity.'[58]

I ask Fríða what advice she would give to women in other countries around the world, and her message is simple. 'Organise, put forward your claims and be persistent. Never give up.'

Share Parenting Responsibilities

It's clear that gender equality at work is only possible if there is also equality at home. Given the huge share of unpaid domestic work that women have historically undertaken, equal pay and greater female workforce participation is unlikely to be possible unless men spend more time at home. Hence, Iceland – through a comprehensive and well-planned paid paternity leave scheme – has intervened to encourage fathers to establish a new relationship between work and parenting.

It's important that they do. The evidence suggests that children of highly involved fathers develop better cognitive abilities, perform better at school, are more resilient and have enhanced social relations. Positive co-parenting relationships also provide a model of the types of skills that children can use in their own relationships.

Mothers benefit from highly involved fathers too. While extended paternity leave allows women to return to work more quickly, involved fathers also lead to mothers experiencing a greater sense of wellbeing and lower rates of post-natal depression.[59]

Reflecting on their experience of parenting in Iceland, Sigurður and Nicole both emphasise the importance of early connections.

'Children are developing most in the early years of life, and being able to connect during that time is priceless,' says Sigurður. 'I hope more fathers will have a chance to build a strong relationship with their children.'

'The initial bonding is just so important,' Nicole says. 'And fun, judging by Siggi's experience.'

Sigurður and Nicole have high hopes for Iceland. 'I would like our children to experience that they are not at a disadvantage because of their gender,' Sigurður says. The fact that Iceland is number one in the world is 'great', Nicole says, 'but I think we still have work to do.'

FIVE THINGS
WE CAN DO NOW

1. **Introduce measures to close the gender wage gap.** Gender parity in wages and employment will not happen overnight, but we can move further towards it from today. Countries could require companies to analyse gender wage gaps and share the results with the public, or they could follow Iceland's lead and require companies to comply with a standard. Government could lead the way on this by revealing and addressing gender pay gaps in their ranks.

2. **Improve paid parental leave.** A generous parental leave scheme helps parents retain a connection with the workforce while taking time out to care for infants. Offering fathers extended paid paternity leave on a 'use it or lose it' basis encourages a more equal sharing of caregiving and allows women to return to work sooner. For countries without a parental leave scheme currently, benefits could start modestly – some in the United States propose twelve weeks of paid leave at 66 per cent of regular wages.

3. **Make childcare affordable.** Access to childcare enables both mothers and fathers to work when children are young. Affordability can be increased through subsidies, benefits, rebates or the provision of free childcare hours for working parents. Regardless of whether the provider is for-profit, government-run or community-based, childcare needs to be delivered by suitably qualified early childhood educators and governed by appropriate quality standards.

4. **Allow men to spend less time at work.** A work–life balance promotes mental and physical wellbeing and more effective sharing of work and domestic duties among couples. This could mean more men working flexibly or part-time, or the standard working week could be reduced for everyone. As a first step, individual businesses could pilot shorter working weeks, as some in Sweden and New Zealand have done with positive results.

5. **Legislate for affirmative action.** Targets and quotas for the proportion of women in senior management roles, on boards and in politics are an effective means of accelerating change. Introducing mandatory or voluntary quotas for private business is one way to achieve this. Similarly, governments can ensure that 50 per cent of all appointments to government committees or boards are women.

5

MULTICULTURAL MELTING POT
How to Build a Successful Immigrant Nation

'He left in the dead of night.'

Hutch Hussein tells me that her father, Niazi, fled to Australia from the Mediterranean island of Cyprus in 1970, when conflict between Turkish and Greek Cypriots was escalating.

'He was an apprentice mechanic and the bus he would take to work would often be hit by gunfire,' she says. 'He knew that his life was in danger and that it was going to be a long time until there was peace and reunification.'

Niazi had an uncle who had migrated to Australia, and he knew there was a community of Turkish Cypriots there. 'So, he decided. He said to his dad he'd just come for six months, visit his uncle and see what life was like.' Biting back tears, Hutch tells me, 'His family knew that he was going to go, but they didn't know when. He left at the end of Ramadan, just before Eid. The whole family woke up joyous the next day, then realised he was gone.'

With close-cropped hair and a beaming grin, Hutch has a personality that fills a room. Her words are tinged with the distinctive accent of a second-generation Australian. We've been friends for twenty years, since university, when we studied Middle Eastern politics together. But I've never heard her tell her family's story in full.

Hutch's father travelled by ship for forty days, eventually docking in Melbourne. 'He arrived on the Friday night, got a job by the Monday at a local mechanic and ended up staying for three years.'

On a trip back to Cyprus to visit family, he met and married Hutch's mother, Nahide, before returning to Australia to set up house. Nine months later, 'Mum arrived, and she worked at a television factory for three years,' Hutch says. 'It was on a processing line and there were other Turkish workers there, so she never had to learn English. They would just speak Turkish. It wasn't until I was born, three years later, that my mother learned English while watching *Play School* with me. So, I got to kindergarten not really being able to speak full sentences of English.'

In 1970s Australia there were not a lot of services for new arrivals. Sunday-morning television show *You Say the Word* aimed to teach English to newly arrived migrants. Beyond that, 'there were ad-hoc ethnic community groups helping their latest arrivals settle,' Hutch says, but nothing government-sponsored. She has since 'acted as interpreter and translator' for her parents when it came to going to the doctor or filling out forms.

Hutch went on to study social work, specialising in settlement services. She worked for a time in London, organising foster placements for the unaccompanied refugee children that would arrive at Heathrow Airport, situating them with families that spoke the right languages and dialects. Back in Melbourne, at the Spectrum Migrant Resource Centre, she would also become familiar with the airport route, picking up newly arrived migrants, settling them into rental accommodation and 'helping them navigate mainstream services with intensive case management for the first six months'.

For the past eight years, Hutch has been at the Brotherhood of St Laurence, a Melbourne-based charity, as senior manager of refugees, immigration and multiculturalism services, 'overseeing our multicultural communities team and the service delivery we do there'. Her role has also involved refugee policy, 'looking at the systemic issues arising from what we're seeing on the ground and advocating to government for better practice, better services and policy reforms'. Hutch has led submissions to parliament arguing for cross-cultural training for police officers and for a national campaign to address racism. A 2018 submission objected to changes that increased the waiting time before new migrants can access welfare payments.[1]

'It was really being able to see the experience of my parents that led me to become a social worker and get involved in settlement services,' Hutch tells me.

Settlement services like those Hutch Hussein administers are just one of the reasons Australia is often termed the most successful multicultural nation in the world. To claim such a title for Australia might seem counterintuitive, given that the country was founded on institutionalised racism in the form of the White Australia policy and still has a long way to go in terms of recognising its First Nations peoples and combating racial prejudice. Yet Australian immigration is taking place on a scale not seen anywhere else in the world. One in every two Australians was born overseas or has at least one overseas-born parent – double the proportion found in countries such as the United States and the United Kingdom. Immigrants and their children settle into Australian society successfully, and surveys show that Australians overwhelmingly believe immigration has been beneficial to the nation. Let's explore this good-news story.

The world's largest island and smallest continent has been home to humanity for well over 65,000 years.[2] Australia's First Nations peoples come from about 500 Indigenous nations, each with different cultures, beliefs and languages. Australia was colonised by the English, not without fierce resistance and frontier wars, in the late eighteenth century to serve as an open-air prison.[3] The initial European migrants were English and Irish convicts.

Since then, more than ten million people have migrated to Australia.[4] This is an awful lot in a country with a population that has just reached 25 million.

The first big wave of migration came with the discovery of gold in the 1850s. Between 1851 and 1861, more than 600,000 people arrived, almost trebling the colony's population. Most of these were from the United Kingdom and Ireland, but there were also many from China. The Chinese population peaked at more than 42,000 over that period, representing 3 per cent of the population. The influx of Chinese caused fear and anxiety among the Anglo community, who blamed them for everything from prostitution and gambling to smallpox. Considerable anti-Chinese sentiment culminated in a number of anti-Chinese riots.[5]

By the dawn of the twentieth century, Australia's population had grown to four million, almost a quarter of whom were born overseas.[6] The colonial settlements dotted across the country were in the process of uniting to become a federation. One of the drivers towards this was a sense of shared national identity, which was intimately associated with a desire to keep Australia white. It was accompanied by underlying fear of an Asian influx, fuelled by a substantial body of propaganda literature, with popular novels such as Kenneth Mackay's *The Yellow Wave* featuring an Asian invasion of the 'empty north' of Australia. In an illustration of the sentiment at the time, parliamentarian Chris Watson, who was later to become prime minister, expressed his anxiety at 'the coloured races insidiously creeping in ... we find that coloured people have gained more than a footing – they have practically secured control'.[7]

The *Immigration Restriction Act 1901* took its lead from similar legislation in South Africa, limiting migration to Australia by those who were not British and formalising the White Australia policy. The legislation didn't mention race specifically, as the government feared this would cause diplomatic offence. However, with the introduction of powers that enabled immigration officers to exclude anyone who failed a dictation test in a European language, that was its intended – and practical – effect. As Australia's first prime minister, Edmund Barton, told the parliament, the legislation was critical 'for the preservation of the purity of the race, and the equality and reasonableness of its standards'.[8]

The White Australia policy operated with little change until the end of World War II. In 1945, immigration minister Arthur Caldwell encapsulated a new policy focus with the phrase 'populate or perish'. The war had made Australia feel strategically vulnerable, given its geographical isolation and small population. While the government enticed many British migrants with the offer of £10 passages, British migration alone was unable to deliver the population growth and labour resources required. As a result, the government broadened the interpretation of 'white' for immigration purposes to encompass Southern and Eastern Europeans. Large groups came from Italy and Greece during the 1950s and 1960s, changing the ethnic composition of Australia forever. The 1971 census shows 289,000 Italian-born residents and 160,000 Greek-born residents, making up about 3.5 per cent of Australia's population at the time.[9]

In the 1960s, Australia experienced a cultural awakening. A new generation of young, internationally engaged activists started to challenge the White Australia policy, and the mood among the bureaucratic and political elite began to shift. With bipartisan support, legislation was introduced in 1966 to begin dismantling the policy, expanding pathways for non-European skilled migrants and creating new rules for citizenship and residence. A year later, Australians voted to overturn centuries of institutional racism by amending the constitution to allow Aboriginal people to be counted in the census and the federal government to make laws for Aboriginal people that could assist in addressing inequalities.

In 1973, with the election of the progressive Whitlam government, the last remnants of the White Australia policy were dismantled. A universal visa scheme was introduced, and citizenship rules were applied to migrants uniformly, regardless of their country of origin. The *Racial Discrimination Act* made it illegal to discriminate on the basis of race. To Whitlam and his government, the White Australia policy was 'dead and buried'.[10]

Not long after, a new wave of people began to arrive. In contrast to the ocean liners that had carried British and European migrants, the first Vietnamese, Cambodian and southern Chinese refugees arrived in leaky fishing boats, before more followed by plane. They have since been followed by waves of other groups fleeing conflict in the Middle East, Sri Lanka and Africa.

Since the 1990s, the focus of Australia's immigration program has shifted to skilled migration. An army of nurses, engineers, electricians and teachers has been welcomed to address labour shortages created by Australia's rapidly growing economy.

Migration incorporates a number of different categories. An asylum seeker has left their country and is seeking protection, while a refugee has already received such protection. A migrant moves country for any other reason, often to seek a better life. A skilled migrant is selected because their skills complement a country's labour-market needs and skills shortages.

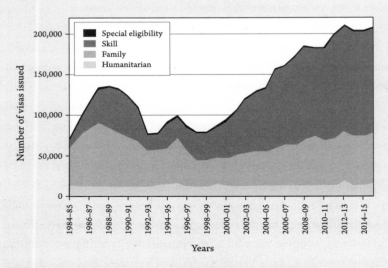

Permanent Migrants to Australia

Figure 12. Due to a focus on skills-based migration, Australia's migrant population is highly educated.

As Figure 12 shows, for the past twenty years skilled immigrants have been the largest category of migrant to Australia. Refugees and those migrating for family reasons – such as joining a partner or relatives already in Australia – are now in the minority. In 2015–16, family migrants were about 28 per cent of the total, and refugees about 8 per cent. While Australia has a substantial humanitarian program, it is far from the most generous in the world. Australia is well down the list, with other wealthy countries, such as Sweden, Germany, Austria, Norway and Switzerland, recognising and resettling more than twice as many refugees per capita as Australia.[11]

Skilled migrants represent almost two out of every three people arriving permanently in Australia. As a result, the migrant population is more highly educated than those born in Australia. Half (52 per cent) of those born overseas have at least some tertiary education, and the figure for recent migrants is 62 per cent. This compares to just 36 per cent for native-born Australians.[12]

Australian cultural commentator George Megalogenis notes that while migrants arriving in the mid-twentieth century were poor, today's migrants largely arrive with money. 'The previous waves from England, Europe and South-East Asia began their Australian journey on the lower rungs of the income ladder,' Megalogenis notes. 'The skilled immigrant lands between the middle and the top.'[13]

Since 2004, immigration has contributed more than half of Australia's population increase. For the past decade, net overseas migration (the number of migrant arrivals minus the number of migrant departures) has increased Australia's population by about 1 per cent each year.[14] On average, a new migrant arrives in Australia every two minutes.

Whereas the United Kingdom and continental Europe were once the source of most Australian immigration, over the past decade China and India have come to dominate as countries of origin. In these nations, growing middle-class, university-educated populations now have the means to search out opportunities internationally. And it's in these countries that Australia has found a reliable source of skilled migrants to fuel its economy and balance its otherwise ageing population. It has been only too happy to welcome them. Between 2006 and 2016, three times as many migrants to Australia arrived from Asia as from the United Kingdom.[15] For a country that just over fifty years ago was still pursuing an immigration policy that privileged skin colour over all else, this is a remarkable turnaround.

With one in seven Australians arriving in the last twenty years, migration is rapidly changing the country. Across the OECD, only tiny Luxembourg has a higher population share of foreign-born or second-generation residents than Australia, and 90 per cent of its immigrants are from elsewhere in Europe.

While people born in England remain the largest group of Australian migrants, China and India are the next-largest source countries. Overall, one in ten Australians was born in Asia, and of those born overseas, there are now more from Asia than from Europe. Just over half (58 per cent) of Australians are of Anglo-Celtic heritage, and a further

Immigrant Population Share

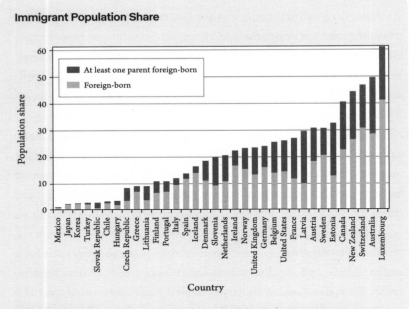

Figure 13. Nearly one in three Australians (29 per cent) was born overseas, and half of Australia's population now has at least one foreign-born parent.

18 per cent have a European background. About one in five (21 per cent) has a non-European background, and 3 per cent are Aboriginal or Torres Strait Islanders.[16]

Australian immigration is largely confined to its big cities. Only 64 per cent of native-born Australians live in densely populated cities, yet 85 per cent of migrants do. One in four Melbournians arrived in the past decade, and in the CBD, two out of every three residents were born overseas. A four-hour drive away, in the dryland farming area of West Wimmera, less than 1 per cent of residents were born in Asia.[17] Megalogenis notes that there are now parts of Australia predominantly populated by those born in Asia. 'Already the Asian-born outnumber the Australian-born in Melbourne's inner city, and in Auburn in Sydney's west,' he writes. 'They match the Australian-born in Melbourne's Dandenong, Sydney's Parramatta and Brisbane's Sunnybank.'[18]

Most Australians feel positively about immigration. According to a major survey by research group the Scanlon Foundation, 68 per cent of

Australians agree with the proposition that 'accepting immigrants from many different countries makes Australia stronger'. Only 6 per cent of Australians nominate immigration and population growth as 'the most important problem facing Australia today', with most far more concerned about economic and environmental issues. A vast majority (85 per cent) agree or strongly agree that multiculturalism has been good for the country. A global survey conducted by the US-based Pew Research Center asked these same questions slightly differently, and found a similar answer: 64 per cent of Australians (including 80 per cent of eighteen- to twenty-nine-year-olds) think that migrants make their country stronger. This is the second-highest approval rate in the world, behind only those friendly Canadians.

In Australia, attitudes towards migration do not change substantially across income groups. But they differ a whole lot based on education levels. Australians with a tertiary qualification are far more likely to be positively disposed towards immigration, with 79 per cent believing immigration makes the country stronger. Just 55 per cent of those without a tertiary qualification share the same view.[19]

The study of second-generation migrants is one way to measure how easily immigrants and their families integrate into their communities. In most countries, the school performance of second-generation migrants lags behind those with a more distant migration background, often by a considerable margin. Across the European Union, the gap is six months. However, second-generation Australians perform far better in standardised testing than their peers with Australian-born parents. In the OECD's Program for International Student Assessment (PISA) test, second-generation Australians have an average reading score more than six months ahead of their classmates with Australian-born parents.[20]

Second-generation Australians perform better academically regardless of their family's socio-economic status or country of origin. These students tend to read more books than their non-migrant peers, despite not having as many in the family home – it's likely that they access libraries much more often. The size and scope of Australia's migration program means that Australian schools are experienced at dealing with students from a diverse range of cultural backgrounds and language groups, and can provide the resources and teaching that students need to overcome academic obstacles they might face.[21]

Esther Rajadurai grew up in Sri Lanka and came to Australia at eighteen to study at Sydney's Macquarie University. Now in her early twenties and on the path to permanent residency, she is employed under a temporary work visa as an economist at the McKell Institute, a left-leaning think tank. She recently authored a paper focusing on why Australia is 'the world's most successful multicultural society'.

Rajadurai tells me that she chose to migrate to Australia 'because I have family and friends here and also because it has a really good education system'. She is convinced the fact that children of migrants do better than those of Australian-born parents 'speaks to a bigger story ... it shows how the children of migrants have been successfully integrated into the culture and have opportunities to grow and thrive and also treat this country as home'.

The statistics she can cite in support of her argument are impressive. The adult literacy level of Australian migrants – both native English speakers and those who grew up speaking a foreign language – is higher than in any OECD country. Over past decades, immigrants have successfully joined the workforce, experiencing an unemployment rate of 6 per cent or less. This is only marginally higher than the unemployment rate of those born in Australia, and long-term unemployment is more likely for native-born Australians than it is for immigrants. And as most come to Australia with skills, migrants are mainly doing valuable work – less than 10 per cent are undertaking low-skilled employment, the lowest rate in the OECD.[22]

Given all this, it's not surprising that the relative poverty rate for migrants in Australia (22 per cent) is similar to the rate for native-born Australians (20 per cent). Immigrants also have the same level of self-reported good health (83 per cent) as native-born Australians. While 8 per cent of immigrants live in overcrowded housing, this is less than half the rate of the OECD average (17 per cent), and compares to 21 per cent in the United States and 14 per cent in the United Kingdom.[23]

Multiculturalism

Since the 1970s, Australia's approach to immigration has been defined by the concept of multiculturalism: respect for a diverse range of cultures, coupled with the expectation of a shared commitment to the values of liberal democracy.

Multiculturalism is a repudiation of the White Australia policy and the assimilationist mindset that governed Australia for so long. Yet at the same time there is no particular emphasis placed on the maintenance of minority cultures. There is an assumption that migrants will gradually adapt to Australian culture, even as they may continue to maintain practices from their traditional culture.

The Australian culture that migrants adapt to is not fixed. The national identity of any country evolves over time – but Australian culture is perhaps more malleable than most, both because its history of white settlement and migration is short, and because of its changing demographics due to immigration. The scale of Australian migration means that the culture migrants adapt to is not entirely Anglo-Celtic. As Sydney-based academic Geoffrey Brahm Levey notes, 'Australia's Anglo culture took hits when coffee overtook tea and wine overtook beer as the preferred hot and cold drinks, respectively, in the 2000s.'[24] These changes occurred almost imperceptibly over decades, through the decisions of millions of Australians in the wake of the nation's consistently large migration program.

This concept of an evolving cultural identity generally has wide support. Even conservative prime minister Scott Morrison has observed that 'as Australians, our nationalism is divorced from ethnicity, race and religion' and has claimed with pride that 'we exchange and adapt the old for the new, bringing what's best, leaving the rest and embracing over time a new national identity'.[25]

Australian migrants come from all over the world, with no single migrant group dominating; immigrants live alongside those from a range of cultural groups. This is quite different to many other countries. In the United States, for example, more than 60 per cent of those who speak a language other than English are native Spanish speakers. In Germany, about 30 per cent of non-European immigrants are from Turkey.[26]

By contrast, those born in China are the largest non-English-speaking migrant group in Australia, but make up just 11 per cent of the total. Another 10 per cent are from India, 5 per cent are from the Philippines, 5 per cent are from Vietnam and 4 per cent each are from Italy and Malaysia. A further 3 per cent each are from Germany, Sri Lanka and Greece. Mandarin is the most frequently spoken language other than English, but is used by less than 3 per cent of the population. It represents less than 10 per cent of those who speak a language other than English at home.[27]

Julian Hill is a federal member of parliament whose electorate, Bruce, in Melbourne's south-east, is one of the most diverse in the country. More than half (53 per cent) of his electorate was born overseas, 57 per cent speak a language other than English at home, and one in five arrived in the country recently. All of these metrics are double the national average.

He speaks with me from a café in the suburb of Dandenong, Melbourne's multicultural epicentre. 'It's a unique place,' he says, 'where we have people from literally every part of the world – from more than 100 faith backgrounds, more than 200 different languages, 154 countries – living side-by-side and working together. The kids attend school together in a slice of suburbia.'

Hill says that while there is 'certainly a strong pattern of people communing in formal associations and gatherings with people of the same background', there are also places in the community where these groups come together. Migrants interact through 'the normal stuff of communities', including in spaces such as kindergartens, schools and workplaces. At Dandenong North Primary School, for instance, 46 per cent of students were born outside Australia, and 80 per cent speak a language other than English at home. In total, fifty-two different languages are spoken by the student population.[28]

Hill also says that local councils play a central role in 'providing spaces and events where different parts of the community can come together and share stuff in common, and also share their cultures with each other'. Each January, the City of Greater Dandenong arranges a multicultural Australia Day festival, bringing together 11,000 people from Dandenong and surrounds with music, performances, an awards ceremony and fireworks.[29]

Settlement Services

One reason for the success of the Australian migration program, according to Hutch Hussein, is the quality of its settlement services. 'We have really good services,' Hutch says, 'and if people are linked into them, they generally do well.'

What began as basic on-arrival accommodation and assistance has evolved substantially over seventy years. Intensive support packages now target the unique needs of those who arrive through the humanitarian program.[30] Refugees are offered hundreds of hours of free English classes and access to the government benefits afforded to all Australian residents, including healthcare.

Hutch's organisation is just one of many, including a vast network of multicultural, ethnic and faith-based groups, with a government contract to deliver settlement services. She says, 'We're navigating people through everything from how to use an ATM to the fact they don't need to place buckets around the house filled with water, because the water's not going to run out.' Also, 'we provide an orientation around the healthcare system and the legal system. Local by-laws too, such as how to understand parking signs.'

'Part of our six months of intense orientation is providing fortnightly information sessions, and the most crucial thing is linking people up to the things that help them feel the most settled. Knowing where to find things that keep them alive as well as connected.' This can involve 'linking them up with their social groups' and showing them 'where to buy food that they're used to eating'.

Hutch says that economic inclusion is a priority: employment support is part of the package of services 'so that people can feel a sense of contribution by being able to earn their own funds, make their savings and start making their own contributions to Australian life'.

Refugees in many well-off countries, such as Sweden and Germany, are offered similar services, yet Hutch tells me that Australia's settlement system has a reputation for being among the best in the world. The Australian Human Rights Commission, an organisation not known for hyperbole, claims that settlement services have been 'integral to the success of multicultural Australia' and are 'well-regarded internationally and represent good practice'. On a visit to Australia in 2012, the then United Nations High Commissioner for Refugees, António Guterres, applauded Australia's approach. 'One of the notable features of Australia's resettlement program is the excellent standard of settlement services provided to new arrivals,' he said. 'NGOs, community and faith-based groups, as well as central and local authorities, undertake essential and meaningful work toward helping new arrivals to integrate and settle into Australian society so that they can begin productive lives in this country.'[31]

Skilled and Temporary Migration

Abul Rizvi gives the impression that he would be comfortable in a suit and tie. As a former long-time public servant, he probably is. However, when I meet with him at his golf club in the Canberra suburbs, the retired Rizvi is dressed casually, in anticipation of a round of golf after we meet.

Indian-born Rizvi, who was the deputy secretary at the federal immigration department for many years, arrived in Canberra as a boy in 1966. His father, who had a PhD from Oxford, took up a position at the Australian National University. Following his retirement from the public service, Rizvi too is completing a PhD, on Australia's immigration policies. He tells me that the key factor driving Australia's migration program is the rapidly ageing population. Economic imperatives mean substantial immigration is needed now and into the future.

The factors that drive economic growth are increases in the rate of workforce participation, increases in productivity and increases in population. However, the share of the population in the workforce is declining due to age, and productivity growth is subdued. 'So they pull the population lever,' he says.

The Australian Bureau of Statistics projects that with low fertility, baby boomers retiring and increased life expectancy, the percentage of the population not of working age (the 'dependency ratio') will increase from fifty-two in 2017 to fifty-eight by 2042. Rizvi explains that 'if the population ages very gradually, the economy and budget is able to adjust', but if the median age rises rapidly, 'the economy finds it hard to adjust quickly, and the budget does too. A lot of people are left dislocated, and the problems are far greater.' By encouraging young and skilled migrants,

Australia hopes to slow the rate at which the population is ageing and guarantee more people working and paying tax to support the growing group of older Australians.[32]

To ensure the skilled migration program attracts those individuals of most benefit to Australia, applications for a skilled visa require a minimum number of points. Points are awarded for things such as age, English language ability, educational qualifications, skilled employment experience and the skills of an accompanying partner.[33] Unlike most countries, Australia's system allows someone to migrate to Australia without a job offer, and to find work once they arrive.

Rizvi feels that Australia's skilled migration program has been extremely successful: it has 'undoubtedly slowed the rate of ageing', he tells me. Other countries with ageing populations – such as Italy, China and Japan – will inevitably copy its focus on skilled migration and attraction of young, skilled migrants, he thinks. Germany, for example, recently changed its immigration laws to encourage skilled migrants, particularly if they work in any of the industries where there is a labour shortage.[34]

According to a report by Australia's Productivity Commission, skilled migrants pay an average of A$8100 (US$5500) in tax each year, about double the average rate of Australians in general. Skilled migrants – who generally arrive as young adults, with their education funded by someone other than the Australian taxpayer – contribute 'more tax revenue over their lifetime and make comparatively lower use of government-funded services'.[35]

In addition to growth in permanent migration, Australia has experienced a huge increase in temporary migration. This has been mainly driven by an influx of international students and those here on business. Education is big business in Australia, and is now its third-largest export, after iron ore and coal.[36] Australian universities have been aggressively targeting students from Asia. China alone accounts for one-third of the sector's revenue.

Temporary migrants are an attractive proposition for the government, as while they make an economic contribution and pay taxes, they are not entitled to government-funded services. As Rizvi says, 'They're a bargain!'

Temporary Migration to Australia

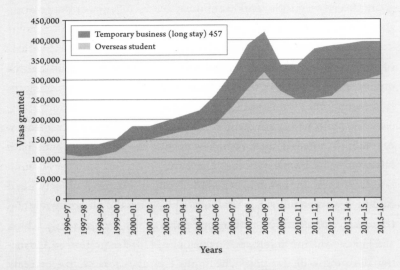

Figure 14. The number of visas granted shows that temporary migration to Australia has almost tripled over the past twenty years.

Temporary migration has historically been the means by which students and working holidaymakers 'could go through a gateway to permanent residency', Rizvi says. This enabled Australia to retain bright international students educated in its own universities, as well as employees from overseas who had proven themselves valuable. However, as we'll explore later in this chapter, the government recently changed the policy settings, and there are now far fewer pathways to permanent migration.

There are now more people living outside their country of birth than at any other time in human history. About 258 million people are migrants, or 3.4 per cent of the global population.[37] While this may sound like a relatively small share, it's equivalent to the combined population of Germany, the United Kingdom, South Korea, Canada and Australia all relocating within a generation.

Migration has been a wonderful success story for humanity.

It has clear benefits for the individual. Migrants generally earn far more abroad than they would at home. For example, migrant workers in the United States earn more than four times what a worker in their home country would for the same job. Those from developing countries also have better education and health outcomes after moving to industrialised countries, including a doubling of school enrolment rates and a sixteen-fold reduction in child mortality.[38]

Migration helps the country of origin, too. It can reduce unemployment, contributing to the alleviation of poverty. Those who have left often send money back home to family members, and these remittances – which amount to hundreds of billions of dollars sent to low- and middle-income countries each year – contribute more than three times the amount of official development assistance.[39]

For destination countries, migration aids economic growth. Changing the profile of the population and the labour force can increase productivity and address skills shortages. In countries such as Australia, where the population is ageing, migration can ensure that the ratio of workers to 'dependents' is maintained.

There is also evidence that migration contributes to innovation. In the United States, immigrants and their children helped found 60 per cent of today's most valuable technology companies. Tech giants such as Apple, Amazon, Google and Facebook were all founded by immigrants or their children.[40] The largest 500 companies in the United States form the S&P 500 Index, and 43 per cent were founded or co-founded by an immigrant or a second-generation migrant. Similarly, 49 per cent of the fastest-growing UK businesses have at least one foreign-born founder, and in Germany, 44 per cent of new businesses are founded by those with non-German heritage.[41]

Rates of migration across the world continue to grow. There are currently three times as many migrants as there were in 1970.[42] Population growth is one contributor – there are simply more people on the globe than at any point in human history. But international relocation is also becoming feasible for a broader range of people, due to reductions in travel costs and the rise of digital communication. Social media is one factor attracting people from their home countries by raising (an often exaggerated) awareness of living conditions in affluent countries. Lively diaspora communities around the world also make migration more attractive to many.[43]

Given the growing scale of international migration, it's no surprise that making relocation safer and better supported is increasingly recognised as an important global challenge.

Over the last decade, there has been a huge increase in the number of people displaced by civil or international conflict across the world. The patterns of refugee migration are influenced by major geopolitical events, such as conflict in Syria.[44] In 2018 there were 25.9 million refugees, and this number will only increase in future given that many poorer countries, such as island nations in the Pacific, are vulnerable to the impacts of climate change. The World Bank predicts that without concrete action to address climate change, around 143 million people will be forced to move by 2050.[45]

The challenges of migration are not only on a global scale. While Australian migration has been an indisputable success story, not everyone is willing to accept that success. There is a significant, and often disproportionately vocal, minority of Australians who are uncomfortable with Australia's immigration program. The Scanlon Foundation survey shows that the issues that evoke the strongest negative reaction are the impact of immigration on (what many perceive to be) overcrowded cities and on house prices, and government failure to adequately manage population growth.[46]

Rebecca Huntley is a researcher who regularly speaks with a range of Australians in focus groups. She points out that the subject of immigration is emotive for Australians. 'While the majority acknowledge increased immigration has brought many benefits in the past, they are worried about the current rate and future consequence of more people coming to Australia,' Huntley writes in the essay *Australia Fair*:

> That equates to a concern not just about the kinds of people who might come here, but also about whether governments are ready and able to invest in the infrastructure needed to service new arrivals. The anxiety is a reflection of lack of trust in our political leaders as much as it is a reflection of anxiety about cultural change.

Part of the problem is that not everyone is convinced by the economic arguments in support of immigration. To some, 'cutting back immigration seems the best way to protect our social safety net, our unique natural environment, our local jobs and our peaceful, suburban neighbourhoods – what we treasure about the Australian lifestyle'.[47]

Infrastructure Australia, Australia's independent infrastructure adviser, argues that more than US$400 billion (A$600 billion) of infrastructure spending is needed over the next fifteen years just to keep up with demand. Belatedly, some Australian governments have caught up to the fact that if a high rate of immigration is to be sustained, it needs to be accompanied by significant investment in infrastructure and services to provide for an expanding population. In Victoria and New South Wales – the states that accommodate the majority of Australia's population growth – governments now have substantial infrastructure programs in place.[48]

Nevertheless, the trust that Australians have for government has been steadily dwindling. According to the OECD, just 45 per cent of Australians report confidence in their national government, down from 53 per cent in 2007. This is marginally better than the OECD average (42 per cent), and substantially above the United States (30 per cent). Yet Australians trust government far less than those in countries such as Switzerland (80 per cent), Norway (66 per cent) and New Zealand (57 per cent).[49]

'There is almost no area of policy in which leadership is more important to allay fears and smooth out anxieties,' writes Huntley. 'We have to build greater faith that the leaders of our institutions, public and private, are planning well for a future where more doesn't equal less.'[50]

While Australians may have very practical concerns about immigration, race is also a factor. A big one. Up to 30 per cent of Australians indicate some measure of support for selecting migrants on the grounds of race, ethnicity or religion. Huntley (again – she's good on these topics) writes that many Australians have 'a sense that ethnic diversity naturally means a distortion, diminishment or outright loss of "Australian identity"'. Yet with one in every two Australians having at least one parent born overseas, 'this "Australian identity" is becoming harder for Australians themselves to define'.[51]

Former Australian prime minister Paul Keating described a country's national identity as 'the way it thinks about itself ... the commonly shared model of what its national values and priorities are'.[52] It's no longer easy to articulate what it means to be Australian, and some argue that Australia's national identity has not kept pace with its changing demography. Its foundation myths are monocultural in nature, involving stories of bushmen, World War I soldiers and cricketers. Australian politician Tim Watts, in his book *The Golden Country*, worries that 'the Australian Legend is no longer fit for purpose' and suggests that 'we need to build something new, with the same kind of emotional and symbolic power, to bind us together'. This goal is, as Watts says, a 'political project' requiring national leadership.[53] Yet it's a tough ask in contemporary Australia. Whereas national identity emphasises unity, multiculturalism emphasises diversity and difference. And it's arguable whether it's even the business of politicians to define national identity. The identity of a nation is something that unfolds and changes over time, the product of everyday human interaction.

It's an awkward, in-between time in Australian history, with national stories that no longer really work in a diverse, multicultural country, but without new narratives that can re-fashion a refreshed national identity. It should be no real surprise that some Australians are feeling unsettled, and yearn for a time when it was clear what it meant to be Australian.

Much of the Australian anxiety about immigration is directed towards asylum seekers, in particular those who arrive by boat. Australian governments have responded to this challenge by adopting an increasingly brutal set of measures. These include turning back boats and indefinitely detaining those captured in facilities located on the Pacific island nation of Nauru and on Papua New Guinea's Manus Island. Several hundred men from Afghanistan, Iran and elsewhere are being held on Manus, a remote landmass in PNG's north. The Australian government has been clear that none of these men will ever be resettled in Australia. While a small number have been resettled in the United States, the others remain there indefinitely. Conditions are desperate: reports of self-harm are frequent, and there have been a number of suicides.[54]

Australians value rules, procedures and fairness. To many Australians, even those who profess to be sympathetic to those fleeing perilous situations, boat turnbacks and offshore detention seem a reasonable response to those seen as 'queue jumpers' and an acceptable way to disrupt the people smugglers who profit from this trade. In a defining moment in contemporary Australian history, conservative prime minister John Howard was re-elected in 2001 after declaring that 'we will decide who comes to this country and the circumstances in which they come'.[55] Since then, political debate about the treatment of asylum seekers has been fraught. An uneasy bipartisan consensus has emerged, with both sides of politics supporting the rather draconian deterrence model of mandatory detention.[56] There are no signs that this consensus will break any time soon.

Asylum seekers arriving by boat exert a force on the Australian imagination – and on Australian politics – that far exceeds their numbers. Those arriving by air are treated with comparative dignity and granted protection visas, which enable them to live, work and access welfare benefits in Australia.

Immigration may be rapidly changing Australia, but there are parts of the country that remain seemingly impervious to this change. As *The New York Times* put it recently, 'in proudly diverse Australia, white people still run almost everything'.[57] The Australian parliament, for example, remains overwhelmingly white. Less than 10 per cent of politicians were born overseas, and less than 4 per cent have one or more parents from a non-European background. This is far lower than the comparable share in the US Congress (where 19 per cent identify as racial or ethnic minorities) and the British parliament (where 10 per cent are black or an ethnic minority). Across the Australian state and federal public service, 98 per cent of management is from an Anglo-Celtic or European background.[58]

The figures are just as bad in the business world. The share of company chief executive officers from a non-European background is just 3 per cent. Of senior managers, the share is 5 per cent. Seventy per cent of the board members of Australia's largest companies have an Anglo-Celtic heritage.[59] It seems that while the composition of Australia's population has shifted dramatically, its established power structures have not.

While immigrants as a whole are employed at much the same rate as those born in Australia, those arriving as refugees face a much harder time finding a job. Eighteen months after arriving in Australia, just 17 per cent of refugees are in paid employment. Although these results improve dramatically with time, helping newly arrived refugees into employment sooner is clearly a goal for Australia.

Part of the issue is that although newly arrived refugees receive a package of tailored settlement services, they are referred to mainstream services for employment support. Many report getting lost in this system and having difficulties in access, as there is little capacity for support.[60]

A number of organisations are now advocating for a program of assistance for humanitarian migrants in the labour market. 'Given the importance of economic inclusion,' Hutch Hussein says, 'that's something we need to do better at.'

One example of how this could look is the Jobs Victoria Employment Network run by the state government of Victoria. This program is aimed at addressing the gap in services for disadvantaged job-seekers, including refugees and asylum seekers. It offers mentorship, training, tailored employment preparation, and job placement and post-placement support. The service providers used by Jobs Victoria specialise in working with disadvantaged groups and leverage their links with employers in target industries to identify and fulfil employment needs.

The enormous increase in migrants from Asia, particularly those on temporary visas, has been the biggest recent transformation to Australian immigration. The government has now made it more difficult for migrants to obtain citizenship, notionally in response to terrorism concerns. The period of time before migrants can become citizens has been lengthened, twice, and the government has introduced a written test for prospective citizens on Australia's national history, values and civic responsibilities. The introduction of a much higher English-language hurdle has also been touted.

Migrants in Australia on temporary visas include international students, skilled workers and working holidaymakers. Temporary migration once provided them an established pathway to permanent residency and citizenship. However, this pathway has now been made less viable, creating a significant group of migrants who have been in the country for an extended period and wish to stay, but have very few options.

Because of the enormous appetite for skilled workers in Australia, it seems likely that, rather than return home at the end of their visa, these temporary migrants will simply have a new temporary visa issued, and perhaps another after that. This will add to what Abul Rizvi describes as the 'continuously growing stock of temporary entrants who can never get permanency'. He estimates this group at about two million and predicts that its number will rise significantly.

Rizvi sees the government's changes as 'a very high-risk strategy'. It could undermine the finely tuned compact that Australia's immigration program has been built on, which has at its heart the notion that legal migrants can seek a permanent home in Australia. How will this work if the country no longer provides this cohort of immigrants with any hope of becoming citizens?

The Australian immigration juggernaut continues apace, but the language used to talk about it has shifted. The story told by the Australian government today is less about Australia's diversity and more about the contribution immigration can make to the nation's economic self-interest.

What Australia Can Teach the World

Immigration is a sensitive topic. It generates fears and anxieties in some. Government needs to show that it can address the practical consequences of immigration, such as the infrastructure demands of a growing population. It is also incumbent on a nation's leaders to explain the reasons for – and benefits of – a large immigration program.

Encourage Skilled Migration

An emphasis on skilled migration is perhaps the important factor that has enabled Australia to welcome so many permanent migrants. These migrants are highly educated and reasonably affluent, speak at least some English and tend to find employment quickly. As a result, they have relatively little need for government services, and collectively they contribute significant tax revenue. Their children often do well at school and generally embrace Australian life. Countries such as Germany and Canada are now following Australia's lead and increasing their intakes of skilled migrants.

Australia has enjoyed largely bipartisan support for migration since the end of World War II. In recent decades, both of Australia's major political parties have supported a large, non-discriminatory skilled migration program. The huge growth in skilled migrants from China and India began under the conservative Liberal–National government from 1996, and has been maintained since then through multiple changes of leadership. This has occurred despite sometimes ugly rhetoric that has leveraged the anxieties of sections of the public, as well as intense debate about Australia's treatment of asylum seekers.

At times, populist voices have threatened to disrupt the bipartisan consensus, and there have been calls to limit Muslim immigration, but these voices remain largely on the margins. At the 2019 election, the only overtly anti-immigration party of any size, One Nation, won just 5.4 per cent of the national vote. Despite some peripheral haggling over the size and focus of Australia's skilled migration program, the consensus seems solid.

Sing the National Benefits

Australia shows that multiculturalism is a multigenerational project. As wave after wave of migrants, and their children and grandchildren, become Australians, the national identity evolves.

This is not as organic a process as it may seem. Some parts of the country don't change quickly. The profile of those occupying elite positions in business and in government will not automatically refresh to match the new demography. National stories and legends only get written over centuries. The demographic profile of the country alters, but a new national identity can be a long way behind.

That's why the stories we tell about migration on a national level are important – they can play a role in speeding up cultural change and social attitudes. Abul Rizvi, in an article co-written with journalist James Button, argues convincingly that support for migration requires a narrative that goes beyond the economic. The two point to 'the dynamism and fresh thinking that migrants bring; the buzz and pride of having global streets and cities, and opportunities for young people to work in them; the bridges to China and India and other countries that migrants can build; the prospect of developing a new and distinct Eurasian society in the most dynamic economic region on Earth'.[61] Telling this national story requires political leaders with the commitment to pull it off, even when faced with what may seem like countervailing public sentiment.

Australian prime ministers Bob Hawke and Paul Keating did just this in the 1980s and 1990s, emphasising Australia's engagement with Asia and opening up a national conversation about what this might mean for a transformation of national identity. Likewise, Canadian prime minister Justin Trudeau prompted debate in his country by suggesting that Canada could be the 'first postnational state' and that 'there is no core identity, no mainstream in Canada'.[62] In welcoming more than one million refugees to Germany in 2015, chancellor Angela Merkel assured Germans, 'Wir schaffen das' ('we can do this'). These leaders have been prepared to support immigration vocally, directing a conversation about the moral case for and social benefits of immigration, as well as the economic profits it may bring.

The Frameworks Institute is a not-for-profit think tank that conducts research on how to frame public debates to achieve social change. It concludes that to foster public support for immigration, leaders should refer to immigrants as 'us', not 'them'. In a country such as Australia, where half the population is a first- or second-generation migrant, this should not be difficult. But given the preponderance of white males dominating federal and state parliaments, inclusive language is something of which Australian leaders still need to be conscious.

Leaders can also gain traction by explaining how the immigration system works, making the positive outcomes for the nation explicit. When it comes to refugees, it is heartening to learn that moral arguments can be effective, tapping into the deeply embedded sense of compassion that most people have. The majority agree with the proposition that no matter where someone is born, they are entitled to basic human rights and to respect.

Logic and pragmatism – emphasising the fact that we need to consider all approaches to immigration and choose the most practical route for the nation – also holds sway with many. As does the use of metaphor to distil what is otherwise a complex topic (the Institute cites the example 'immigration is the wind in our nation's sails').[63]

Migrants themselves are assets in promoting this national story. Many are enthusiastic to support their new homeland, often becoming among the most patriotic of residents. Four out of every five (81 per cent) settled immigrants take out Australian citizenship.[64] 'I've noticed firsthand and with delight the fierce pride that new migrants have in Australia,' federal parliamentarian Julian Hill says. 'Their commitment and celebration of democratic values and free elections and the freedom that they enjoy becomes at times, in a lovely way, almost evangelical. Those diaspora communities then fuel and provide energy to those advocating for democratic reforms and human rights in their home countries, be it Afghanistan, Cambodia or Vietnam. Because their experience of it is so positive.'

Foster Inclusive Communities

Partly by design, and partly due to its location in the Asia-Pacific, Australia has been able to source migrants from an enormously diverse range of countries. As a result, it has largely avoided ethnic enclaves, and no single migrant group is able to claim status as Australia's predominant minority. Countries such as the United States, bordering Latin America, are likely to find it difficult to replicate this pattern. However, countries in Europe and elsewhere could, with a concerted effort, encourage migrants from a greater range of nations within their region.

Australian migrants live side-by-side with people from all around the world. As a result, with almost half of all Australians a first- or second-generation immigrant, migration is familiar. Everyone has a migration story. The ubiquity of Australian migration makes it accepted and understood, and today widely celebrated. Towns and cities host a busy calendar of cultural festivals, schoolchildren wear orange for Harmony Day, and immigration museums document the country's migrant history for citizens and tourists.

The Scanlon Foundation survey finds that for most Australians, multiculturalism is a two-way process of change, 'requiring adaptation by Australians to immigrants and immigrants to Australia'.[65] In practice, that seems to be happening. 'Overall, Australia's settlement model has served us incredibly well, because we've broadly got very integrated communities,' Hill says. 'Sure, some people might worship together with their own culture and language traditions. But their kids are pretty familiar with Greek Orthodox, or Serbian Orthodox, or Italian or Armenian, churches. It's not a threat, it's just kind of normal. We have people of all different races broadly living next to each other. It kind of works.'

Marriage between people of different cultures has long been regarded by sociologists as a key indicator of inclusive communities. As academic Geoffrey Brahm Levey notes, 'intermarriage is more likely in multicultural societies where different ethnic groups are more likely to come into daily contact with one another in schools, workplaces and social and community activities than in societies where ethnic minorities are residentially and/or socially more segregated'. In a study of census data, researchers from the Australia National University and Monash University found that in Australia, 'many ethnic groups show low levels of intermarriage in the first generation, but that by the third generation, rates of intermarriage are high'.[66]

About one in three marriages in Australia are between people who are born in different countries, and one in four between a person born overseas and a person born in Australia. A further 7 per cent are between partners born in different overseas countries who have each migrated to Australia.[67] More-inclusive communities, with fewer social and cultural barriers limiting citizens' interactions, is one of the great success stories of Australian multiculturalism.

Plan for a Larger Population

Much of the discussion about immigration in Australia defaults to talk about the economy. Successive Australian governments have built a consensus case that emphasises migration's importance to the national economy. Australians increasingly understand that with a rapidly ageing population, the country benefits from the energy displayed and contributions made by young and skilled migrants. A nation such as Japan, which has an ageing population but negligible immigration, represents a cautionary tale, with ageing dragging down Japan's GDP growth.[68]

Nevertheless, there are parts of Australia that feel as though they don't reap these economic benefits. Instead, all they see are clogged roads, expensive housing and neighbours to whom they can't relate. Migration programs need to be accompanied by new infrastructure. In the state of Victoria, there are now $70 billion of infrastructure projects underway, with much of Melbourne a giant construction zone as massive road and rail projects are completed. Sydney, too, is awash with infrastructure projects; trams have returned to the streets after more than fifty years, and a new metro project will deliver thirty-one new train stations.

Embrace Difference

Australia's migration program is enormous and sustained, and the government is understandably still grappling with some of the challenges it poses. Yet in a little over seventy years, Australia has transformed from a small, insular nation with a racist immigration policy to a cosmopolitan country that seeks to embrace diversity.

'We've had generations and different waves of migration,' Hutch Hussein says, 'and we've benefited from the diversity that each of those cultures have brought to our country. It's been enriching.'

Julian Hill feels that Australia's diversity is one of its greatest strengths. 'When I'm seeing all these incredible things, people so generously sharing their cultural traditions, I just wish that the people who are fearful of that diversity could understand what's happening in the suburbs, and how truly special and unique it is. It's not something to be feared, it's something to be celebrated and engaged with.'

Ultimately, everyone, migrant or not, aspires to much the same thing: quality of life. 'The prime motivation that has led people to board that boat or get on that plane has been the aspiration for a better life,' Hutch says. 'That's something that all parents aspire to for their kids and themselves. Fundamentally, migrants want to feel Australian. They want to feel a sense of belonging.'

Since Hutch's father first arrived in Australia fifty years ago, she and her family have been on a momentous journey. As Australia was edging slowly towards legalising same-sex marriage, she met and fell in love with her partner, Ariadne, who is of Celtic heritage. The two of them celebrated their love with an enormous ceremony attended by hundreds, including Hutch's extended family. They now have two young boys, who are growing up fast – the third generation in yet another Australian immigration success story.

FIVE THINGS WE CAN DO NOW

1. **Target migrants who have the skills the country needs.**
   The best way to ensure that immigration does not lower wages and employment is to use migrants to address labour shortages. Bringing a new set of talents and motivations, skilled migrants contribute to the economy in needed ways, thereby raising income and employment rates. Migration programs and laws governing immigration should make it easy for skilled workers to resettle in a host country. Skilled migrants may not only mean white-collar workers, either. Germany, for example, is lacking in nurses, caregivers and skilled labourers such as electricians and carpenters.

2. **Use temporary migration to address critical labour shortages.**
   If well designed, temporary migration programs are an effective way to alleviate labour shortages and minimise the risk of individuals over-staying their visas. New Zealand's temporary labour scheme allows workers from Pacific Island states to work on a seasonal basis, for no longer than seven months at a time. As there is an incentive to comply if workers would like to return in following years, it has an overstay rate of less than 1 per cent.

3. **Offer legal pathways for migration.** Irregular migration (for instance, asylum seekers arriving via boat) is not in anyone's interest. But a person only gets on a leaky boat if they have no other option. While physical barriers and enhanced enforcement can be effective deterrents to unauthorised migrants, evidence indicates that deterrence is most effective when coupled with sufficient legal pathways for migration. For example, between 1954 and 1964 the United States supported up to 400,000 seasonal workers to enter the country from Mexico each year. During this time, unauthorised migration from Mexico to the United States was nearly zero. Following the closure of this legal pathway, the demand for workers remained and unauthorised immigration spiked.

4. **Invest in quality support services.** Tailored, intensive support services help migrants – particularly humanitarian migrants – integrate quickly into mainstream society, minimising alienation and improving social cohesion. Pre-departure cultural orientation programs should be offered to refugees and other migrants, providing practical information, managing expectations and addressing questions they may have. From the point of arrival, immigrants should be supported with interpreters, housing and an introduction to relevant services. Longer-term, access to English-language classes, social and cultural orientation and help to navigate services such as healthcare and education are critical.

5. **Develop employment assistance for migrants.** The best way to ensure migrants settle into their host country quickly is to make sure they have a job. But many migrants have unique needs that are not readily addressed by mainstream employment services. Tailored employment services include specialised interpretive services; sessions to build a cultural and social understanding of labour market norms; capacity building, such as mock interviews; feedback and debriefs after failed employment outcomes; and linkages with other migrant support services. The Jobs Victoria Employment Network in the Australian state of Victoria is an example of this type of support.

6

PARADISE IN THE SNOW

How to Reduce Inequality and Raise Living Standards

t's snowing heavily when I talk with Gunnar Garfors in the Norwegian city of Oslo. Mid-morning in the middle of winter, it's minus five degrees (23 degrees Fahrenheit) and has only been light for less than two hours. In just a couple more, the sun will start to set again.

This doesn't faze Garfors, though. 'I love the Norwegian weather,' he says. 'The climate always changes here. We have a very clear four seasons, which means you never get bored. We have this saying that Norwegians are born with skis on their feet, and there might be some truth to that. We love skiing. We love going into nature.'

Garfors works at the Norwegian Broadcasting Corporation in central Oslo, surrounded by mountains, not too far from the waterfront on the Oslo fjord. He's settling back into a daily routine after travelling to all 198 of the world's countries. Twice.

Garfors grew up in the small village of Naustdal, on Norway's west coast. His father was a doctor on cruise ships, who regularly sent home cassette-tape missives of his travel adventures to Garfors and his six younger siblings. 'I remember those stories having such an impact on me,' Garfors says. 'He told us tales from the Philippines, from Japan, from China, from the United States, from Canada, and I was gobsmacked. And I promised myself that when I became as big as my dad, I would visit many countries as well. And so, I think that's where it started.'

The travel bug took hold in earnest in 2004, when Garfors travelled to Kazakhstan and Kyrgyzstan for a conference. 'The hospitality we received was incredible,' Garfors says. 'I resolved to visit all seven "stan" countries [Kazakhstan, Tajikistan, Uzbekistan, Kyrgyzstan, Turkmenistan, Afghanistan and Pakistan] to see if they were similar. When I ran out of stans, I decided I needed another goal, and that became visiting every country in the world. I finished five years later. And now I've done it twice.'

Garfors has been to all 193 countries that are members of the United Nations, as well as two UN observer countries (The Vatican and Palestine) and three other widely recognised countries – Kosovo, Western Sahara and Taiwan. He has written two books about his travels[1] and spent time reflecting on the qualities of each place. He is convinced that Norway's unique characteristics make it among the world's best. 'Naturally I am biased, but I'd say that Norway is one of the best countries in the world to live in,' he says. 'Not only do we have a democracy, free education, healthcare for all, good infrastructure and fair wages, but also a non-hierarchical society where solidarity and equality are important. Equality brings happiness, and this is a priority in Norway.'

Garfors' view is unsurprising, as it aligns with a host of studies reaching the same conclusion. Norway has extremely low social and economic inequality while maintaining the highest living standards in the world. Its democracy is ranked the strongest in the world and its residents are among the happiest. How does Norway do it?

Inequality in income and wealth is typically measured by something known as the gini coefficient, with 1 representing perfect inequality (one individual earns all the income) and 0, perfect equality (everyone earns the same). Once taxes and welfare payments are taken into account, Norway has a net income gini coefficient of 0.249, the second-lowest in the world, behind Iceland (0.244). It is markedly ahead of Australia (0.332), New Zealand (0.325) and the United Kingdom (0.328). The greatest inequality among the advanced economies is found in the United States (0.378), and Singapore (0.398), which have worse income inequality than the African countries of Malawi, Senegal and Uganda.[2]

Given its low rate of inequality, Norway also has relatively little poverty. Just 8.2 per cent of Norwegians live below the poverty line, which

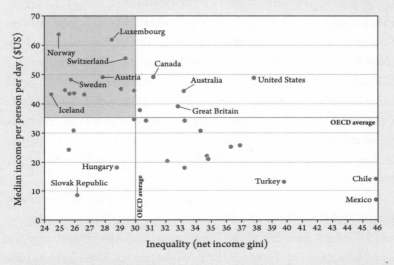

Figure 15. Norwegians have the highest incomes in the world, along with the second-lowest rate of income inequality.

the OECD defines as living on less than half the average national income. This is the fifth-lowest rate in the world, behind Iceland, Denmark, the Czech Republic and Finland. Countries such as the United Kingdom (11.1 per cent), Australia (12.1 per cent) and Canada (12.4 per cent) do far worse. The poverty rate in the United States (17.8 per cent) is more than double that of Norway.[3]

As Figure 15 shows, Norway manages to combine this relatively equal income distribution with the highest living standards in the world. At least partly underpinned by income from the country's huge oil and gas sector, Norway's GDP per capita in 2018 was US$67,614, higher than the United States' (US$62,853).[4]

Norway is ranked first on the World Economic Forum's Inclusive Development Index, which measures economic growth and development, inclusion and intergenerational equity, and on the Social Progress Index, which measures social and environmental performance. It also tops the United Nations Human Development Index, an aggregate measure of health, life expectancy, education and living standards, and ranks second (behind Denmark) on the Legatum Prosperity Index, an aggregate measure of wealth and life satisfaction. The World Economic Forum's Global Gender Gap Report ranks Norway second (behind Iceland), as does UNICEF (behind Denmark) in a recent report into childhood equality.[5] While much of Europe has struggled to rebound after the 2008 financial crisis, Norway is booming. According to UK think tank The Resolution Foundation, only Norway has seen generation-on-generation progress since the crisis. Whereas in the United States a typical thirty-year-old millennial is 5 per cent worse off than a Gen X-er was at the same age, in Norway they are 13 per cent better off.[6]

It manages all this while also being extremely democratic. Norway is ranked first on the Economist Intelligence Unit Democracy Index, and US-based democracy watchdog Freedom House gives the nation a perfect score in its 'Freedom in the World' report. These indexes take into account free and fair elections, government functioning, political participation, political culture and civil liberties.[7]

With impressive outcomes across such a range of measures, it's no surprise that Norwegians are a happy lot. According to the World Happiness Report, Norway has the third-highest 'subjective wellbeing' ranking in the world, just behind Finland and Denmark. When asked to rate their general satisfaction with life on a scale of 1 to 10, Norwegians give an average of 7.6, quite a bit higher than the British (6.8), Americans (6.9) and Australians (7.4).[8]

Dr Kristian Heggebø is a senior researcher at the Norwegian Social Research Institute. He is particularly interested in 'how vulnerable groups fare on the labour market, and in which institutional settings they perform better or worse'.

In person Heggebø, in his early thirties, has a friendly enthusiasm. Like Garfors, he grew up in 'a really small town on the west coast of Norway'. He argues that the structure of the labour market has underpinned Norway's success. Participation in employment is key, with work regarded as an expectation of every citizen. Although there is no minimum wage set by law, 70 per cent of Norway's workers are covered by collective agreements that specify wage floors. As a result, the minimum wage for a hospitality worker is US$19.50 per hour, and cleaning staff receive at least US$21.80 per hour.[9]

'In Norway, we've been very, very keen on trying to ensure that even for jobs on the lower end of the hierarchy, the wages are high enough that people are allowed to have a decent living,' Heggebø says. 'I think that's one of the key components – paying people a decent enough salary so that they can participate actively in an economic sense, and also in a social sense, in all of the activities that are available in the local community.'

Norway's 'compressed wage structure' allows people to 'participate actively in society, and also to take good care of their health', Heggebø says. 'You don't have to continually worry about making ends meet, so people's mental health and wellbeing will hopefully be improved as well.'

This wage structure means that the difference in pay between the average employee and their boss can be quite small. 'If you compare it to the United States, the United Kingdom and Australia, it's much, much smaller than many of these countries,' Heggebø says. In Norway, the average chief executive officer of a large publicly-traded company is paid twenty times the average worker's income. This ratio is far lower than in most other countries. For example, in the United Kingdom, CEO salaries are 201 times the average income.[10]

The Norwegian wage structure is made possible by strong collective bargaining. Unions play an important role. In Norway, 52 per cent of workers are union members, compared with 25 per cent in the United Kingdom, 14 per cent in Australia and 11 per cent in the United States. Unlike most industrialised countries, which have seen a substantial fall in union membership, the membership ratio in Norway has largely held steady over the past twenty years.[11] Unions and employers conduct talks on a bi-annual basis. In contrast to the adversarial collective-bargaining process in some countries, these are 'very, very tight collective efforts, where employers and employee representatives talk together and try to figure out how we can ensure a wage development that's both sustainable and fair', Heggebø says. In the 2017 negotiation round, for example, the unions' objective was long-term sustainable job growth and an increase in real wages. With Norwegian wages already among the highest in Europe, the employer association argued that wage increases needed to be modest to keep Norwegian companies competitive. After three days of negotiation – and no industrial action – an agreement was reached that provided for wage rises slightly above inflation.[12]

Heggebø says that the emphasis in Norway is on permanent contracts. 'This ensures that people have more stability, and they don't have to fear for their income levels when their temporary contract is about to run out.' Only 8 per cent of employees are on fixed-term contracts, below the OECD average of 11 per cent.[13] 'The average employee in Norway is quite strongly protected, and so, at least compared to other countries, the employers have less power.' Norwegian employers can only use temporary employees for up to twelve months, and the share of temporary employees cannot exceed 15 per cent of total staff.[14] 'We have devoted quite a lot of resources to ensuring that the negotiation position of individual employees is improved. So, this is also something that I personally believe is really important for how well we've done in recent years.'

Garfors agrees with this proposition, though he puts it a little differently. 'Norway is probably one of the worst countries in which to fire people,' he says. Employees have extensive protections against unfair dismissal.[15] 'If you have a job, it's thought a permanent position. It's really hard to fire you.'

Working Hours and Welfare

Residents of Norway enjoy shorter working hours than those in almost any country in the world – only Germans and Danes work less. Norwegians work an annual average of 1416 hours, which is 370 hours, or about nine and a half weeks, less than the average American.[16]

'We work seven and a half hours a day,' Garfors says. 'Normally you start at eight and finish at four. A lot of it is because both parents typically work, while the kids must be somewhere, and that's usually in kindergarten. If you're not there when the kindergarten closes, you'll have some really upset staff. So, there's some sort of self-regulation there. You have to pick up your kid.'

While a thirty-eight-hour work week is common to many countries, the difference in Norway is that people typically don't work overtime. In most OECD countries, the majority of employees work more than forty hours per week. Overtime in Norway can only be undertaken if the need is exceptional, and must be compensated with an hourly rate at least 40 per cent higher than normal. It can't exceed ten hours per week, twenty-five hours a month or 200 hours a year. As a result, most employees (65 per cent of Norwegian men and 55 per cent of women) work between thirty-five and thirty-nine hours per week. Very few work longer than forty hours a week.[17] Norwegians also enjoy five weeks of annual leave, which factors into these figures.

While Norwegians might not work as many hours as their international counterparts, they are extremely productive. 'People work hard when they are at their jobs,' Heggebø says. 'On average, I think the common Norwegian works rather hard while at work, and then goes home rather early.'

Norway has the second-highest labour productivity rate in the world, behind only Ireland. For every hour worked in Norway, US$80.80 of economic output is generated. This is substantially more than the United States ($63.50), Australia ($52.50), Canada ($49.80) and the United Kingdom ($48.50).[18] Investment in equipment, technology and the education and skills of employees all contribute to productivity. As Figure 16 on the next page shows, countries with lower annual hours tend to have higher labour productivity.

Around the world, this phenomenon is increasingly catching the interest of researchers, who think that stress, fatigue and factors such as sleep deprivation may make overworked employees substantially less productive. For example, a recent study found that in a Dutch call centre, as the number of hours worked increased, so did the average handling time for a call, meaning staff became less efficient.[19] Long hours also leave little time for necessary life tasks, such as paying bills or running errands, so employees may attempt to fit these into their work day.

Companies around the world are experimenting with shorter working hours. In 2018, New Zealand's Perpetual Guardian, which manages trusts, wills and estates, trialled a four-day work week, with 250 staff

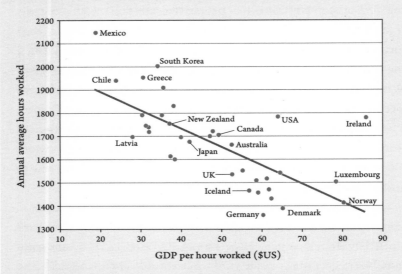

Figure 16. Norway has an exceptionally high level of economic output per hour worked compared to other OECD countries.

getting paid for five days. They reported lower stress levels, greater job satisfaction and an improved work–life balance during the trial. The results showed that productivity over the four-day week increased by 20 per cent, so the overall rate of work completed in a week was the same. The company decided to adopt the schedule permanently.[20]

Residents of Norway are also assisted by a strong welfare system. Unemployment subsidies provide security for those looking for work, allowing people to claim around 60 per cent of their previous salary (up to a capped amount) for two years while they are job-hunting. 'We have quite a lot of active labour market policies that will help people to hopefully be reintegrated into the labour markets if they're unemployed,' Heggebø says. The assistance provided includes employment services, as well as training schemes that help the unemployed to improve their skills. Temporary wage subsidies are also made available to help job-seekers build up experience in the labour market.[21]

These initiatives appear to be working. A study by Norwegian researchers found that these programs have a significant effect on employment and earnings for those who participate, both in the short term and five years later.[22] Norway has one of the lowest long-term unemployment rates in the world. As of 2018, just 14.4 per cent of those unemployed had been out of work for more than twelve months, which is less than half the average rate across the OECD.[23]

'We try to be as inclusive as possible,' Heggebø says. 'So, if people have a health condition – or if you're a newly arrived migrant – we try really hard to integrate you into the labour market if that's possible. If not, we have comparatively generous disability benefits, that will enable people to participate – at least to some extent – effectively in society. You don't run the risk of getting kicked out onto the streets.'

To illustrate this point, Heggebø refers to his aunt, who has the rare genetic disorder spinal muscular atrophy. The nerve cells that service her muscles don't work properly, leading to progressive muscle weakening. Her condition has, in part, motivated his research into health and well-being issues. 'She's in a wheelchair, and I see that she's unable to do all the things she would like, but nonetheless she doesn't go hungry.'

The provision of universal welfare services is at the heart of the Norwegian approach, as in most of the Nordic states. Means testing is unusual. Free services include parental leave, family allowance, education (including higher education) and training. Generous support is provided for the elderly, including subsidised home help. Everyone is covered by public health insurance – meaning healthcare is free at the point of access.

Around the world, some politicians have expressed a fear that extensive welfare creates a disincentive to work, as some will choose to live on benefits. This is the language of 'dole-bludgers' or 'leaners'. For example, former UK prime minister Margaret Thatcher felt that generous provision for unemployment and sickness sapped 'some working-class people's drive to work.'[24]

Heggebø dismisses this argument quickly. 'The overwhelming majority really want to participate in some sense,' he says. 'This is clear in cases of unemployment and how unhappy people often tend to become after just a short while relying on unemployment benefits.'

There's certainly no obvious evidence that Norway's generous welfare provision is creating any disincentive to work. Seventy-five per cent of the working-age population are employed, which is a higher proportion than in the United States (71 per cent) and Australia (74 per cent). At the same time, the unemployment rate in Norway is less than 4 per cent – a rate most economists would consider full employment and significantly below the OECD average (5.3 per cent).[25] Women's workforce participation is particularly high: for every 100 men in Norway's workforce, there are ninety-five women, and on average women working full-time earn just 7 per cent less than men (compared to 14–18 per cent in Australia, the United Kingdom and the United States).[26]

To aid workforce participation, heavily subsidised kindergarten is provided for children up to age five. Low-income parents of children aged three to five have access to twenty hours free childcare each week, allowing them more freedom to work or study.[27] Norway also provides forty-nine weeks of parental leave at full pay or fifty-nine weeks at 80 per cent of earnings. At least fourteen weeks must be taken by the father.[28]

Norway also invests heavily in education. Kindergarten children learn through a play-based program (much of which occurs outdoors – regardless of snow, rain or winter dark, kids spend most of their time outside) delivered by university-trained staff with expertise in preschool education.[29] The nation spends more per student on primary and secondary education than any other in the OECD, and as a result there is almost no private expenditure. In the average Norwegian primary school, there are just ten students per teacher, compared to fifteen in the United States and Australia, seventeen in the United Kingdom and twenty in France. Educational outcomes across science, reading and maths may not rival Singapore, but are substantially higher than the OECD average.[30]

This state investment continues beyond compulsory schooling. University students in Norway graduate with very little debt. Lina Gjerde studied at the University of Oslo for nine years, becoming a licensed psychology clinician and earning her PhD. She did not incur any debt from course fees. She does owe about US$37,000 in loans for living expenses, but she paid no interest on this debt while she was studying, and she's now on a repayment plan of US$245 per month – an amount she can manage easily on her salary from the Institute of Public Health, where she works as a postdoctoral researcher.

'I am happy with the way things turned out for me after earning my degrees,' she says, speaking with *Fast Company* magazine. 'I earn enough to support myself. There are many people here who do not enjoy paying their taxes, but I actually do enjoy it because we get so much back.'[31]

Norway provides higher education free of charge to both domestic and international students. Unlike higher education systems in many countries, the Norwegian university sector is almost entirely publicly funded, and revenue from international students is not pursued as a business opportunity. On all these education and welfare measures, the country is truly remarkable.

Taxing the Rich, Giving to the Poor

Over past decades, there has been incredible progress in reducing poverty around the world. In the decade to 2018, the share of the world's population living on less than US$1.90 per day fell from 18.1 to 8.6 per cent. In 2015, more than one billion fewer people were living in extreme poverty than in 1990.[32]

While global rates of extreme poverty are falling quickly, the gap between rich and poor continues to grow. According to Oxfam, just twenty-six billionaires now control as much wealth as the 3.8 billion people that make up the poorest half of humanity.[33] The economies of rising countries such as China and India are growing much faster than the nations in the OECD. So inequality between countries is decreasing – the gap between the richest and poorest countries is smaller than it was. But the World Inequality Report shows that the gap between rich and poor *within* countries has been increasing nearly everywhere. The United Nations Development Programme reports that between the early 1990s and the late 2000s, inequality within countries increased by 9 per cent in high-income countries, and by 11 per cent in low- and middle-income countries.[34]

It was not long ago that some in economic policy referred to a need to choose between 'sharing the pie' and 'growing the pie'. Now we know that the best way to grow the pie may be to share it more equally. There is

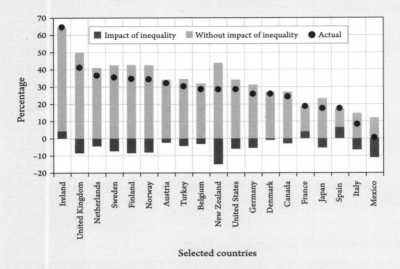

Estimated Consequences of Increased Inequality on Economic Growth

Figure 17. According to the OECD, growth in economic output between 1990 and 2010 would have increased materially had inequality not worsened between 1985 and 2005.

a solid consensus across key global economic bodies, such as the World Bank, the OECD and the International Monetary Fund, that rising inequality has damaged economic growth.

Inequality hurts economic growth because people from disadvantaged backgrounds under-invest in their education. The nation does not benefit from the productivity that a more highly educated population would generate. The OECD advises countries to target redistribution efforts towards children and teenagers, as families are where key decisions on education are made.[35]

Our understanding of best-practice economic policy has shifted in the last decade. Even the International Monetary Fund, once a staunch advocate of economic neoliberalism – an ideology that promotes free markets, free trade and small government – has changed its thinking. It now argues that neoliberal economic policies have increased inequality and stunted economic growth.[36] Consequently, a serious effort to address inequality needs to be at the heart of any effort to grow the economy.

The Relationship Between Income Inequality and Social Mobility

Figure 18. The Great Gatsby curve shows that countries with low income inequality, such as the Nordic states, have higher social mobility.

Inequality not only impacts on economic growth; it also hurts social and economic mobility. Miles Corak, a professor of economics at City University of New York, developed what is known as the 'Great Gatsby curve' – a reference to F. Scott Fitzgerald's best-known novel and its depiction of inequality and class in 1920s America. The term was popularised in a speech by Alan Krueger, chairman of former US president Barack Obama's Council of Economic Advisers.[37] The Great Gatsby curve shows the relationship between the concentration of income and wealth in one generation and the ability of those in the next generation to move up the economic ladder. Higher levels of income inequality among parents make it less likely that their children can improve their socio-economic status. Families become trapped in a multigenerational cycle of poverty.

As we can see in Figure 18, countries such as the United States, the United Kingdom and Italy have relatively high income inequality and low social mobility. Countries with low income inequality, such as Denmark, Norway and Finland, have relatively high social mobility. It seems the American Dream of upward social mobility through hard work is more likely to be achieved in the Nordic states than in the United States!

The best way to reduce inequality is through a progressive taxation system – where the rate of tax increases according to income – along with economic redistribution through the welfare system.

In general, countries that generate more revenue from tax achieve more redistribution. For example, most Nordic countries reduce more than 35 per cent of the inequality generated by the market through redistribution, whereas Chile reduces only 5 per cent. Norway reduces 30 per cent of market inequality through taxes and welfare payments, above the OECD average of about 26 per cent. Countries such as New Zealand (17 per cent), the United States (18 per cent), the United Kingdom (23 per cent) and Australia (25 per cent) redistribute less than the OECD average.[38]

There's lots of scope to increase taxes without hurting the economy. Most of the countries with the highest living standards are high-tax nations. Of the fifteen nations in the world where the average person has an after-tax income of more than US$40 per day, eleven collect more tax than the OECD average.[39]

The International Monetary Fund argues that there is 'no strong empirical evidence that progressivity has been harmful for growth' and that progressive taxation can be implemented 'without significantly hurting growth'. It claims 'optimal tax theory suggests significantly higher marginal tax rates on top income earners than current rates'.[40] There is also support among economists for the notion that 'very high earners should be subject to high and rising marginal tax rates on earnings'.[41]

A more progressive taxation system might seem impossible in some countries. However, there is hope. Once stripped of its ideological framing, people around the world consistently express a preference for more-equal distribution of wealth.

Michael Norton and Dan Ariely are academics at Harvard and Duke universities. They interviewed thousands of Americans and asked them to describe their ideal distribution of wealth. There was a surprising level

Tax Revenue of the Top 15 OECD Countries for Median Income

Country	Median Income (US$ per person per day adjusted for purchasing power parity)	Tax Revenue as a Percentage of GDP	OECD Average Tax Revenue
Norway	$63.80	39.0%	Above
Luxembourg	$61.80	40.1%	Above
Switzerland	$55.60	27.9%	Below
Austria	$49.20	42.2%	Above
Canada	$49.20	33.0%	Below
United States	$48.90	24.3%	Below
Sweden	$48.30	43.9%	Above
Germany	$45.30	38.2%	Above
France	$44.70	46.1%	Above
Denmark	$44.70	44.9%	Above
Australia	$44.40	28.5%	Below
Belgium	$43.80	44.9%	Above
Finland	$43.50	42.7%	Above
Iceland	$43.40	36.7%	Above
Netherlands	$43.30	38.8%	Above
OECD average	**$30.30**	**34.3%**	

Sources: Median income from 'The Inclusive Development Index 2018: Summary and Data Highlights', World Economic Forum, Geneva, 2018, pp. 18–22. Tax revenue as a percentage of GDP from 'Tax Revenue, Total, % of GDP, 2018 or Latest Available', OECD, Paris, 2019.

of consensus. An overwhelming majority of all demographics (including Republican Party voters and the wealthy) preferred a distribution of wealth considerably more equal than the status quo. When asked to choose between a distribution of wealth mirroring that found in Sweden and the current pattern in the United States, 92 per cent of Americans chose the Swedish model. Similarly, in a 2019 poll of Americans, Fox News found that 'increasing tax rates on families earning over a million dollars a year' enjoyed broad support, with 65 per cent in favour.[42] Based on these studies, it seems that pressure on governments to keep taxes low may be coming from those with vested interests, such as those in business and at the top end of town, rather than from the average voter.

Norway is small. With just over five million people, it is marginally bigger than Ireland or New Zealand. The stunning Scandinavian nation is defined by its extraordinary coastlines, with steep-sided fjords and glaciers snaking down from ice fields. Home to the northernmost towns in the world, parts of Norway enjoy twenty-four-hour daylight during summer and the surreal lights of *aurora borealis* in the winter darkness.

Equality runs deep in Norwegian culture. It has never had a nobility, and class differences have historically been small.[43] 'We have been a rather flat society in terms of hierarchies,' Garfors says. 'It's very uncommon for one person to be the big boss. Even in some offices, in some workplaces, it's difficult to find who is actually the boss. Of course, there is always a boss somewhere, but delegation of responsibilities is important here.'

This is represented in the language, too. Along with the other Scandinavian countries, Norway has more or less dropped the formal version of 'you' (equivalent to *Sie* in German or *vous* in French). While an initial introduction may involve a handshake and full names, first names are generally used beyond that. Few Norwegians would think to refer to anyone as 'sir'.

This egalitarian attitude manifests in its citizens' aspirations. The Norwegian version of the American Dream is a little different, with less emphasis on self-realisation. 'If there is a Norwegian Dream,' Garfors says, 'it's probably that you should get a nice education and you should get a nice job. And you raise your kids and they're cross-country skiing and playing football.'

A high level of trust is an important feature of Norwegian society, as in all Scandinavian countries. More than 70 per cent of Norwegians report that they trust others. This is the second-highest rate in the world, marginally behind Denmark.[44] 'Bosses trust their workers,' Garfors says. 'If it turns out that you abuse this trust, of course that's a different story. But as a rule people are trusted, and I think that's very important in terms of equality. Responsibilities are delegated, and that's probably the best way to show you trust someone. A lot of people leave work at twelve and do half the day at home, or if they want to work in a coffee shop or in the library or wherever, they can. So that's quite common as well. I think this makes us happier, just knowing that you're trusted.'

Together with this trust comes a level of openness that some in other countries would find confronting. For example, everyone's tax returns are publicly available.

Heggebø supports this. 'Personally, I think it's great that we have that openness,' he says. 'You should be allowed to know what people who do similar work to you earn.'

But while it might be good for salary benchmarking, research has found that this transparency has increased the gap in life satisfaction between rich and poor. In other words, because people were acutely aware of their income relative to others, rich people felt happier, and the poor less happy.[45]

Perhaps as a consequence, the policy settings were tweaked in 2014. Citizens can now see who has looked at their tax return. So if one is inclined to search the income and financial history of colleagues, lovers or in-laws, these individuals will receive an alert letting them know that their records have been accessed. This change has led to a dramatic reduction in the number of people viewing private citizens' tax returns, although no reduction in the scrutiny applied to high-profile people such as politicians.

Norwegians pay high taxes, but perhaps not as much as we might suspect. Overall tax collections in Norway amount to 39 per cent of GDP, which is above the OECD average (34.3 per cent), and higher than those in the English-speaking countries are used to. However, eight countries in the OECD collect more tax than Norway, and France and Denmark collect a much higher proportion (46.1 and 44.9 per cent respectively).[46]

Income tax in Norway is not particularly high. The average income tax for a single person with no child is 27.6 per cent, not much more than the US rate of 26 per cent.[47] Norway's top marginal rate is 39 per cent, which is lower than in Australia, where the top rate is 45 per cent. But with a 25 per cent value-added tax on most goods and services, it costs a lot to live in Norway.

Heggebø says that those he knows are happy to pay tax. 'People see that the taxes are well spent,' he says, pointing to free healthcare, free or affordable higher education and generous sickness benefits. 'There are, of course, some – most often the wealthiest individuals – who complain about high tax levels in Norway, but the majority are more preoccupied with other political issues.'

Government is *big* in Norway. Government spending adds up to just over half of GDP (50.8 per cent). National, county and municipal governments spend a collective total of US$30,754 per person a year – far more than the OECD average of US$18,231. In comparison, UK government spending is just US$17,760, and Australia spends US$18,334 per person. Government spending in the United States is a little higher, at US$22,685 per person, partly due to its enormous defence budget.[48]

Norway can afford to be generous because it generates substantial revenues from oil and gas production. It ranks fifteenth on the list of oil-producing nations, which is topped by the United States and Russia. But only the Middle Eastern Gulf states (Kuwait, Saudi Arabia, Qatar and the United Arab Emirates) produce more oil on a per capita basis.[49]

Rather than hand over extraction licences to the big oil companies a generation ago, the Norwegian government set up its own company and has been an equity partner in profitable oilfields. It has also implemented an aggressive petroleum taxation regime that slugs oil companies with a tax of 78 per cent on profits.[50] As a result, Norway has been able to secure enormous revenues and preserve the benefits for future generations. In 2018, the Norwegian government received about US$31 billion from petroleum activities – around $6000 per person. Ten years ago, it received almost double this amount.[51]

Revenue from oil and gas has enabled Norway to maintain huge government surpluses over more than twenty years. In 2018, the national surplus was 7.3 per cent of GDP – easily the highest in the OECD (the next highest was South Korea, at 2.8 per cent). Nevertheless, this was nearly the lowest it has been in almost twenty years. Past surpluses have been as high as 19 per cent.[52]

This has led Norway to amass the world's largest sovereign wealth fund, worth more than US$1 trillion, or two and a half times the size of the Norwegian economy. The figure equates to about $US190,000 for every person in Norway. To guard against a downturn in oil and gas prices that would impact Norway's exchange rate, this fund is invested entirely offshore, including in tech companies such as Apple, Alphabet, Microsoft and Amazon.[53] Returns from the fund will contribute to future government revenue as income from oil phases down.

'It's not fair to spend all of this money just in one generation,' Heggebø says, 'because oil and gas resources have been built up over several thousands of years. It belongs to not just the current generation, but also to the ones that come after us.'

Access to resources might seem like a lucky break, but throughout history they have also been a curse, bringing high inflation, extreme levels of indebtedness and sometimes corruption or civil war. This negative relationship appears to hold regardless of a nation's initial wealth. Between 1960 and 1990, the economies of countries poor in natural resources actually grew three times faster than resource-rich nations. Researchers point out that during the twentieth century, newly industrialising – and resource-poor – nations such as South Korea, Taiwan, Hong Kong and Singapore grew extremely quickly at the same time as oil-rich countries such as Mexico, Nigeria and Venezuela went bankrupt.[54] Nobel laureate Joseph Stiglitz concludes that 'the extraction of resources lowers the wealth of a country' and even that 'if a country is unable to use the funds well, it may be preferable to leave the resources in the ground'.[55]

Other countries have largely squandered the windfall from their resources. For example, the Australian government earnt about US$135 billion over a decade from a mining boom. According to think tank The Grattan Institute, it spent 90 per cent of this on tax cuts and spending increases that cannot be sustained into the future, creating a substantial underlying budget deficit.[56]

Given the dismal history of resources-led economic development, the way Norway has managed its oil and gas resources is impressive. To Norwegians, it's a source of great pride. According to the government, 'Norwegian oil policy is based on the principle that our petroleum resources belong to the nation and should be developed under full national control as an integral development of the nation as a whole.'[57] That egalitarian attitude at work again.

Like all countries, Norway has its challenges. A common misperception is that it is culturally homogenous, but the proportion of the population that is foreign-born (13.9 per cent) is actually higher than in the United States (13.1 per cent).[58] Most migrants are from nearby countries within the European Union, such as Poland, Lithuania and Sweden. However, there are also significant populations born in the war-torn regions of Somalia, Iraq-Kurdistan and Syria.[59] Heggebø says that in Norway, immigration 'is a rather recent phenomenon' (at least from countries other than Scandinavian neighbours), and it's not been an easy social adjustment. Over the past few years there has been a rise in anti-immigration sentiment, and in the 2017 elections the anti-immigration, populist Progress Party gained more than 15 per cent of the vote, to form part of the governing coalition with prime minister Erna Solberg's Conservative Party.[60] Government ministers have expressed concern that unless immigrants can be successfully integrated into the workforce, large humanitarian intakes may place pressure on Norway's welfare state, forcing the government to raise taxes or reduce benefits. It has since taken several small steps to tighten immigration to Norway. Asylum applications to Norway are now at their lowest level in more than twenty years, though it seems this is due less to government policy and more to a broader trend of fewer asylum seekers coming to Europe.[61]

Unemployment among Norway's foreign-born population is high, at about 9 per cent. Although it is lower than the foreign-born unemployment average across Europe (14 per cent), it is much higher than most English-speaking OECD countries.[62] Heggebø says that immigrants with non-European backgrounds 'have a considerably lower employment rate compared to native Norwegians and immigrants from European countries'. Some of this is due to discrimination by Norwegian employers; it is also because the skills of migrants aren't matching the skills that are in demand.[63] 'Norway has a rather highly educated workforce, with high qualifications required in most sectors,' he says. 'It's difficult to achieve the educational qualifications in demand if you come from a refugee situation and you have had very, very little education in your source country.'

Garfors introduces me to a friend, Nathkai Safi, who arrived in Norway at age twelve as a refugee from Afghanistan. Her parents were highly educated and politically active in Afghanistan, resisting the Russians during the Soviet–Afghan war. She tells me of the difficult transition to Norway: her parents deeply depressed, 'far, far away' from the country they loved, feeling a burden to their host nation. Yet the small town to which they moved was extremely welcoming, and over time they adjusted. Safi has built a successful career as a vascular surgeon. Now a Norwegian citizen, she is positive about her experience, saying she has not experienced 'racism or discrimination in any way'.

Yet I also speak with Hazem Ali, a refugee from Gaza in his late thirties. While he says he has never faced overt racism, he has experienced subtle forms of discrimination. Despite being an engineer, with multiple degrees and extensive work experience, Ali found the process of getting a job in Norway extremely difficult. He applied for 'maybe two or three hundred positions'. He now works with Garfors at NRK, the government-owned radio and television broadcast service.

While oil and gas extraction has made Norway extremely wealthy, burning of fossil fuels is the key contributor to climate change. This sits uneasily with progressive Norwegians. According to advocacy group Oil Change International, Norway is the world's seventh-largest exporter of emissions. Norway has been a vocal advocate on climate action in international forums, concerned about the melting Arctic, yet it continues to open up the Norwegian Arctic for oil exploration. 'There is significant cognitive dissonance as the country fails to address the impact of its oil and gas extraction,' the report says.[64]

Given the dire warnings of climate scientists, Norway's role as one of the world's largest fossil fuel producers risks putting it at odds with the global community. Some of its recently opened oilfields are due to produce for another fifty years. Its plans for further exploration and oil extraction are incompatible with a global warming limit of 1.5 degrees Celsius. As Garfors says, 'We provide 2.1 per cent of all the oil in the world and 3 per cent of all the gas. And we're 0.07 per cent of the world population. We pump up all this gas and oil, and we sell most of it. So, looking at it that way, we are really awful as polluters of the world. But the oil, the gas, that's what's made us wealthy, and most of it has been used for the people: for healthcare, for education. Pretty decent infrastructure as well.' As the contradiction at the heart of the Norwegian miracle becomes more apparent, it's difficult to see how Norway can continue on this path indefinitely.

There *are* signs that Norway might be disentangling from its reliance on oil and gas. Its sovereign wealth fund is selling off stakes in coal companies, as well as those that explore for oil and gas. Instead, it is investing in renewable energy, a growth sector. Grants from Innovation Norway – a government-funded agency supporting industry development – are helping start-ups to develop renewable energy technology.[65]

While the country remains committed to the oil and gas industry, the parliament voted to keep key parts of the Arctic off-limits from drilling, despite significant opposition from oil companies and unions. In this, Norway is effectively walking away from billions of dollars in oil revenue.[66]

Is Norway truly an economy miracle, or just the fortunate beneficiary of the rivers of gold that have flown from its natural resources? This is not an unreasonable question, Heggebø says, because 'the oil industry makes up such a large proportion of our economy'. Yet Norway's economy is fuelled by several industries, including hydropower, which it exports to the rest of Europe, and aquaculture, in which it is a world leader. Norway has the world's fifth-largest shipping fleet by dollar value, and tourism contributes to 9 per cent of its economy and nearly 13 per cent of its jobs.[67]

Heggebø is confident that Norway would have been successful regardless of oil. 'The way that we have chosen to structure our welfare state and our economy, I think that would ensure reasonably good outcomes, even without the oil industry.' He points to neighbouring Denmark and Sweden, neither of which has access to oil resources at any scale, but nonetheless achieve similar outcomes to Norway in living standards and poverty rates. 'They are not as good as Norway in these domains,' he says, 'but they're nearly as good.'

What Norway Can Teach the World

Norway shows that it is possible to build a strong economy without high inequality. While there are factors unique to Norway – not every country has access to vast oil and gas resources, for example – there are some ideas we can take away.

Encourage Participation

'Norwegian society is among the richest in the world because of high social inclusion and economic participation,' Heggebø says. 'Even people holding "low-skill" jobs and those unable to participate in the labour market can be active members of the local community.'

Norway has been able to enjoy economic success for such a prolonged period because of its 'continually high employment rate', according to Heggebø. 'This implies that everyone of working age contributes with tax revenue.' By making it easier for parents to work – through paid parental leave, heavily subsidised childcare and shorter hours – women's participation in the workforce has risen extraordinarily. By investing heavily in programs that support people to enter the labour market, Norway assists otherwise vulnerable groups – such as those from disadvantaged backgrounds or with health problems – into work. 'Limiting social exclusion is a cornerstone in the Norwegian welfare state model,' Heggebø says.

Invest in Education

Quality kindergarten, schooling, vocational education and tertiary studies help disadvantaged young people to 'beat the odds'. A more-educated population means that more people are able to make an economic contribution. There is evidence that performance at school as a fifteen-year-old is a good indicator of outcomes in early adulthood, with higher school performance associated with university completion and an increased likelihood of a job that requires a tertiary education.

No country can claim to have eliminated socio-economic inequalities from education. Across the OECD, students from disadvantaged backgrounds are about three years behind students from advantaged backgrounds. But Norway is one of the world's leaders in addressing inequity in education, with socio-economic status only explaining a small part of the variance in student outcomes. Only Iceland and Estonia do better. Estonia achieves its results with free early childhood education, and schools that usually have rich and poor students in the same classroom.[68]

Inequality in education is often already observed by age ten, so investing in high-quality early childhood education for kids from disadvantaged backgrounds is key, as this sets a pattern for educational engagement into the future. Overall educational outcomes will be improved if targeted support is given to low-performing students from disadvantaged backgrounds and to schools in low socio-economic areas.

Given that about two-thirds of a country's population is already of working age, governments, businesses and communities also need to work together to provide learning opportunities to disadvantaged groups, such as refugees and migrants, to increase employability. Norway demonstrates how this can be done not just through formal education, but also through structured on-the-job training that helps unemployed people to learn new skills.

High Tax Can Exist Alongside Economic Growth
High taxes in Norway have not hurt the economy. In fact, by smoothing out the income distribution and providing universal services, Norway has benefited economically. This is a lesson we can learn not just from Norway, but from many of the world's richest countries that collect a greater share of tax than the OECD average. Average incomes in places such as Austria, Sweden, Germany, France and Denmark are among the highest in the world, yet they collect revenue from taxation equivalent to 37–46 per cent of GDP, substantially more than Australia and the United States, which generate tax revenue of about 27 per cent of GDP.

Norway may have high taxes and relatively little inequality, but it's also quite competitive, with the sort of conditions likely to lead to sustained economic growth. The World Economic Forum ranks Norway at number seventeen on its Global Competitiveness Index, one place behind Australia. The Forum itself is not afraid of taxation, arguing that 'restoring greater tax progressivity with higher top tax rates should allow for more equitable income distribution without much impact on economic activity or productivity'.[69] More important than the overall tax rate in driving competitiveness is a country's performance across a range of policy areas, such as technology adoption, economic stability and innovation capability.

Make Smart Investments (And Keep Making Them)

Norway has been fortunate to have access to the immense wealth of its North Sea oil and gas fields. However, while other resource-rich countries have squandered their profits, Norway has shown extraordinary foresight in constructing a regulatory and taxation regime that means it is not just multinational oil companies which benefit from the nation's bounty. Norway's sovereign wealth fund acts as a hedge against a global downturn in oil and gas prices and ensures that future generations also benefit from the industry's proceeds.

Other countries have taken inspiration from Norway's experience. Timor-Leste established the Timor-Leste Petroleum Fund to invest the tiny country's petroleum and gas income. At the end of 2017, the fund had a balance of about US$17 billion, which is rather a lot for a developing country of just 1.3 million people.[70]

Around the world there are more than sixty sovereign wealth funds, which are government-owned and may invest in foreign assets. They exist in places as diverse as Singapore, Botswana, Chile and Alaska. They may be created – as in Norway – as an endowment for future generations, or they may serve as a 'rainy-day fund' for use in an economic downturn. Regardless of their purpose, saving some of the proceeds of natural resource extraction in this way is clearly a better strategy than succumbing to the 'resource curse' that many resource-rich countries throughout history have experienced.

After travelling around the world, Garfors is home for now. 'I'm very lucky,' he says. 'My mum still lives in Naustdal, and she has the most beautiful view in the world, overlooking a fjord, islands, mountains, glaciers, a river and everything. So I jokingly say the reason I travelled around the world was to see if I could find an equally good view anywhere else in the world. I keep saying I have not succeeded.'

Although he's out of new countries, Garfors is not entirely finished with travel. 'I could live anywhere for a while, and I probably will have addresses abroad from time to time,' he says. 'Still, I believe that Norway will remain home for the largest part of my future. I am very fond of the clean air, how nature is accessible to anyone and the relatively inclusive society here in Norway.'

The nation has some challenges ahead. 'The government needs to do much more about the future of this country and the world. To keep pumping up oil and gas uncritically is not a viable solution, for the short, medium or long run,' Garfors says. But he is confident that the country can succeed. 'We should invest a lot of the money we have made on oil and gas in research to find sustainable and futureproof ways to make a living. If we manage this, the future is bright – and not only because of the Northern Lights and the midnight sun.'

FIVE THINGS WE CAN DO NOW

1. **Move towards progressive taxation.** One of the best ways to reduce inequality is progressive taxation – where the tax rate increases according to income. Low-taxing countries such as the United States, Australia and South Korea could consider raising taxes incrementally. There is an emerging consensus among economists that increasing taxes does not hurt economic growth.

2. **Begin to redistribute resources.** Redistribution of the proceeds of taxation through the welfare system helps groups such as families, the unemployed, the sick or disabled and aged pensioners. It is an important way to ensure that all people are able to participate meaningfully in society regardless of their individual circumstances, and together with progressive taxation is a key way to keep inequality to a minimum. Redistribution can involve cash benefits, direct provision of goods or services, or tax breaks that have a similar effect.

3. **Reduce working hours.** Working less provides employees with more time to care for children, exercise or socialise. Shorter working hours are associated with greater productivity, as workers who are not exhausted or stressed tend to get more done. Reducing working hours is also likely to lead to greater gender equality in the home, as it enables more effective balancing of work and family responsibilities. Limiting overtime, increasing the length of paid annual leave (or, in the case of the United States, introducing statutory annual leave) or incrementally reducing the standard working week are ways to achieve this.

4. **Create a fund for the future.** All countries that are drawing on the windfall gains associated with resource extraction would be wise to accept that the revenue is unlikely to continue forever. Global prices can change and resources can deplete. The creation of a sovereign wealth fund is a hedge against this eventuality and also ensures that the benefits of prosperity are shared with future generations.

5. **Help people into work.** Everyone wins when more people are in work. Some groups – such as people with a disability, refugees and the long-term unemployed – are likely to require extra assistance to find a job. Assistance can involve training programs that help people develop their skills and temporary wage subsidies to make it easier for employers to take on job-seekers while they build work experience.

7

FROM DICTATORSHIP TO DEMOCRACY
How to Have a Fairer Political System

Mid-May 1998: Indonesia is in chaos. Its capital city, Jakarta, has experienced three days of riots. Buildings have been razed and shops looted, rioters encouraged by the absence of security forces. More than one thousand people are dead, many burned alive in shopping malls. Women are being raped. Reports suggest the military itself has coordinated, led and orchestrated the violence.

A few days earlier, at the elite Trisakti University in Jakarta, police shot at students who were calling for the resignation of Indonesia's president, Suharto. Four were killed and dozens injured. The turmoil spread across the entire country. In the city of Medan, in North Sumatra, student protests escalated into riots. Clashes between police and rioters led to the deaths of six protesters and injuries to more than 100. Extensive rioting also took place in the cities of Surakarta, Surabaya, Padang and Palembang.[1]

The economy was in deep trouble, with the Asian financial crisis hitting Indonesia particularly hard. Over the previous year, the Indonesian rupiah had lost 80 per cent of its value against the US dollar, many local companies had gone bankrupt and an estimated US$150 billion in capital had been withdrawn from the country. During 1998, Indonesia lost an incredible 13.5 per cent of its GDP.[2]

President Suharto had just attained another five years in office after his Golkar Party won elections widely known to be rigged – as it had won every election since he came to power thirty-one years earlier. Suharto ensured victory by deploying tactics such as forcing political opponents to merge their campaigns, preventing opposition parties from criticising the government and coercing civil servants to vote for Golkar. A system of rewards, punishments and violence meted out by thugs helped warrant compliance.[3] The dictator had stacked his cabinet with family members and business associates. His daughter Tutut became Minister of Social Affairs, while Bob Hassan, a long-time friend and business associate, was made Minister of Trade and Industry.

Vedi Hadiz was living in Jakarta at the time. He had returned to Indonesia in 1997 after completing his PhD at Murdoch University in Perth, Western Australia. Through the 1980s and early 1990s, he worked for various non-government organisations while campaigning against Suharto. He is now a highly respected academic, publishing a slew of books and journal articles on Indonesian politics. Speaking to me in his office at the University of Melbourne, where he is director of the Asia Institute, Hadiz recalls the period vividly. 'I remember a lot of people who looked mysteriously like soldiers but weren't dressed as soldiers attacking neighbourhoods and so on,' he says. 'I saw truckloads of people being transported back and forth between neighbourhoods to attack them, and frankly that would not have been possible without the connivance of security forces.'

Less than a week later, half a million Indonesians marched in the city of Yogyakarta, and there were large demonstrations around the country calling for Suharto's resignation. Thousands of students occupied the grounds, lobby and roof of the parliament building in Jakarta.[4] 'A couple of times I went there,' Hadiz says. 'I remember one time at night I went there after a meeting with some activists. I just wanted to see whether everybody was all right, talk to the students, because by that time there was a whole new generation that I didn't personally know, having only returned a year earlier.

'I was chatting with them and it seemed all right, and I thought, *Well, okay, nothing's gonna happen tonight,* so I took a cab and went home. When I got home, I switched on the TV and I saw that those same students had been attacked by soldiers not long after I left. So, I missed being bashed by about five minutes.'

Pressure was mounting on Suharto. At a press conference, Harmoko, a Suharto loyalist and Speaker of the Parliament, called for his resignation. Amien Rais, the leader of Muhammadiyah – one of Indonesia's two largest Islamic organisations – threatened to mobilise more than a million people to do the same.

In an attempt to alleviate tensions, Suharto outlined to the public plans that would involve reshuffling the cabinet and, ultimately, a new election.

But this move did not play out as he anticipated. Suharto received a letter signed by fourteen cabinet members rejecting the formation of a new cabinet. With his ministers' support eroding, and facing the threat of impeachment from Harmoko, Suharto's position became increasingly untenable. On 21 May, in a short statement, Suharto announced his resignation, effective immediately. Vice-president BJ Habibie became president.

'I was at home when Suharto made his resignation speech,' Hadiz says. 'I remember that although I couldn't really afford it at the time, I opened a bottle of wine to celebrate that he had finally gone.

'It was a very, very strange feeling, because I grew up in a generation that thought Suharto would probably die in office. It was really hard to fathom that he could be ousted. It actually took me quite a long time to come to terms that it was happening, after so many years being in the anti-Suharto movement. When it was actually happening it seemed surreal.'

Indonesia has since enjoyed almost twenty years as the third-largest democracy in the world. In the period generally referred to as the *Era Reformasi* (reform era), it has run numerous free and fair elections for all levels of government. Freedom House rates Indonesia's political process highly, giving it a score of eleven out of twelve for 'electoral process' (higher than the United States, which receives ten out of twelve) and a score of thirteen out of sixteen for 'political pluralism and participation'.[5]

The scale of Indonesia's democratic system is staggering. The presidential election held in April 2019 was the world's largest-ever single-day election, with 154 million Indonesians peacefully casting votes at 800,000 polling stations staffed by six million election workers. More than 20,000 seats were contested by over 245,000 candidates.[6] The turnout was the highest on Indonesian record, with about 80 per cent of eligible voters participating. This was much higher than in the United Kingdom, which saw 67 per cent of the population attend a voting booth in the 2019 elections, and in the United States, which saw 56 per cent of enrolled voters cast a ballot in the 2016 presidential election.[7]

Importantly, Indonesian civilians now have supremacy over the military. There is also a legally enshrined separation of power between the executive, legislative and judicial arms of the state, and for the most part Indonesia enjoys a vibrant civil society. Considering it is a nation of 17,000 islands, with a diversity of strong faith-based cultures (from Arabic-style cultures in Aceh in the west through to Pacific Islander Papua in the east), this is a remarkable achievement.

Indonesia's relatively smooth transition from authoritarianism to democracy has been especially impressive given the dashed democratic hopes of the 2011 Arab Spring. In Libya, Syria and Yemen, protest movements have morphed into full-scale civil war. In Bahrain, pro-democracy protests were violently crushed, and the country is now one of the Middle East's most repressive states. In Egypt, the toppling of President Mubarak failed to bring democratic reform, and authoritarian rule has since returned.

Similarly, over the same period in which Indonesia's democracy has flourished, its neighbours in South-East Asia have become increasingly autocratic. Thailand is ruled by a military junta that came to power in a coup in 2014, Cambodia is run by an authoritarian regime, Laos is a one-party state, and Myanmar's transition from military dictatorship to democracy has stalled.

In this context, Indonesia is a shining light in Asia and the world. While its democratic system is by no means perfect – more on that later – Indonesia demonstrates that it is possible to make, and sustain, a transition from dictatorship to democracy.

Suharto's regime was centralised, and dominated by the military. Cronyism was at its heart. His friends controlled huge monopolies and held valuable concessions (such as the right to operate tollways or log forests), while his children acquired assets worth billions of dollars. Political opponents were killed, jailed or sent to labour camps. Tens of thousands died in East Timor alone following its illegal annexation to Indonesia in 1975.[8] Nevertheless, the regime largely enjoyed the support of Western countries such as the United States, thanks to Suharto's focus on the suppression of communism.

Under Suharto's regime, election results were more or less a foregone conclusion. Suharto was able to play factions off against one another. His talent was in manipulating military leaders to ensure he was able to rely on them to divide and rule.[9] He would intimidate, jail or execute those considered a threat. The legacy of that period still haunts Indonesians today.

During the country's only other leadership transition, in 1967, when Suharto came to power, 500,000 (and possibly more than a million) people were massacred. Large-scale killings – instigated by the armed forces and government – began as an anti-communist purge, but ended up targeting ethnic Chinese, alleged leftists and many others.

One of those jailed during that time was Dr Ken Setiawan's father, Hersri, who was detained as a political prisoner from 1969 to 1978. Setiawan, who has a doctorate in law, researches human rights in Indonesia and Malaysia. From Yogyakarta, Setiawan tells me via Skype that her father was imprisoned because he was a member of Lekra, a literary and social movement associated with the Indonesian Communist Party. He was never formally charged or convicted of any 'crime'.

In 2015, Setiawan accompanied her father when he returned to the island where he was imprisoned. 'It's something that is obviously very central to the identity of our family,' she says, 'and to me on a very personal level. To be able to return at some point with your child, I think that was meaningful for him, but it was for me too. To stand on that land where he was really just thrown away to die, but then to come back ... I think there's power in that. It's not hard power, but it's meaningful. We are here. We're still here. We know the story, we're told the story, and in a way it's really all that we have got, but it's a lot.

'As an academic it was interesting to be there, but in the end it was a deeply personal, personal journey.'

With the atrocities of 1965 still very much alive in the memory of Indonesians, many worried that the 1998 transition could end in bloodshed of a similar scale. Some were concerned Indonesia faced potential disintegration, similar to that which destroyed the Soviet Union and Yugoslavia.[10]

'Indonesia in 1998 was actually on the brink of collapse,' Setiawan says. 'We saw increasing ethnic unrest, the rise of political militant Islam, separatism.'

Those involved in negotiations following Suharto's resignation were acutely aware of two particular threats. First, it was not clear what the military would do during the transition. Prabowo Subianto was head of Kostrad, the army's 27,000-strong Strategic Reserve Command. This was the same position held by Suharto in 1965, when he used it to seize power. 'I remember Prabowo was being chased around,' Vedi Hadiz says. 'People didn't know where he was. They were afraid he would actually launch a coup.'

Second, Indonesia was facing widespread ethnic, religious and separatist violence. Some Islamist forces were agitating for a state based on sharia law, the moral, legal and religious code followed by Muslims. In debates about potential changes to the constitution, three Islamic factions were advocating for an amendment to make sharia law obligatory for Muslims. These proposals were eventually voted down almost unanimously.

Extensive negotiations to reach democracy took place over the five years following Suharto's resignation. They incorporated a diverse range of voices, including surviving elites, oligarchs and emerging leaders of civil society. 'I was part of some of the meetings and discussions about new political laws, new legislation on elections and parties, parliaments and so on,' Hadiz says. 'They were always inviting intellectuals. And also, international development agencies came around and provided advice. It was an interesting time to be in Indonesia.' Drawing on a long-suppressed desire for *Negara hukum* (the rule of law) and human rights, the new system had ambitions to become a fully fledged liberal democracy.

Restructuring the System

To defuse communal and ethnic tensions and ensure a range of voices were heard in Indonesian democracy, the electoral system was built upon proportional representation. This means parties are elected to parliament in proportion to the number of votes they receive.

Single-member electorates found in countries such as Australia, the United States and the United Kingdom mean that the winner takes all. It often leads to two dominant parties in parliament. By contrast, the multi-member electorates in Indonesia mean a variety of political parties can be elected in each electorate, and there is less chance of a single party being able to dominate. Cross-party alliances have become common, along with a preparedness to make deals. This has not necessarily been conducive to good government, with the sharing of power between major parties meaning that clearly identifiable opposition parties have not been able to emerge.[11] Nevertheless, it has meant that pluralism has been maintained, and tensions between groups have not escalated, which is a significant factor given Indonesia's cultural make-up.

Another feature of the Indonesian electoral system is that purely local parties are excluded.[12] To participate in a national election, parties need to demonstrate that they have a national reach. This requirement means that smaller secessionist movements have not been able to gain widespread political momentum.

Under the Suharto regime, the executive arm of government was clearly dominant. However, Indonesia's new democratic system established a clear separation of power between the executive, legislative and judicial arms, in the same manner as most Western democracies. The legal system operates independently of the executive; the executive, which consists of the president, ministers and their departments, is responsible for administering the laws made by parliament, with funds approved by a parliamentary budget process.

The separation of powers has been supported by the establishment of the Constitutional Court, whose role is to safeguard democracy and the constitution according to the rule of law. It performs many of the functions of the Supreme Court of the United States, the High Court of Australia or the myriad of constitutional courts that exist throughout the world. Setiawan rates the establishment of Indonesia's Constitutional Court as one of 'the biggest achievements'. When political parties or individual politicians have challenged the electoral laws, the Constitutional Court has made a number of key decisions and extended a range of political rights, changing the shape of Indonesia's electoral system. For example, the court ruled that provisions banning former members of the Communist Party from standing for election were invalid; it also ruled that those whose names did not appear on the electoral roll could vote provided they could prove their residency, such as with a valid identity card.[13]

In 1995, Transparency International rated Indonesia as the worst country in the world in its corruption index.[14] Since then, new institutions have been established to combat the endemic dishonesty that characterised the Suharto regime, such as the Corruption Eradication Commission, whose remit is to investigate and prosecute cases of bribery, fraud and exploitation. The commission has confronted this legacy of the pre-Reformasi era aggressively, prosecuting a number of cases involving politicians and other senior officials. The Indonesian public has delighted in media broadcasts of wiretaps revealing detail of quite sleazy behaviour. The Corruption Commission has a conviction rate of almost 100 per cent, with more than 1000 corrupt public officials sentenced to date.[15]

This development is clearly working. In Transparency International's latest report, Indonesia was ranked mid-pack, at eighty-ninth, with a score of thirty-eight out of 100. While this is a very long way off the country ranked least corrupt, Denmark, which has a score of eighty-eight out of 100, it's also a long way ahead of the country at the bottom of the list, Somalia, which has a score of ten out of 100.[16]

Hadiz describes the commission as 'the most successful product of Indonesian democracy', noting that from time to time 'it's been politicised, it's been defanged and so on, but it is the symbol of Indonesian Reformasi'.

G iven the local conflict and secessionist movements across Indonesia, and the very real fear that the country would implode, one of the first steps taken by the Habibie government in 1999 was the radical devolution of government power. While the Suharto regime was highly centralised in Jakarta, the new arrangements saw the widening of governmental and fiscal responsibility to local representatives at the district and municipality level.

The federal government now has full authority over only seven areas of policy: foreign affairs, defence, security, justice, religion, monetary policy and fiscal policy. The provinces of Aceh and Papua were given special autonomy at the provincial level, allowing them to keep more of their revenue and adopt elements of local culture into their legislative processes, such as sharia law in Aceh. (Indonesia's still heavy hand in these provinces has not been unproblematic, particularly in Papua, as we will see later in the chapter.) Decentralisation has reduced separatist agitation, increased budget transparency and improved policies as competition at the regional level for investment has grown.[17]

Edward Aspinall, an academic at the Australia National University, writes that 'devolution has greatly expanded the capacity of the political structure to absorb, neutralise and buy off potential democratic spoilers'. However, he also points to the corruption that has flourished as a result: 'The effects on conflict amelioration have been positive: the impact on corruption control and improving government performance has not.'[18]

Hadiz agrees, saying that while 'decentralisation in and of itself is a good idea', the context in which it took place in Indonesia 'facilitated the development, really, of corrupt mini-regimes'. It seems that decentralisation of political power also led to the decentralisation of corruption.

Given the central role the military played in the Suharto regime, civilian control over the military is a necessary guard against a future dictatorship. Active military personnel are now banned from taking public office; if officers want to run for parliament, they need to resign first.

The military has also been separated from the police forces, with the military primarily responsible for national defence and the police for domestic security, as is the case in most democratic countries. The military can only assist the police at the government's request.

Although this was an important move, Aspinall argues that it was 'a process marked by an urge to accommodate the military as much as to reform it'.[19] Hence, there has been a lack of progress in two key areas.

First, there has been no serious effort to punish perpetrators of the human rights violations that occurred during the Suharto years. The result is that Indonesian soldiers still sometimes behave brutally when they act against civilians. Amnesty International reports the continued use of excessive force and unlawful killings by Indonesian soldiers and police. It estimates that over eight years, Indonesian security forces have unlawfully killed at least 95 people in the provinces of Papua and West Papua.[20]

Second, there have been no institutional reforms to dismantle the military's territorial hold. Consequently, although the military is no longer a direct player in day-to-day politics, Aspinall argues 'it retains the institutional capacity and the mindset that could allow it to intervene in the future'.[21]

Civil and Political Liberties

Since Suharto was forced from office, Indonesian democracy has succeeded in fending off three potentially powerful complicating forces. The military has retreated. Many of the most severe ethnic and religious conflicts have receded. And Islamist groups are being increasingly incorporated into the mainstream, with many now pursuing their agenda through democratic methods.

As a consequence, Indonesians have experienced almost twenty years of democracy. Figure 19 on the next page shows Indonesia's democracy levels over more than forty years, as measured by US-based not-for-profit organisation Freedom House, which assesses 'the real world rights and freedoms enjoyed by individuals'.[22] While Indonesia is an imperfect democracy, the level of democratic engagement its population has experienced since 1998 has been a stunning, sustained improvement on the Suharto years. Indonesia is the world's largest Muslim country, with Muslims accounting for 87 per cent of its 260 million people.[23] There's a striking absence of militant Islamism in Indonesian politics. Aspinall observes that 'no political party that openly proclaims – or at least emphasises – a goal of dramatically overhauling Indonesia's social and political

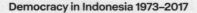

Democracy in Indonesia 1973–2017

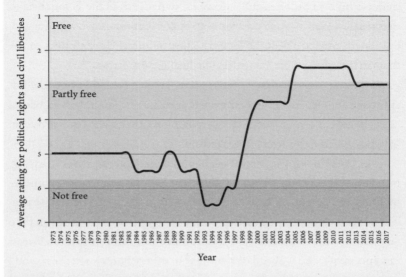

Figure 19. Freedom House research shows that the Suharto dictatorship before the 1970s has given way to a far more democratic era in Indonesia, measured by the rating for political rights and civil liberties.

system in line with sharia now represents a significant force'.[24] It appears that in Indonesia, the majority of voters prioritise economic and welfare issues over religiosity.

Indonesian democracy has also been successful in co-opting and absorbing Islamic voices. For example, in the 2019 presidential election President Jokowi chose as his running mate Maruf Amin, the nation's top Muslim cleric, who is now the country's vice-president. Political Islam in Indonesia largely acknowledges the rules of the democratic system, and is pursuing its conservative agenda through democratic participation. In 2019, five Islamic-leaning political parties contested the election, winning a combined total of about 29 per cent of the vote, which was the lowest share since 2004.[25]

Indonesia has a lively press, and not-for-profit organisations are active in community development, advocacy and policy formation. Indonesians are not shy about airing their views in public: there is no shortage of vocal labour unions, and citizens are avid users of social media. More than 150 million Indonesians – or about 56 per cent of the population – spend an average of three hours and twenty-six minutes each day logged onto social media. This is the fourth highest usage rate in the world, more than an hour longer each day than the average American.[26]

'I grew up in an authoritarian regime,' Hadiz says, 'so I can't take for granted things like freedom of the press, freedom of association, freedom of expression. I used to write things and my mother would be horrified: "Are you going to be arrested tomorrow?"'

Another hopeful sign for Indonesian democracy is the increasing number of women in politics. About 17.4 per cent of the seats in the national parliament are held by women. While this is clearly well shy of equal representation, women's representation in Indonesia is not all that far behind countries such as Ireland (22.2 per cent) and the United States (23.5 per cent), and is ahead of a number of other countries in the region, including Malaysia (14.4 per cent) and Thailand (16.2 per cent).[27]

The Democratic Ideal

Two hundred years ago, almost no one lived in a democracy. While Americans had begun to enjoy the democratic freedoms that came with the 1788 ratification of their constitution, they represented less than 1 per cent of the global population. Others lived in a monarchy, a colony, a dictatorship or some sort of autocratic regime. The United Kingdom had a parliament, but less than 5 per cent of adults were entitled to vote.[28]

Democracy and democratic institutions have made enormous progress over the intervening period. Today, about 39 per cent of the world's population live in the eighty-six countries that Freedom House rates as 'free' and enjoying democratic values.

Yet much of the world still does not reap the benefits of democracy. More than a third of the global population (37 per cent) live in the fifty countries rated as 'not free'; of these, over half live in China. The Economist Intelligence Unit Democracy Index is even more pessimistic than Freedom House, arguing that only twenty countries (home to just 4.5 per cent of the world's population) are considered 'full democracies', with substantial political freedoms and civil liberties, and only limited

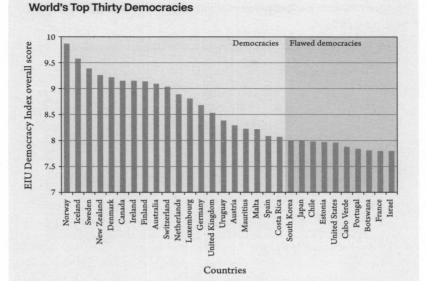

World's Top Thirty Democracies

Figure 20. According to the Economist Intelligence Unit's 2018 World Democracy Index, countries such as Uruguay and Mauritius are more democratic than the United States and Japan.

problems in the functioning of their systems. A further fifty-five countries (home to 43 per cent of the world's population) are rated 'flawed democracies'. This includes Indonesia, which is ranked sixty-fifth out of the 167 countries assessed. More than a third of the world's population across fifty-three countries live under 'authoritarian regime'.[29]

Figure 20 shows the world's top democracies as assessed by the Economist Intelligence Unit. We can see it is headed up, unsurprisingly, by the Nordic countries of Norway, Iceland and Sweden. What is also noticeable is how few countries are considered full democracies, and that some of the world's oldest, such as the United States and France, are now considered 'flawed', ranking lower than countries such as Estonia and Chile.

Far from extending its reach, democracy around the world seems to be under threat. As Figure 21 on the next page shows, in 2018 a total of sixty-eight countries suffered net declines in political rights and civil liberties, compared with fifty that registered gains. This was the thirteenth consecutive year in which declines outnumbered improvements.

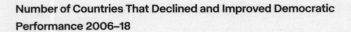

Number of Countries That Declined and Improved Democratic Performance 2006–18

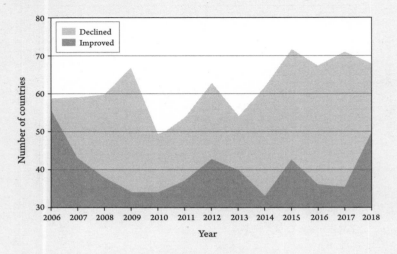

Figure 21. Thirteen years of democratic decline shows that Indonesia is bucking a trend.

The challenges of democracy aren't limited to the developing world. Some of the oldest democracies, in Western Europe and the United States, have seen major decreases in political participation. Larry Diamond, one of the world's leading democracy scholars, argues that we have been going through a 'democracy recession'. He says this is shown in the form of declining voter numbers, diminishing trust in institutions and the dwindling appeal of mainstream, representative parties.[30] Freedom House despairs that 'young people, who have little memory of the long struggles against fascism and communism, may be losing faith and interest in the democratic project'.[31]

Around the Western world, many voters seem to feel that the economic and political system has let them down. This has manifested in populist movements that have seen the election of President Trump in the United States and support for Brexit in the United Kingdom. English journalist Edward Luce argues that the crux of the West's democratic crisis is that 'our societies are split between the will of the people and

The Relationship Between Democracy and Life Satisfaction in the OECD

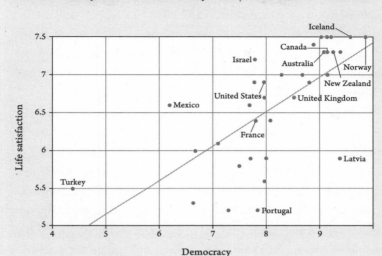

Figure 22. The 2018 Democracy Index and the OECD Better Life Index indicate that the more democratic their country, the more generally satisfied individuals are with their lives.

self-serving insiders; Britain versus Brussels; West Virginia versus Washington'.[32] This deepening polarisation between the political class and alienated voters in the West is ensuring that, as former *New York Times* book critic Michiko Kakutani put it, 'democracy is defeating itself'.[33] It is clear that we can't take democracy for granted.

Why is democracy such a great system anyway? Well, on average, democracies are richer, less likely to go to war and better at fighting corruption. No country that is an autocracy has an average income of more than US$15,000 per annum – unless that country is a fossil fuel exporter.[34]

Among the rich countries of the OECD, democracy is associated with less poverty and better health outcomes. People in more-democratic countries live longer, are more innovative and productive, wealthier and happier. Given a choice, I suspect most of us would want to live in a democracy.

Okay, so democracy is *associated* with a wide range of positive outcomes. But what is the causal link? Here the experts differ. Does democracy cause more economic development, longer lives or greater levels of innovation? Or could it be that factors such as economic development mean that democratic conditions are more likely to take hold and thrive?

The weight of recent evidence seems to tip towards the idea that democracy is indeed positive for economic growth. One 2019 study found that democratisation increases GDP per capita by about 20 per cent over time. This appears to be because democracies have greater investment in capital, schooling and health.[35] Democracy also contributes to factors such as strengthened protection of property rights, the formation of human capital and strong civil societies – aspects important for economic development. As a consequence, one could argue that countries remain poor precisely because of their autocratic political structures.[36]

Whether or not you accept the emerging balance of evidence, we do have some insight into what causes countries to become democracies.

We know that countries with oil are less likely to be democratic. The pattern is not limited to the Middle East – think of Nigeria, Venezuela and the oil-rich countries in central Asia. As the world's most democratic country and a big oil exporter, Norway is an anomaly. Explanations for this pattern are varied. I've read of the following: resource-rich countries use low tax rates and patronage to dampen democratic pressures; resource wealth allows regimes to strengthen their domestic security forces to repress popular movements; and economic growth based on oil exports is different from other types of economic growth so doesn't bring about the economic and cultural changes that tend to lead to democratic government.[37]

Countries with majority Muslim populations are also less likely to be democratic. This is despite the fact that research shows individual Muslims value democracy more than non-Muslims. The lack of religious freedom in Muslim countries may be one reason for the democratic deficit.[38] It makes Indonesia's political transition even more impressive.

Countries with highly educated populations are more likely to be democratic, with the democratising effects of education strongest in poorer countries. This is because, researchers say, education 'teaches people to interact with others and raises the benefits of civic participation, including voting and organising'.[39]

Inequality also represents a threat to democracy. One study of forty democracies found that higher levels of income inequality reduces support for democracy. Excessive financial inequality has implications for a number of attitudes and behaviours that support democracy, including civic involvement, social trust and belief in institutions. It should be no surprise that the OECD countries with the highest levels of inequality – Chile, Mexico, Turkey and the United States – are all considered to be 'flawed democracies' by The Economist Intelligence Unit.[40]

Corruption – dishonesty or fraudulent behaviour by those in power – undermines democracy by diverting resources from those who need them. It also undermines the rule of law and lowers citizens' trust in political institutions and processes. While democracy reduces corruption, all democracies continue to struggle against it in some form.[41] In the United Kingdom, widespread misuse of parliamentary allowances and expenses led to several MPs being jailed. In the United States, impeachment proceedings are underway for President Trump, who has seemingly abused the powers of his office to advance his personal political interests. And in Australia, a number of former state politicians and party officials are serving jail sentences for corruption offences.[42]

While no democratic system is perfect, it's worth reminding ourselves of the intrinsic benefits of democracy. Liberal democracy is built on a core philosophy that calls for the guarantee of the rights of the individual. These include freedom from arbitrary authority, freedom of religion, the right to own and exchange private property, rights to equal opportunity in healthcare, education and employment, and rights to political participation and representation.[43] These benefits are incredibly valuable and in many countries of the world, including Indonesia, hard-won.

Indonesia's shift towards democratic ideals has been sustained over an extended period, despite frustrations and setbacks. The scale of the achievement is truly incredible, and makes this one of the world's great political success stories. Yet Indonesia's democratic transition has been long and messy, and remains incomplete. The experience shows how chaotic, contradictory and ugly such a transition can be. Democracy is hard to achieve.

Vedi Hadiz is worried about Indonesia's future democratic progress. 'What's concerning to me is that whatever progress was made in the first few years of Reformasi is now being pushed back.' To Hadiz it seems 'there's a kind of democratic regression going on, which you could think of as being part of a worldwide phenomenon'. This is due partly to the voices of radical Islam in Indonesian life. While these groups are not in a position to take power, Hadiz says 'their discourse is powerful, and it has an effect on the other competitors, so what we've seen is actually the mainstreaming of ideas associated with radical Islam being normalised. Ideas that were crackpot ten years ago are suddenly normal.'

The voices of Islam have been able to gain traction because of a growing 'distrust and disenchantment with the institutions of democracy', Hadiz says. This is assisting people outside these institutions to gain vocal support. It's the same phenomenon in Western democracies, which has led to support for Nigel Farage's Brexit Party in Britain, Marine Le Pen's National Rally in France and the Republican Party under Donald Trump.

Part of this disenchantment is due to the ongoing presence of corruption in Indonesia, which remains despite the Corruption Eradication Commission's valiant work. According to Indonesia Corruption Watch, at least forty-six candidates in the 2019 elections had been previously convicted of corruption offences.[44]

Yet in a particularly concerning development, after the 2019 elections the Indonesian parliament passed a law that severely weakens the Corruption Eradication Commission. It makes wiretaps, searches and seizures impossible without the permission of a new supervisory board appointed by the president. It is widely expected that the new board will block many corruption investigations. Other measures in the legislation include restrictions on the types of cases that can be investigated and a requirement for the Commission to only employ investigators from the (notoriously corrupt) police force. These changes appear to weaken the commission to the extent that it will no longer be able to pursue corruption cases without fear or favour.[45]

Hadiz argues that there are also economic underpinnings to the growing disenchantment with democracy in Indonesia, with inequality in the country close to an all-time high. The population is more educated and urbanised than ever before, with higher aspirations, but 'these aspirations are very hard to translate to reality'. Consequently, Hadiz says, this has led to 'disenchanted youths hanging round, who can be easily recruited into gangs or paramilitaries, or any group that gives them a sense of belonging and promises them something'.

In the face of developments such as these, Ken Setiawan is ambivalent about Indonesia's democratic journey. 'Democracy is not without its challenges, and there's still so much to be done,' she says. In particular, she points to the lack of progress in achieving justice for past human rights violations, current discrimination against and persecution of minorities, and repeated crackdowns on liberal civil-society groups. Indonesia now has a comprehensive legal framework protecting human rights. Setiawan says that 'on paper they [the policies] look good, but implementing them, that's a whole different question'. And while official censorship has now receded, she says there are still 'a lot of problems around press freedom in Indonesia' and 'we still see the persecution of journalists'. Dozens of assaults, arrests and threats targeting journalists have been reported in recent years, with perpetrators including police, politicians and military officials. Journalists recount extreme difficulty accessing Papua and West Papua to report on the ongoing campaign for independence.[46]

Ambivalence is the strong flavour that emerges in any discussion about Indonesia. Enormous progress has been made, with formal legal and institutional frameworks in place. As Setiawan says, 'compared to what was there, almost everything is better'. But 'if you dig a little bit deeper, then I think you can see that there's still a lot of problems.'

What Indonesia Can Teach the World

With democracy waning across the world over the past decade or more, there is much that we can learn from Indonesia's experience, imperfect as it may be.

Democratic Transition Is Possible

A transition from authoritarianism to democracy is a long, messy process for any country. It requires patience and persistence, and a preparedness to keep fighting for democratic reform. As we've seen in places such as the United States, there are forces that, if left unrestrained by legislation or healthy checks and balances, can lead to democratic regression.

While most of the world's population does not live in a democracy, over past decades there have been many successful democratic transitions, in countries such as Brazil, Chile, Ghana, Poland and South Africa. Indonesia's experience further reinforces that a transition is possible. If a large, complex, geographically diverse, predominantly Muslim country can sustain a democratic system over an extended period, there is nothing to say that others can't, too.

In Crisis Lies Opportunity

Democratic transition is not a 'smooth, linear process', Vedi Hadiz says. 'I think there needs to be something that shakes it up.'

Although democracy is linked to economic growth, research shows that growth is not in itself enough to prompt a transition from an autocratic regime to democracy. Rather, the evidence suggests that regime change is most likely to be brought about as a result of economic crisis.[47] In the South American countries of Brazil and Bolivia, for example, soaring debt, enormous inflation and economic mismanagement was the catalyst for democratic transition in the 1980s.

In Indonesia, the 1997 Asian financial crisis – which began in Thailand and spread throughout much of South-East Asia and other parts of Asia – was a key catalyst for the end of Suharto's reign and the beginning of Indonesia's democratic transition. Economic crises have the capacity to up-end the status quo and galvanise the populace, creating the conditions required for fundamental political and social change.[48]

While Indonesia did take advantage of the crisis, Hadiz thinks that not enough advantage was taken, as while 'we all wanted to oust Suharto, we had no idea what would replace him'. 'For the first six months of the post-Suharto period, there was a sort of vacuum,' he says. 'History only ever gives you a very small window of opportunity. That window closes very quickly.'

Democracy Is Sticky

What are the prospects for Indonesian democracy? While there are certain dark clouds brewing, overall Indonesia's democratic system is well-placed to endure into the future.

There's a body of academic research indicating that once a country has experienced democratic rule for a lengthy period it is unlikely to regress towards authoritarianism. One scholar, Milan Svolik, puts the figure at seventeen to twenty years, arguing that 'our confidence that an existing democracy is consolidated increases with its age'.[49] By that measure, Indonesia stands a good chance.

Hadiz says that Indonesian democracy is robust because the country's elites are on side. 'They're democrats now,' he says. 'They've figured out that they don't need an authoritarian regime anymore to protect their interests, that democracy, no matter how messy and chaotic it can be, is good enough in terms of protecting their interests.'

Ken Setiawan, too, is confident Indonesia has a democratic future. She says that while there are 'things that are really concerning', they are 'not concerning to the extent that you see the system as a whole collapsing. I can't really see that happening.'

'If you look at most civil society groups – whether they are on the liberal side or the illiberal side – they are actually not arguing against the macro structures of how Indonesia is organised,' she says. 'People generally do support democracy.'

As democracy wanes in many parts of the world, Indonesia's democratic transition is cause for optimism. This mostly Muslim nation of 268 million people has wrestled out from the grips of authoritarianism, casting a light for those who wish to follow.

FIVE THINGS WE CAN DO NOW

1. **Establish anti-corruption measures.** Anti-corruption agencies seek to expose official corruption and head off any emergent risks. To hold even the most powerful people to account, they need to be independent of government and properly empowered to investigate allegations. Countries such as Australia, which lacks a national authority like Indonesia's Corruption Eradication Commission, should establish a body empowered to investigate all public officials, including politicians.

2. **Legislate democratic checks and balances.** Because organisations such as intelligence agencies largely operate in secret, oversight bodies independent of the executive branch of government are necessary to ensure that these authorities are acting in accordance with the law. Oversight mechanisms, without impinging on the capacity of these organisations to act independently of government, help to prevent abuses or arbitrary exercises of power. For example, through its committee structure the US Congress regulates and monitors intelligence programs and approves top intelligence appointments. In Germany, a parliamentary committee reviews the legality of intelligence agencies' actions and investigates citizens' complaints.

3. **Spread power widely.** Devolving responsibilities from a centralised federal government to local regions has democratic benefits, as it helps dilute the dangerous concentration of power authoritarian regimes use to spread tyranny. Shifting responsibilities to the lowest appropriate level of government is good practice for established democracies too, ensuring that decisions are made closer to the people, communities and businesses they affect.

4. **Back non-violent demonstrations.** Non-violent mass mobilisations are more likely to lay the groundwork for democratic change than armed rebellions. Liberal democracies are also strengthened when people have the right to protest. Countries such as Australia, which do not have a constitutional right to peaceful protest, should ensure that this right is enshrined in law, as it is in the United States.

5. **Be a good neighbour.** Foreign policy plays a role in supporting democracy. Connections with other democratic countries within a region can strengthen domestic support for reform and help the process of democratic transition. Existing democracies in Europe, South-East Asia and South America can help by building strong relationships with and supporting emerging democracies in their region.

8

WINNING FROM GLOBALISATION
How to Keep Manufacturing Alive

I n 2012, the Olympic sailing events were held off the coast of Dorset in the United Kingdom. The local police had a massive task in keeping the coastline secure from terrorists and wayward spectator craft – this was the largest on-water security operation in the history of UK policing. As part of their preparations, Dorset Police needed eyewear for several hundred officers who would spend twelve hours a day on the water, travelling at up to 110 kilometres per hour in boats or on jetskis.

Not far away, in London, the Hochtief Murphy Joint Venture was constructing twin railway tunnels under the Thames River and found that the boots it had supplied to workers were uncomfortable and causing blisters. What's more, they were falling apart after just two months. The company needed a better solution.

At Denby Pottery in the English Midlands – where ceramics have been made by hand for more than 200 years – management was seeking to supply its 500 employees with safety footwear, gloves and respiratory and hearing protection. Its factory is a harsh environment, with wet and dry conditions and products that eat away at leather. In one glazing process workers need to run their hands along the pottery, which can cause cuts without proper protection. Some employees are on their feet for twelve hours a day, so comfort is key.

All three organisations turned to Uvex, a family-owned company headquartered in a small town in southern Germany, which produces some of the world's best protective equipment for the workplace.

Uvex supplied Dorset Police with safety glasses bearing a 100 per cent ultraviolet filter and a specialised coating to keep the lens cleaner for longer while at sea. Hochtief Murphy found that while Uvex's boots cost twice as much as those they were replacing, they were far more comfortable and lasted more than six times as long, so there were significant savings. Denby Pottery was supplied with a full range of Uvex safety gear, including earplugs that adapt to the shape of the ear and gloves that have excellent grip in wet and oily conditions. Like Hochtief Murphy, they found that the high quality of the products meant a longer life, saving the company money.[1]

Soon to be celebrating its centenary, Uvex has been owned by three generations of the Winter family; it is now headed by Michael Winter, the founder's grandson. Uvex has invested significantly in innovation and the skills of its workers. Its business model is built on high-tech manufacturing in Germany and other European countries, where it produces the world's best safety products. Companies all around the world are turning to Uvex to supply gear for their employees – from UK ambulance services to Japanese carmakers to US mining businesses. The company has grown strongly and now generates an annual revenue of more than US$500 million.

Uvex is just one of thousands of successful manufacturing businesses in Germany. In absolute terms, German manufacturing has grown substantially, and as a share of its economy it remains just as big as it was twenty years ago.

In many parts of the Western world, manufacturing is in decline, due – at least in part – to low-cost competitors in Asia. Countries such as Australia and the United States, which have traditionally relied on manufacturing as a key sector of the economy, have simply been unable to compete with countries such as China, where wages and production costs are lower. This is leading to the collapse of businesses and the community structures in the towns and cities built around manufacturing, such as Detroit. Yet Germany has benefited from China's rapid industrialisation, finding that Chinese consumers have an appetite for quality German products. Germany is proving that it is possible to have a thriving manufacturing sector in a high-tax, high-cost and highly regulated economy. Let's explore the secrets of Germany's success.

Stefan Brück is the chief executive officer of Uvex's safety products division, Uvex Safety, which employs some 1800 people. Bespectacled and in a suit that looks expensive, on first appearance Brück seems every centimetre the traditional senior executive he is. Yet he surprises me with his animation – perhaps a legacy of his upbringing in Italy, where his German father ran a business trading in steel. Brück is clearly proud of what Uvex has achieved. But he also says that Uvex is typical of what hundreds of manufacturing businesses are achieving across Germany.

After finishing school in Italy, Brück moved to Germany, where he studied management and economics in the south-eastern city of Regensburg, on the Danube River. Upon graduating, he spent a couple of years working for a large pulp and paper company in Düsseldorf, before joining Uvex in 1991 as an 'assistant to the managing director'. Building up experience in sales, product management and the international side of the business, he became managing director of the Uvex Safety Group in 1999. He's been its CEO since 2010.

We speak in his office as he explains the company's strategy, leaving me with the sense that Uvex has carefully planned all that it does. 'Innovation is part of our DNA,' Brück says, meaning that new ideas and technological development runs through the business. Uvex is not interested in simply producing different versions of products already on the market. 'Everything we launch, everything we do, needs to have a measurable innovation component.'

Almost all of Uvex's products are manufactured in Germany or elsewhere in Western Europe. 'We have built up a know-how in our factories that is really second to none,' Brück tells me. 'While we don't necessarily need to produce everything ourselves, our clear strategy is to focus on our own manufacturing units in Germany and in Europe. Our manufacturing competence and the "Made in Germany" brand is part of our business model.'

The company's roots are in Germany, and it has no plans to move production to a lower-cost location. About 80 per cent of its sales are in Europe. 'We can provide a really first-class service to those customers by being close to our manufacturing bases,' Brück says.

Another key reason to remain in Germany is the company's focus on sustainability. Despite a booming economy, Germany's carbon emissions have fallen substantially in both per capita and absolute terms over the past decade.[2] The nation's reputation for environmental leadership in energy, urban infrastructure and transportation is an asset to a company such as Uvex. 'We just feel that the potential environmental improvements in Germany and in Europe are much more attractive than in many other countries in the world,' Brück says. 'It's part of our strategy to improve our carbon footprint every year.'

Uvex is headquartered in Fürth, a town of 126,000 residents, where it was founded. 'The owner's family have their roots here,' Brück says. 'For them, it's very important to continue to invest in the region, and to expand, so that we provide opportunities for the population here.'

With many of the company's employees living in the same town as the owners, the firm has a relationship of trust with its workers. For a number of years, the company has been rated a 'top national employer' by *Focus*, a German-language news magazine.[3] 'The worker is a fully integrated part of the organisation, and a big contributor to its success,' Brück says. 'They are rewarded and treated accordingly.'

I speak with Salvatore Fratantonio, one of the workers at Uvex's eyewear plant in Fürth. Reserved at first, but soon revealing a dry sense of humour, Fratantonio tells me that he likes working at Uvex because of the 'philosophy and strategy of Uvex, the fact that it's a family business and the orientation of the firm towards technology and innovation. And, of course, the salary package!'

Fratantonio migrated to Germany from Italy with his parents when he was twelve years old, and went on to do an apprenticeship in plastics manufacturing. He started with Uvex eighteen years ago as a shift manager, and is now a team leader, overseeing thirty-five workers who coat the lenses of Uvex safety glasses. Noticing Fratantonio's keen interest in technology, management recently supported him to gain certification in robotic technology. He says there has been a 'technological explosion' since he's been at Uvex, with each new product line incorporating new technology, innovation and efficiency measures, all developed in-house.

Like most German companies of a similar size, Uvex works closely with the works council, or shop-floor workers group, at each of the major manufacturing plants. Works councils complement trade unions – members are elected by employees for four-year terms, and they ensure that the national agreements negotiated by the unions are geared to the individual workplace. 'It's a partnership relationship, on equal levels,' Brück says. 'Our target is to have all our employees fully informed about the strategy of the business, the performance of the business and why we make certain decisions. I think it's much easier to make decisions if the workforce knows the background.'

Uvex's goal is not extremely fast growth, funded by equity investment or by debt, which carries a high degree of risk. 'The preference of the family is to have sustainable and profit-oriented growth,' Brück says. 'This will ensure the long-term existence of the business and is a much better guarantee for employees than faster, quicker growth in a short period of time.'

Nevertheless, over the past fifty years the safety group has seen annual growth of about 5.5 per cent, which roughly equates to the company doubling in size every thirteen years. 'A strong and solid number,' says Brück. 'The family invests most of the earnings back into the business. It's interested to keep and maintain the heritage we have built over the years, and to grow the strength that we have.'

Across the developed world, there is a very real fear that increased global competition will lead inexorably to a 'race to the bottom' in wages, labour rights, employment practices and environmental sustainability.[4]

Since the 1990s, a rising share of trade in industrialised countries has been with emerging economies, and this is having a disruptive effect on labour markets. Economists broadly accept that trade with low-wage countries has contributed to the decline of manufacturing in many developed countries.[5] As Figure 23 on page 191 shows, in the United States, Australia, France, Canada and the United Kingdom, manufacturing's share of economic activity has been declining dramatically. Its contribution to the Australian economy has fallen from 14 per cent of output in

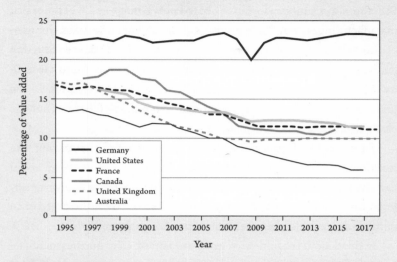

Manufacturing's Contribution to the Economy

Figure 23. Germany is bucking the trend common to Western economies, which has seen a decline in manufacturing. This downturn is particularly apparent in Australia.

1995 to 6 per cent in 2017, while in the United Kingdom it has fallen from 17 per cent in 1995 to 10 per cent in 2018. In the United States, manufacturing's share of economic activity has dropped from 17 per cent in 1997 to 12 per cent in 2017. Between 1979 and 2009, the United States lost 41 per cent of all its manufacturing jobs.[6] This decline is hitting some places hard. For example, suburbs in the Australian city of Adelaide have had an unemployment rate of more than 30 per cent since the closure of the automotive manufacturing industry. Towns in the American rust belt, such as Erie, Pennsylvania, have lost thousands of manufacturing jobs, as well as the white-collar jobs that supported them.[7] This shift is decimating communities and an entire way of life.

Some economists argue that the loss of manufacturing in developed economies is not concerning in the context of overall economic performance, as it is a result of rapid productivity growth (a good thing), and service industries can be just as productive and innovative as manufacturing.[8] The counterview – which has academic, political and popular support – is that manufacturing absolutely matters. For example, the Brookings Institution, a think tank based in Washington, DC, argues that manufacturing is important because 'it provides high wage jobs, commercial innovation (the nation's largest source), a key to trade deficit reduction and a disproportionately large contribution to environmental sustainability'. Manufacturing is particularly important for the 'clean economy' – the production of goods or services with an environmental benefit, such as electric vehicles, water-efficient products and wind energy.[9]

Because manufacturing has been a good source of high-paying jobs for medium- to low-skilled workers, its decline has raised fears about the impact on inequality. In a 2018 report, the International Monetary Fund found that the loss of jobs in manufacturing had contributed to an increase in inequality between the 1980s and the 2000s.[10]

In contrast to the decline in many industrialised countries, manufacturing's share of the German economy has been holding steady at about 23 per cent since 1993.[11] Dr Jeromin Zettelmeyer notes that the sector is thriving across the nation. 'It has the kind of model which usually you would think cannot work, but somehow it does,' he says.

Zettelmeyer, an economist, was until recently a senior official in Germany's Ministry for Economic Affairs and Energy. He is now deputy director of the Strategy and Policy Review Department at the International Monetary Fund, based in Washington, DC. Having worked in Germany, the United Kingdom and the United States, he brings a well-qualified perspective to the discussion.

As an example of the highly regulated environment in Germany, Zettelmeyer points out that companies are obliged to join German chambers of industry and commerce, which promote foreign trade, deliver vocational training, support regional economic development and provide other member services. 'They have a monopoly and are allowed to levy a compulsory members fee,' he says. 'Effectively, it's a tax.'[12]

Germany's taxation revenue is equivalent to 38.2 per cent of its GDP, which is higher than the OECD average of 34.3 per cent. Yet corporate taxes are relatively low, accounting for only 5.6 per cent of all tax revenue.[13] When various national and local taxes are taken into account, the effective corporate tax rate in Germany is about 27 per cent. This is lower

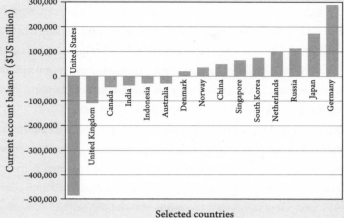

Figure 24. At just under three hundred billion dollars, Germany's 2018 surplus was the biggest in the world.

than Australia (31 per cent) and the United States (37 per cent), although substantially higher than countries such as the United Kingdom (19 per cent), Singapore (16 per cent) and Ireland (12 per cent).[14]

The growth of trade with China has been beneficial to Germany. According to Zettelmeyer, China 'is more important as a market for German industrial products than it is as a competitor in third markets, or as an importer'. Germany's comparative advantage is in machine tools – that is, the machines used in manufacturing. Zettelmeyer says these are 'something that industrialising countries need. These are investment goods rather than consumption goods.'

Similarly, Germany's car industry – with brands such as BMW, Mercedes Benz, Audi and Porsche – focuses on the high end, so it occupies a niche, in which it has become a global leader. Around the world, if they can afford it, people still prefer a German car to a Chinese one.

While Uvex produces some products in China for the Chinese market, it also sells them products made in Germany and in Europe. The German-made products sell at a substantially higher price point, but

Brück says 'the Chinese customers very often prefer products made in Germany to products made in China'.

The growth of trade between Germany and China (as well as between Germany and Eastern Europe) in the period between 1988 and 2008 impacted different regions differently, but overall created 493,000 additional jobs in the German economy. These new jobs were mostly in manufacturing, but they were also in complementary business-related services such as accounting and consultancy.[15]

German manufacturing has been so successful that the country now exports far more than it imports. Germany has 1 per cent of the world's labour force yet produces 10 per cent of the world's exports.

A nation's transactions with the world are recorded in its current account, and Germany's is enormous. In simple terms, the current account is the difference between a country's imports and its exports. 'The German current account is the biggest in the world in absolute terms,' says Zettelmeyer.[16]

As Figure 24 shows, Germany had a US$291 million *surplus* in 2018, substantially bigger than that of China (US$49 million). In the same year, the United States had a deficit of US$488 million – the world's largest. There were also deficits of US$109 million in the United Kingdom, US$45 million in Canada and US$31 million in Australia.[17]

Countries that run current account deficits are consuming more than they produce. To finance their deficits, these countries are effectively borrowing from the rest of the world. One way that current account deficits are financed is through foreign investment, such as into domestic housing or share markets. While this approach can work well, some economists argue that large inflows of foreign capital without appropriate checks and balances can be problematic, and in the United States this may have contributed to the financial bubble that led to the 2008 global financial crisis.[18]

The other way in which current account deficits are financed is by borrowing from foreign lenders. In the United States, foreign loans amount to nearly US$10 trillion (US$10,000,000,000,000).[19]

Countries with large current account deficits may find that at a certain point, their level of global borrowing becomes unsustainable.

This would be associated with sharp currency depreciations rapidly driving up the cost of imports, causing severe financial stress.[20] German leaders do not have to worry about this possibility for their own economy.

Investing in Workers

Uvex is just one of hundreds of German manufacturing businesses that make up what is known as the *Mittelstand* – a literal translation is the 'middle estate' or 'middle class'. These medium-sized companies thrived in the aftermath of World War II, when German manufacturing boomed due to efforts to rebuild the economy.

Mittelstand companies focus on quality products and long-term success. Export-oriented, they are often market leaders in very specific products – think music stands, de-icing fluids or machinery for producing corrugated cardboard. Focusing on niche products and markets means they do not typically compete with multinationals. A study undertaken by Swiss professor Christof Müller found that 461 German companies are global leaders. These companies have the highest or second-highest market share in their category, generate annual sales of more than €50 million (US$56 million), operate on at least three continents and generate at least half of their sales abroad. Over half of these companies are still owned by their founding families.[21]

Uvex is a typical *Mittelstand* company. It is family-owned and headquartered in a small town, where it has strong connections with workers and the local community. This means it is less likely to move production offshore. Its roots stretch back a long way, and not being beholden to investors, it is able to plan for the long-term.

The success of the *Mittelstand,* and of the German manufacturing industry in general, is partly due to a unique system of industrial relations. Through a works council, employees participate in the company's decision-making along with management. This system, known as *mitbestimmung* (co-determination), is embedded in German law.

Unions and employer associations negotiate wages at the industry level, and these agreements are applied nationwide. Manufacturing wages in Germany are among the highest in Europe, with workers paid an average of €40 per hour (US$44), which is about 50 per cent more than in the United Kingdom.[22] But it is possible to deviate from these conditions if the works council for an individual company agrees to do so. The management needs to prove that a temporary stop on wage rises or a more modest increase is necessary to prevent bankruptcy or to remain competitive. With the threat of production relocation to Eastern Europe, German workers are often willing to accept a lower wage than the union-negotiated rate. 'The success of Germany in export markets is a national prerogative. So many jobs depend on it,' Jeromin Zettelmeyer says. 'As a result, you tend to have unions, both at the company level and the sector level, that are happy to prioritise competitiveness over wage increases.'[23]

Stefan Brück describes how this worked at Uvex during the challenging times of the financial crisis in 2008 and 2009. 'We made sure that we could keep the employees but reduce the hours,' he says. 'The works council has the authority to agree to reduce hours in extraordinary times. Everything went very smoothly because of the positive relationship.'

German companies have a two-board structure. A 'management board', consisting of senior management, typically meets frequently to deal with operational issues. The 'supervisory board' appoints the CEO, guides and monitors the management board and is involved in long-term strategic planning. Germany requires that the supervisory boards of all firms listed on the stock exchange with more than 500 employees have one-third employee representatives. For listed companies with more than 2000 employees, this increases to 50 per cent employee representation.[24]

The German model might seem crazy to those used to the Anglo-American model of corporate governance, which sees companies overseen by a board made up of shareholder representatives.[25] Can you imagine Australian mining company BHP with half its board made up of representatives from the CFMMEU (the mining union)? How about members of the United Food and Commercial Workers International Union making up half the board of US-based retailer Costco? No? Neither can I.

The Anglo-American model is based on the notion that the primary purpose of the company is to serve the interests of the shareholders. By contrast, the German model takes into account the broader interest of stakeholders as well as shareholders.[26]

Trust levels in Germany, although not as high as in the Scandinavian countries, are much higher than in Anglo countries such as the United States and the United Kingdom. As a consequence, trust permeates German companies far beyond the industrial relations context. For example, German CEOs are more willing than those in other countries to grant decision-making power to lower management.[27]

Trust between workers and firms has been one of Germany's greatest strengths, and a key reason for the strong performance of the German economy. German firms have been able to fulfil broader social obligations and focus on long-term value creation. They can invest without the worry that unions will hold them to ransom.[28] Trust has also seen many German companies place less emphasis on short-term profits for shareholders, and give consideration to the concerns of workers, such as job security.

Another benefit of the German approach to corporate governance is that the gap in wages between CEOs and the average worker is significantly lower. In Germany, a CEO of a large public company is paid around 136 times the average German income. This sounds like an enormous amount (and it is!), but American CEOs are paid almost twice as much – 265 times the average American income.[29] German workers, with their seat at the table, have the capacity to influence the CEO-to-worker pay ratio. CEO remuneration discussions are likely somewhat different with employee representatives in the room!

But arguably the most important contributor to Germany's success is its training system. That's 'the big one', says Zettelmeyer.

About half a million Germans enter the workforce through apprenticeship schemes every year. There is a lot of prestige attached to vocational education. This 'ensures a flow of relatively talented young people into industry that might not even consider industry in other countries', says Zettelmeyer. The apprenticeship system means employees don't just acquire company-specific skills, they also develop skills and qualifications relevant to an occupation or industry. This means that if their employer goes broke, employees will have an easier time finding a new job.

Zettelmeyer points to the vocational training system as evidence of a particularly 'German way' of 'blurring the distinction between the state and the private sector': 'The state provides the schools that these kids go to, and then industry provides commitments to supply training jobs, which are not paid very well, but often come with a permanent job at the end,' he says. 'There is in effect an employment subsidy through the fact that the state provides educational services for free, which enable firms to hire young people at very low wages.'[30]

This is exactly how things work at Uvex. Brück says the company 'offers a number of students per year the chance to do the practical part of their education at our company. We offer a job to almost 100 per cent of those who finish in our organisation.'

Unlike other countries with a tradition of apprenticeships, such as Australia and the United Kingdom, there is a long history in Germany of providing apprenticeship pathways for all sorts of occupations, not just the standard trades.[31] German apprentices in manufacturing companies learn a variety of roles, from machine and systems operator to technical product designer to industrial clerk. This enables an apprentice to do a range of jobs, from materials purchasing to marketing. With this approach, Germany is producing a flood of highly qualified, flexible industrial workers who help to maintain the strength of its manufacturing sector.

Following the financial crisis in 2008, when the manufacturing sector was faced with a sudden, severe downturn, Germany took action that perfectly illustrates the unique relationship between government and the private sector. Rather than laying off workers, German businesses negotiated with unions and employees to reduce hours.

Through the *kurzarbeit* (short-work) initiative, employees were able to reduce their hours by up to 50 per cent, with the government reimbursing them between 60 and 67 per cent of their foregone wages.[32] A full-time worker who cut their hours in half continued to receive more than 80 per cent of their pay. More than 1.4 million – or about one in every thirty – German workers participated in the scheme.[33]

Ultimately, the German economy benefited as many workers used the spare time to undertake training and gain additional qualifications. Another benefit was that because workers were still being paid, they continued to spend on goods and services. This meant the German economy wasn't as badly impacted by the recession as it might otherwise have been.

After the crisis, the German manufacturing sector was able to scale back up quickly, as workers – many of whom were now more highly trained – returned to their regular hours. For example, at one point industrial giant Siemens had 19,000 employees on reduced hours, but by 2010 these employees were all working full-time again.[34]

The OECD estimates that the *kurzarbeit* scheme saved some 500,000 jobs. While the unemployment rate in countries such as the United States rose dramatically during the recession (from 4.5 per cent in 2007 to 9.9 per cent in 2010), Germany managed to prevent a large increase in unemployment, with the rate rising only slightly, from a low of 7.3 per cent in 2008 to 7.9 per cent in 2009.[35]

Focusing on Research and Development

Another uniquely German collaboration between industry and government is the network of Fraunhofer institutes. These take their name from Joseph von Fraunhofer, a prominent German researcher, investor and entrepreneur who died in 1926. The institutes are partly publicly funded and provide applied science for companies that would otherwise find it cost-prohibitive.[36] This helps small- and medium-sized businesses to continually upgrade their processes and products to keep ahead of the competition.

The Fraunhofer network is huge. It has a US$2.6 billion budget and 25,000 employees across seventy-two institutes and research units who collectively have more than 250 business focuses and core competencies. With an emphasis on applied research with industrial value, Fraunhofer institutes undertake 6000 to 8000 projects annually. Most of these are short-term projects of less than two years' duration that focus on practical industrial applications. The institutes retain patent and other intellectual property rights at the end of a project.

Each of the Fraunhofer institutes is associated with a university and selects its own research field and projects, and decides how to handle results. Contract research generates more than 85 per cent of its revenue. The balance of funding is received from state and national governments. Most institutes operate pilot manufacturing plants and demonstration facilities. German machine tool and equipment suppliers regularly provide equipment for testing and training.[37]

Brück says Uvex has significant in-house research and development capability, but also partners with a range of German research institutes, including Fraunhofer. 'We tend to do only very complicated or unknown stuff with Fraunhofer,' Brück says. 'At the moment we are collaborating with them on the digital and sensor side, where they are very advanced and have a high degree of knowledge.'

About a third of Fraunhofer's research and development projects are conducted with companies employing less than 250 people. Given the high financial costs and uncertain outcomes, it's unlikely these projects would have otherwise proceeded.

There are strong staff links between Fraunhofer, academia and manufacturing. The institutes employ part-time master's and PhD candidates, who gain experience while pursuing their studies. Graduates typically spend three to six years at Fraunhofer before moving to industry or academia.[38] In this way, a German researcher typically has a strong engagement with industry. Whereas researchers in some countries largely remain in a research setting, in Germany it is common for researchers to move from academia to industry and back again. This is a key strength of the German system, as it allows for a generally seamless transfer of knowledge between industry and researchers.

German companies, research institutes, universities and governments collectively spend 3 per cent of GDP on research and development. This falls well short of South Korea (4.6 per cent) and Israel (4.5 per cent), but is far ahead of countries such as Australia (1.9 per cent) and the United Kingdom (1.7 per cent).[39] Through its High Tech Strategy 2025, the German government has set itself the goal of reaching 3.5 per cent funding by 2025, with one-third of this expenditure from government and two-thirds from the private sector. It is focusing on areas such as the digital economy, sustainable energy, changes in the workplace, healthy living, improved transportation and secure infrastructure. In 2018, the German government announced plans to set up a dedicated agency to support breakthrough innovations. With funding of €1 billion over ten years, it will run innovation competitions and fund multi-year projects in cutting-edge areas with potential for technological breakthroughs.[40]

The biggest strength of the German economy is also its weakness. Its focus on remaining competitive in established sectors, such as manufacturing, has kept it from pioneering new technologies. There are no German counterparts to US-based tech companies such as Apple, Google, Facebook or Amazon. Nor is Germany spawning biotechnology companies at near the rate of the United States and others.[41]

Jeromin Zettelmeyer says the German economy 'is geared towards supporting incumbents'. Close links between industry and the banking sector ensure long-term funding for established businesses. 'In that sense, market discipline is limited,' he says. It's a relatively comfortable environment for businesses to operate in, and companies are not going out of business at the rate they might in other countries. Zettelmeyer points out that 'what you do not have are large pools of labour that have been shed by exiting firms that you can then easily transfer and draw on'. This lack of labour mobility is not conducive to the establishment of new businesses. 'All of this makes for a society that's not terribly dynamic,' Zettelmeyer says.

However, he also points out that 'some of the factors that slow down exit are also good for entrance, in the sense that they make it less risky to enter'. Germany's high-quality education system, for example, is free. This provides a comfortable safety net and ensures that the cost of failure is not as high as it would otherwise be. As a strategy to tackle the risk-averse German culture, scientists in German universities are provided with up to €3000 per month if they want to turn their discoveries into start-up businesses. Additional funding of up to €30,000 is available for equipment and €5000 for coaching. This support provides scientists with assistance for up to one year while they establish their businesses.[42]

A shortage of skills is emerging as one of Germany's biggest challenges. Already, following a decade-long boom, many *Mittelstand* companies report that they are struggling to find staff to fill vacancies.[43] Yet due to a looming demographic crisis, the real impact will be felt over the medium- to long-term. With 21 per cent of its population aged over sixty-five, and a low fertility rate of just 1.5 births per woman, the German population is projected to decline by over ten million people as it moves closer to the end of the twenty-first century. There are now fewer

Germans aged under thirty than there are over sixty.[44] This demographic change means relatively fewer workers contributing the taxes that fund the German welfare system.

The government is endeavouring to address this challenge through immigration. One study found that Germany needs an additional 260,000 immigrants a year to address labour shortages. Germany has accepted hundreds of thousands of refugees in the last few years, and it recently changed its immigration laws to encourage skilled migrants.[45] Many companies are also endeavouring to attract more women into their workforces by offering family-friendly practices such as flexible working hours. All of this represents a sizeable challenge. If Germany doesn't manage its demographic transition effectively, the lack of skilled workers risks hurting the country's economic growth and may prompt businesses to send skilled work offshore.

What Germany Can Teach the World

Germany's success in sustaining a vibrant manufacturing sector offers other countries many insights. While much of the industrialised world has witnessed the progressive decline of manufacturing, Germany has seen it evolve into a high-tech industry offering products that are in demand all over the world.

Prioritise Planning Over Profit

Germany's success is a consequence of companies that have thrived over the longer-term. Rather than obsessing about short-term profits or fluctuations in share price, many *Mittelstand* businesses plan for sustainable growth to ensure they will still be operational twenty, thirty or forty years into the future. This type of thinking is due to the preponderance of small- to medium-sized family-owned companies with strong community connections. These businesses are less interested in searching offshore for lower-cost production opportunities to maximise profits.

Manufacturing in Germany has been the beneficiary of a steady flow of resources, and supported by well-funded, well-led government initiatives. 'It's important to understand the national benefits of a manufacturing base in a country,' says Brück. '"Made in Germany" is an asset.

Germany has that confidence, so Germany is known positively for manufacturing, for quality.'

Germany shows that management of manufacturing can't be left to the private sector alone. Jeromin Zettelmeyer notes that 'the government has played a role creating a good environment for manufacturing production'. It has developed a system in which company executives, workers and legislation all contribute in complementary ways to the nation's thriving manufacturing sector.

Germany's greatest strength is its workers, and their importance is reflected at every step. Zettelmeyer notes 'the skills angle' and how it has contributed to long-term success. Germany's vocational training system ensures that workers receive the technical qualifications they need to develop transferable skills. It also supplies a pipeline of vocationally trained workers to growing manufacturing businesses.

Likewise, employees' contributions are recognised through a well-planned and sustainable industrial relations model that protects workers and provides them with seats at the boardroom table. With employees – and their unions – integrally involved in the challenge of maintaining competitiveness, in times of crisis there is a shared focus on developing innovative solutions, such as wage flexibility. German manufacturing workers have not only an enormous stake in but also a shared responsibility for success.

Skilled Workers Are the Future

The future of manufacturing perhaps lies more with countries such as Germany than with low-cost Asian nations. Automation means that the cost of labour is becoming less relevant, and developing countries are losing their competitive edge. What's increasingly important is a highly skilled workforce. This is enabling 'onshoring' of production – bringing production back to developed countries such as Germany. One study found that the more prevalent robots are in the manufacturing process, the more likely production is to move back to advanced industrial nations such as Germany.[46]

Stefan Brück says that local manufacturing also reduces the cost of moving parts and products around the world. 'The complexity of a value chain that is split all over the world creates challenges and issues,' he says. 'To focus everything in one place does have an attraction and an efficiency aspect.'

As a potential example of what the future holds, we can look to German shoe manufacturer Adidas. Until recently, it ran most of its production from low-wage countries in Asia, such as Vietnam and China. However, in 2017 Adidas built a large-scale, highly automated production facility in Germany. It is turning out one million shoes each year, with just 160 staff. Robots are doing the bulk of the work.[47] The automation is enabling shoes to be made faster, meaning customers get the latest designs sooner. Adidas plans to open similar facilities in the United States, France and the United Kingdom.

The automation of basic manufacturing means there are fewer jobs than before. It's unlikely we'll ever see a return to the share of manufacturing jobs that peaked in the 1970s and 1980s.[48] Yet jobs in manufacturing are now highly skilled and highly paid.

Of course, while highly skilled workers are better off, lower-skilled workers do not benefit if their jobs can easily be done by robots. Germany is addressing this by training hundreds of thousands of people through apprenticeships and vocational programs. Those who are low-skilled in Germany have otherwise benefited from favourable conditions in the labour market – though they are more likely to be working in the services sector than they are to be in manufacturing. And with one of the highest minimum wages in Europe, Germany ensures that low-skilled workers are at least able to earn a living wage.[49]

Innovate Within Your Niche

The best route to manufacturing success is to produce quality, in-demand products. Rather than competing with low-cost countries, Germany's manufacturers have thrived by developing the world's best products in specialised areas and attracting a reputation for quality. By focusing on niches and becoming known for certain products, German manufacturers have been able to develop reasonably exclusive lines of supply to other countries. This protects against competition and opens up global export markets.

But remaining a world leader doesn't happen without an enormous investment in innovation – both to develop new products and to make continual improvements to existing products. Germany's unique network of industrial research organisations, led by the Fraunhofer institutes, partner with and support manufacturers, enabling them to stay at the global forefront.

Uvex has high hopes for the future. It aims to continue its global expansion, and in particular to take on the United States by building on its recent acquisition of US-based company HexArmor. 'To become a real global player, that's our plan,' Brück says.

It is also undergoing a digital transformation, to improve automation and to be able to track inputs and products seamlessly throughout the production process. 'We are already very advanced, so we have a high degree of automation, connectivity and data analysis of our manufacturing process,' Brück says. 'But it's a work in progress. We do see lots of opportunities with the digital transformation.'

Only by investing in new technology will Uvex be able to 'remain the technology leader in the personal protective equipment business', Brück says. The next round of Uvex products is likely to integrate digital functions. 'Adding sensor technology and more features to the products, which will contribute to a safer workplace, that's the vision,' he says. Think helmets that can detect imminent collisions, safety glasses that can visualise information in a display, or gloves that can operate devices without contact through motion detection.[50]

Brück is optimistic about manufacturing's future in Germany. 'It's a whole world of opportunity,' he says. 'We are creating something positive for the country.'

FIVE THINGS WE CAN DO NOW

1. **Encourage niche production.** Companies – and clusters of companies – stand the best chance of global leadership if they focus on specialised areas of strength. Rather than operating large-scale, all-purpose factories, manufacturing businesses may do best to seek to become the undisputed global leaders in a specific niche. This is likely to require investment in innovation, including partnerships with external suppliers of research and development, such as universities or product development specialists.

2. **Support small- and medium-sized businesses.** These companies typically have strong community connections and are less likely to move offshore. Governments can help these businesses to thrive by providing them with the expertise, training and resources they need to adopt new technologies. In Australia, for example, the Medicines Manufacturing Innovation Centre helps local pharmaceutical manufacturers with specialist services and skills to optimise processes and develop new products.

3. **Involve employees in decision-making.** When workers have a sense of involvement in the company's future, it can reduce industrial conflict and lead to a long-term focus on success. It also creates more-motivated employees, driving innovation and performance. Involving workers in decision-making can range from worker's committees that speak with management through to employee representatives on company boards.

4. **Invest in apprentices.** Apprenticeships are a great way of building a pipeline of workers with skills and experience. They also ensure that these junior workers have qualifications which will enable them to find a new job faster if a company goes out of business. While many countries have apprenticeships in the traditional trades, expanding apprenticeships to a broader range of occupations will benefit both employers and workers. Industry, training providers and government can work together to identify the skills profiles of emerging occupations, so that apprenticeships can be developed for jobs that are likely to be in demand in the future.

5. **Reduce barriers to research and development.** The relatively high costs of research and development make it challenging for small- and medium-sized companies to innovate and experiment. Businesses could be supported with incentives such as tax credits, 'innovation vouchers' (which encourage companies to engage with certain research and development or technology providers) and free or discounted fees to access state-of-the-art equipment based at research institutions.

9

URBAN REVIVAL
How to Create Smart Cities

n 2008, Phoenix, Arizona, was in a bad way. House prices had tanked and construction had stopped. Once one of the fastest-growing cities in the United States, its economy had been built on construction, tourism and retiree spending. But when the global financial crisis took hold, all this ground to a halt. Unemployment rose in the south-western desert city, and per capita incomes fell for the first time in more than forty years.

As Phoenix's leaders scrambled to respond, they realised they 'had to do something to ensure we developed an economy that wasn't built solely on population growth', says Christine MacKay, director of economic development at the City of Phoenix.

MacKay is a lifelong Phoenix resident, now approaching the end of her career. She talks up the city's charms earnestly and with conviction. When she mentions the economic challenges, I have the clear impression that she feels them personally.

MacKay describes how she and her team looked to other cities for inspiration. 'We would see these really incredible spaces in Washington, DC and New York and San Francisco, where innovation districts had started to grow almost organically.' Communities of fast-growing fledgling businesses – startups – were working and collaborating together.

They realised that a genuinely innovative economy needed 'a really densely populated area where people had spontaneous collisions'. The sort of place where you could walk across the street and meet with someone who was developing a technology similar to yours or who could help move yours forward.

In sprawling, car-dominated Phoenix, this was a tall order. The metropolitan area is suburbs to the horizon. Yet MacKay says that downtown is quite densely populated and had all the right ingredients to grow into an innovation district. 'It's filled with high-rises and a high-density major university campus. We have the Arizona Science Center, the Children's Museum, the Phoenix Symphony. We have the opera and the ballet. Light rail connects all of the assets and runs through the entire district.'

MacKay brought together the property developers that owned most of the buildings in downtown Phoenix and pitched the idea of an innovation district to them. They loved it, and in a show of goodwill, committed vacant floors in office buildings to serve as incubation spaces. To set the tone and provide guidance, MacKay and the council established an Innovation District Steering Committee 'made up of building owners, the startup community, our coworking spaces, our universities, our government sector'.

The south end of what is now known as PHX Core has a gritty, urban feel, with technology businesses occupying converted warehouses. The north end is distinctly different, with Arizona State's downtown campus and the green lawns of Civic Space Park. The district is now home to 24,000 employees and more than 130 startups.

There are ambitious plans to increase the focus on bioscience and grow additional clusters of innovative businesses. In 2018, the council brought in Baltimore-based developer Wexford Science and Technology to work with Arizona State University in developing seven acres of land for its biomedical campus.

Tom Osha is vice-president of innovation and economic development at Wexford. 'It looked like we would have a good three-way partnership,' he says. 'We had a city that was highly engaged, a university that was innovative, and the skills and experience of Wexford.'

A 224,000 square foot (21,000 square metre) building is now under construction. In addition to room for university research, when it opens in late 2020 it will have 'space for companies, for entrepreneurs – it'll have programs for innovation that include not only Arizona State, but the University of Arizona, Northern Arizona University, the community college, the entrepreneurial community,' says Osha. 'In a lot of ways, it will become a centre of congregation, in addition to being a centre of gravity for the region.'

Phoenix's efforts are working. The Brookings Institution reports that Phoenix added nearly 8000 tech jobs in just two years.[1] The city now ranks thirty-eighth in the world for the number of venture capital deals, and twenty-fifth in the world for angel investment and seed-stage deals – the type of investments that startups need to grow. More than US$800 million in venture capital was invested between 2015 and 2017. Washington-based think tank The Center for American Entrepreneurship has labelled Phoenix a 'distinguished' global startup hub. This is a kind of fourth-tier global startup city, behind the 'superstars' (such as San Francisco and New York), the 'elite' (such as Austin and Singapore) and the 'advanced' (such as Washington, DC, and Sydney).[2] It may well progress up these ranks in the future.

Phoenix's efforts are indicative of a trend across the United States. A significant number of American cities are leading the world in innovation. Globally, more than half of all venture capital investments are made in American cities. Star cities, such as Silicon Valley, New York, Los Angeles and Boston, continue to dominate the globe in this.

It's not every city in the country, of course. There are enormous economic disparities between the prosperous coastal cities and the struggling 'heartland'. Yet the United States is experiencing the rise of a group of small and second-tier urban centres that are fast becoming among the most innovative in the world.

The strength of the innovation found in American cities is one of the main reasons Americans have the world's highest average household disposable income.[3] But these hubs haven't emerged by chance; government interventions have shaped and enabled their evolution.

Cities and Innovation

The United States hasn't always dominated global innovation. In the nineteenth century, British engineering led the Industrial Revolution, while German scientists were advancing key principles in the natural sciences.

American innovation really started in the late 1800s, when the United States began to innovate rapidly in applied science. Samuel Morse created the telegraph, Thomas Edison refined the lightbulb, the Wright brothers undertook the world's first flight, and Alexander Graham Bell and Elisha Gray invented telephony. American scientists excelled at building on the work of others to develop products with practical application; they were often the last link in the chain of invention. By the late nineteenth and early twentieth century, the United States had become the world's pre-eminent industrial nation. This reputation was consolidated when several leading European scientists, such as Albert Einstein (who developed the theory of relativity) and Enrico Fermi (who produced the first nuclear reactor), moved to the United States in the 1930s to escape the rise of fascism in Germany and Italy.

Silicon Valley – the undisputed epicentre of global innovation – was initially created by the military. In 1933, the navy purchased Moffett Airfield, near San Jose, which became an early hub for the aerospace industry. Professor Stuart Leslie, who specialises in the history of science and technology, writes that Silicon Valley 'owes its present configuration to patterns of federal spending, corporate strategies, industry–university relationships, and technological innovation shaped by the assumptions and priorities of Cold War defence policy'.

In 1951, Stanford University and the City of Palo Alto established Stanford Research Park, a suburban business park now home to iconic companies such as Hewlett-Packard, Skype and Tesla. From 2008 to 2011 it housed Facebook's headquarters. Many people regard it as the heart of Silicon Valley. One urban planner tells me that in the 1950s, 'there was this suburbanisation phenomenon of innovation, with the movement of many R&D facilities and company leadership out to the suburbs to make things easier, more efficient'. This is the Silicon Valley model. The power and promise of this approach led to 'a plethora of science parks and science corridors that dot the landscape in many countries, including the United States'.

Julie Wagner is an urban planner who moves between field work and research with the Brookings Institution and the ESADE Business School in Barcelona. She is also president of the newly established Global

Institute on Innovation Districts. Sporting a pair of semi-rimless glasses, smiling generously, Wagner shares that while innovation was once concentrated in suburban hubs, there has been a 'collapse back of innovation into cities'. Science and business parks have yielded a significant share of innovation since the 1950s, but they are 'spatially isolated corporate campuses, accessible only by car, with little emphasis on the quality of life or on integrating work, housing and recreation'.[4] Today, 'the level of collaboration required to innovate is all the more paramount' and in urban environments 'the physical landscape – the proximity, the density, the higher levels of accessibility, the mixing of different actors in a small geographic area' is a value-add.

The 1970s saw the emergence of the US biotechnology industry. The phrase is often used more or less interchangeably with the term 'life sciences'. In 1976, Cambridge City Council in Greater Boston decided to regulate the industry, which created certainty. This had the unintended effect of fuelling investment in the sector, and Boston has since gone on to become the world's most important city for biotech.

Travis McCready is the president and chief executive officer of the Massachusetts Life Sciences Center, a government-funded economic development agency that has spent nearly US$700 million to support the biotechnology sector in Boston and surrounds. He tells me that government support – in the form of direct funding or tax incentives – to help companies locate or develop in the state has been critical to its success. As an example, McCready tells me that in the early 2000s the state provided 'tens of millions of dollars' to entice pharmaceutical giant Bristol-Myers Squibb to locate a US$750 million manufacturing facility in the state.

Today, the Massachusetts Life Sciences Center provides funding for infrastructure to strengthen the biotechnology 'ecosystem', such as large-scale laboratories, equipment and coworking spaces. It continues to offer tax incentives to attract new companies or help existing companies expand, and it provides seed funding to help startup businesses grow to a stage where they are attractive to investors. It also supports the development of the biotechnology workforce through 'the largest life-science internship program in the United States', which each year trains 550 college and 150 high-school students. Massachusetts now employs as many people in the biotechnology sector as it does in the construction industry.[5]

McCready says that the growth of biotechnology in Boston accelerated when industry began to be attracted to the idea of working in densely populated urban areas, where they could collaborate closely with academics, investors and other companies. Firms 'started to migrate towards having their R&D operations or translational operations located in a dense innovation environment'.

A small precinct known as Kendall Square is now the most innovative square mile on the planet, with the highest concentration of biotechnology companies in the world. After stepping off the train at Kendall Square subway station, it's a few hundred metres to everything needed to start and grow a biotechnology company. Technology can be licensed from Massachusetts Institute of Technology (MIT); workspace rented from LabCentral, a biotech co-working facility; ideas pitched to any number of venture capital firms to raise capital and grow a team. Successful start-ups can be sold to multinational companies such as Novartis, Pfizer or Takeda, which all have large headquarters in the precinct.

Kendall Square's epicentre is MIT, which is deeply committed to 'transferring our scholarship into the economy'.[6] Its professors are encouraged to spend time outside of the university, by founding a startup, serving on a board or acting as an adviser to a young business.

The innovative neighbourhood now has about 50,000 people who work there on a daily basis, more than 250 biotech companies, a growing residential population and several hotels. Life sciences office space in the precinct has expanded from 3.8 million square feet (350,000 square metres) in 2000 to 8.8 million square feet (817,000 square metres) in 2017. Kendall Square is the epicentre of life sciences in the state of Massachusetts, which has seen venture capital investment rise from US$900 million in 2012 to US$3.1 billion in 2017.[7] It's a pretty great story.

More than 55 per cent of the world's population now lives in cities. The number of urban residents has increased from 750 million in 1950 to 4.2 billion today. By 2050, two out of every three people will most likely live in a city. North America is the most urbanised part of the planet, with four out of five people residing in urban areas.[8]

People around the world are moving to cities because it enables them to live better lives, with jobs that are better paid and greater access to services. Cities are the key points of connection to the global economy and the key drivers of improved productivity, including through innovation.[9] How well a city functions influences the material wellbeing of its inhabitants.

In recent years, the way that innovation is undertaken has been changing, making cities – and global engagement – even more important. Once, ideas were researched, developed and commercialised within the secure walls of a company, typically located remotely from competitors. However, the growing cost of innovation and increased competition from other markets has led companies to adopt a different approach.

Many large companies have shifted towards an open innovation model, where they look beyond their internal capabilities to source ideas, technologies and intellectual property. Open innovation favours extensive sharing of intellectual property and research and development capabilities between organisations. An analysis by consulting firm Deloitte found that biotechnology or pharmaceutical companies were three times more likely to achieve success when their new products were developed through open innovation.[10]

This model has profound implications for the way cities need to organise themselves.

Professor Bruce Katz is a lawyer by training who spent twenty-two years at the Brookings Institution in Washington, DC, where he established the Metropolitan Policy Program. Before this, he was chief of staff to Henry Cisneros, a secretary of housing and urban development during the Clinton administration. 'Innovation needs an ecosystem of companies, universities, investors, startups, scale-ups and intermediaries,' he says. 'That ecosystem is more and more likely to be located in the cores of cities, because that's where you can really have a mashup of ideas, a seamless exchange of ideas, by which innovation occurs. Innovation is a team sport, and can't really be programmed, or dependent on one discipline, but manifests when you have this environment for chaotic collision. That's what cities really represent.'

The race to build competitive startup ecosystems is important because startups are increasingly the source of job growth. A report by Australia's Office of the Chief Economist found that young firms make the greatest contribution to job creation. The Congressional Research Service in the United States reached a similar conclusion, finding that 'high impact' businesses such as startups 'account for almost all [net] job creation in the economy'.[11]

While a small number of superstar cities have so far dominated, it seems likely there is room for more than just a handful of cities to thrive in future. Research firm Startup Genome's 'Global Startup Ecosystem Report 2019' predicts there will not be one single innovation hub like Silicon Valley. Rather, there will be '30 "next" hubs, distributed around the world, reaching critical mass driven by either regional (e.g. Singapore in Southeast Asia) or Sub-Sector leadership (e.g. San Diego in Life Sciences)'.[12]

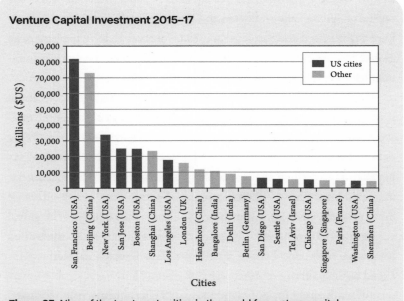

Venture Capital Investment 2015–17

Figure 25. Nine of the top twenty cities in the world for venture capital investment are in the United States.

Beyond the Superstar Cities

Like Boston with biotechnology, US cities dominate innovation in startup activity and through venture capital.

According to the World Economic Forum, the United States is the second-most economically competitive country in the world (behind Singapore). While the Forum ranks Germany slightly higher on innovation, the United States ranks first for scientific publications and the prominence of research institutions.[13]

In its Tech Cities index, global real estate company Savills lists five US cities – New York, San Francisco, Boston, Los Angeles and Austin – in the world's top ten. Similarly, Startup Genome finds that four of the top ten startup hubs are in the United States, with Silicon Valley and New York first and second. The nation is also home to twelve of the top thirty startup ecosystems globally.[14]

Venture capital is a form of private equity funding invested in emerging companies with high growth potential. The Center for American Entrepreneurship reveals that five of the top ten homes for global startups are in the United States: San Francisco, New York, San Jose – the capital of Silicon Valley – Boston and Los Angeles. Silicon Valley (including San Francisco and San Jose) accounts for more than 20 per cent of all global venture capital investment, and remains 'by far the world's dominant location for startup activity'.

Cities in the United States secure 52 per cent of all venture capital invested globally. This percentage has decreased markedly since the mid-1990s, when 95 per cent of venture capital investments were made in the nation. The reduction is not because US venture capital has declined. It's because of growth, as the size of the global venture capital market has increased from US$52 billion in 2010 to US$171 billion in 2017 – a rise of more than 200 per cent. China now has more than a quarter of all global venture capital investment. Other key countries include India, the United Kingdom, Germany, Canada, France and Israel, which have all experienced fast-expanding venture capital markets.[15]

After adjusting for population size, US cities clearly still dominate. For venture capital invested per capita, the United States has thirteen of the top twenty cities globally, including seven of the top ten. These include San Francisco, San Jose, Durham (in North Carolina), Boston, Boulder (in the foothills of the Rocky Mountains), Provo (an hour's drive from Salt Lake City) and Santa Barbara (on the California coast, north of Los Angeles).

While big cities, such as New York and Boston, attract most of the venture capital, there are a number of second-tier American cities now emerging as places to watch.

Bruce Katz is also the co-author (with Jeremy Nowak) of the book *The New Localism*, which discusses the rise of smaller cities across the American heartland. He tells me that this next tier of cities in the United States 'have enormous assets, are more affordable, and have a higher quality of life and a higher level of liveability'. Urban centres across the nation 'are recognising that they have particular assets – sometimes advanced research institutions, sometimes an entrepreneurial culture – that really enables innovation to occur at a large scale'. And while venture capital has historically been invested in the superstar cities on the coast, Katz says that much of the wealth flowing into venture capital funds is actually coming from elsewhere in the country – from university endowments, pension funds or wealthy families across America. This represents an opportunity for smaller cities. 'They have wealth that has been generated locally that now can be reinvested locally,' he says.

In Milwaukee, insurance company Northwestern Mutual has invested in an innovation space called Cream City Labs, designed for 'mentoring, co-location and innovation-focused events, such as hackathons, community meetups, STEM programming and training workshops'. In Detroit, following a recession that sent the city into bankruptcy, a group of ten philanthropic foundations developed an economic development agenda called The New Economy Initiative and invested more than US\$96 million in organisations and programs that support entrepreneurs and small businesses in the city.[16]

Julie Wagner identifies a renaissance among middle-tier cities in the United States, pointing to places such as Pittsburgh, Chattanooga, Phoenix and Salt Lake City. 'Their price points are lower,' she says, 'but we are witnessing a growing concentration of R&D and a talented workforce, and they are creatively leveraging one asset, or several assets together (such as affordable, creative workspaces next to an increasingly ambitious anchor institution), to create new competitive advantages. This is helping to lure talent from larger cities.'

Thanks to Uncle Sam

There's a perception of the United States as the embodiment of corporate wealth, its economic success due largely to government staying out of the way. There's certainly an element of truth to the idea of American entrepreneurialism – for example, the World Economic Forum finds that US executives have among the world's most positive attitudes towards entrepreneurial risk.[17] But successive US governments have played an enormous role supporting entrepreneurial risk-taking. Without government support, it seems unlikely that the United States would be the innovation nation it is today.

Over many decades, the US government has invested billions of dollars into research and development. Investment from the defence budget leads to new technology, as well as a steady stream of well-trained scientists and engineers, while most new pharmaceuticals originate with research done by the taxpayer-funded National Institutes of Health.[18]

The government has a number of bodies to support research and development. Among the most successful is the Defense Advanced Research Projects Agency (DARPA), which is charged with 'making pivotal investments in breakthrough technologies for national security'.[19] It has no direct involvement with defence procurement or military programs, and no laboratories of its own. Rather, it funds and supports new companies conducting relevant research and development. The success of DARPA has led to the establishment of a smaller agency called Advanced Research Projects Agency – Energy (ARPA-E), which is adopting a similar approach in the energy industry.

Professor Mariana Mazzucato is an American-Italian economist based at University College London. In her 2013 book *The Entrepreneurial State*, she writes that 'nearly all the technological revolutions in the past – from the internet to today's green tech revolution' required a massive state push. For example, much of the technology in the iPhone was originally developed by government. DARPA oversaw innovations that led to the internet. GPS began as a US military program called Navstar. The company that created the touchscreen was founded by a professor and his doctoral student, with funding from the National Science Foundation and the CIA, and Siri was a spinoff of a government-led artificial intelligence project.[20]

The state has also played a role in the commercial viability of new technology. It has developed innovative programs to ensure that government organisations and departments, such as the National Institutes of Health and the Department of Defense, allocate part of their research funding to small firms, who will then ultimately have the potential to supply goods and services to government along with larger companies.

For example, the Small Business Innovation Research (SBIR) program is the first place many entrepreneurs seek funding. Each federal department – including Agriculture, Commerce, Defense, Education, Energy, and Health and Human Services – administers its own SBIR program and outlines the research and development topics it will consider.[21] The SBIR program collectively provides more than US$2 billion a year to high-tech firms, over two phases. In Phase 1, companies receive up to US$150,000 for up to six months to establish the technical feasibility and commercial potential of their project. In Phase 2, companies receive up to $2 million for two years to build their product or service.

One study conducted by academics from George Mason and Harvard universities found that government programs such as SBIR provide 20 to 25 per cent of funding to US early-stage technology firms. It also found that government funding for early-stage technology firms is equal to the total investments from business angels (individuals who invest very early in a company's life) and about two to eight times the investment from private venture capitalists.[22]

Phase 3 is commercialisation, which does not involve SBIR funding, although it could involve other research and development support or a government contract for provision of goods or services. There is also the federal Research & Experimentation Tax Credit, which enables companies to claim a credit on tax for expenses they incur for research and development. This credit provides US companies with billions of dollars of subsidy each year towards their research and development costs.[23]

In addition, there are federal venture funds to facilitate technology development. For example, through the energy portfolio the US government makes about US$40 billion in loans and guarantees available to support large-scale energy infrastructure projects. This has assisted the growth of some of America's tech giants, such as Tesla, which in 2010 was loaned US$465 million to scale up production of its Model S sedan.[24] Across the country, state governments have also established venture funds to support startups in their early stages. For example, the New York state government established the Accelerate NY Seed Fund, while the Massachusetts Life Sciences Center Seed Fund invests up to US$250,000 in early-stage life sciences companies.[25]

The US Food and Drug Administration (FDA) has adopted an innovative regulatory model that has accelerated treatments for rare diseases and further fuelled biotechnology. The Orphan Drug program includes tax incentives and subsidies to treat diseases that affect less than 200,000 people in the country. Companies are also granted several years of exclusivity for their product, meaning there is no competition from generic brands. Given the small market for drugs and therapies for these conditions, together with the high cost of development, it's likely that without financial incentives these illnesses would remain 'orphans'. Since 1983, the program has enabled the development of more than 600 drugs and therapies to treat rare diseases.[26] In turn, orphan drugs have generated substantial revenues, which have played a role in igniting the development of the biotechnology sector.

Another innovative FDA measure is a 'priority review voucher' – awarded to companies that receive approval for a drug or therapy to treat a rare disease affecting children or a neglected tropical disease, or for products that may be used in the event of a public health emergency. These vouchers grant the recipients FDA fast-tracking for subsequent products they may wish to register, and can be on-sold to other companies. They can sell for hundreds of millions of dollars,[27] and are further incentive for companies to develop treatments for diseases with a limited pharmaceutical market.

The United States has a long tradition of suspicion towards interventionist government. Given the history of white settlement in the country, with pilgrims throwing off the shackles of the English monarchy, this is not surprising. US political institutions were designed with checks and balances to limit governments' ability to impose their will on ordinary people. While the United States has generally had weak systems of government, it has had a strong civil society, built on a culture of volunteerism, collaboration and philanthropy.

It is because of this culture that the United States finds itself in a rather fortuitous position, since collaborative networks are the best way of organising cities. Bruce Katz says, 'Cities are not governments. They're networks. If you can cohere networks – public, private, civic, institution, university, community groups, et cetera – and you can collaborate to compete, you can have a two-plus-two-equals-five effect.' While many cities in the nation practise collaboration informally, formal governance networks are becoming common. 'They are well capitalised, have enormous capacity, and can project economic power globally and put it to good, inclusive use locally,' says Katz.

'The US has always been more of a network society than other countries in the world. We don't have a central government like in Britain or Israel that is really dictating from on high. It's a federal republic, power is already distributed in the governmental sector, and it's a large country. When you go to see the mayor in an American city, it's likely that philanthropy, or the business chamber, or the university, or the hospitals are at the table. There's an informality in some respects, a familiarity and an ease of working across sectors, that I think is quite remarkable.'

Across America, city-based leadership groups like those in Phoenix have been overseeing the transformation of depressed inner-urban areas into innovation districts. Bruce Katz and Julie Wagner first wrote of this trend in an influential Brookings Institution paper, in which they defined innovation districts as physically compact areas serviced by public transport that involve a clustering of universities, companies, startups, incubators (companies that help startups by offering mentoring or workspaces) and accelerators (programs for groups of startups to provide education and connections; they usually culminate in a public pitch or demonstration event). They typically offer mixed-use housing, office and retail space, all accessible by foot.[28]

Kendall Square in Boston is a perfect example of an innovation district. 'It serves as the meeting place for the life sciences ecosystem,' says Travis McCready. 'You can go there today, get a coffee at any number of coffee shops and bump into some of the most accomplished scientists in the world – exchange ideas while you're waiting for your double espresso. Bump into another set of engineers to help you commercialise that technology while you're waiting for a burrito.'

Katz says the concept is a response to how markets operate today. 'If you have a niche in a next-generation technology or an advanced sector of the economy, you basically want to embellish that,' he says. 'Not just through attracting companies or growing companies, but by building sectors of excellence in your universities, and even in your high schools and community colleges, so that it's really a robust ecosystem.' Because innovation districts are small, 'they shrink the geography' into 'a magic square mile or half square mile where exchanges among researchers and entrepreneurs and investors can occur'.

To help create an innovation district, city leadership can reimagine the types of institutions and buildings that might best service the precinct. This involves considering the type of technology that may be needed, such as advanced connectivity or specialised laboratories. Local capital, such as from universities or philanthropists, is another factor. Land owned by institutional partners is often used as a catalyst for investment. A key factor is the ability to attract and retain talent, and cities such as Nashville, Raleigh and Louisville have developed bespoke campaigns to target individuals with skills and specialisations in specific niches.[29] And because US innovation districts are often located close to disadvantaged urban areas, many local governments see them as a way to provide new jobs in hospitality, administration and technology for low-income residents of the area.[30]

Cities are living organisms. As they grow, there is an exponentially positive impact on a range of measures, such as patents generated, economic output and levels of creativity and innovation.[31] Bigger cities are more productive and generate more innovation.

Why are we more innovative when we live in cities? It's all about people. Wei Pan and colleagues at MIT find that the density of cities increases opportunities to be exposed to different ideas. The bigger the city, the more opportunities we have. The cities in the United States and elsewhere that are working hard to develop innovation districts are effectively trying to intervene to engineer the conditions that generate more connections than would otherwise occur.

However, urbanisation is not a panacea. Megacities in Africa, Asia and Latin America do not seem to experience the upside of increased density. Pan and colleagues argue this is likely because transport is so poor that it's not possible to connect with people in different parts of the city. Poor infrastructure can potentially wipe out the benefits of density.[32] Many of these cities also have weaker institutions and poor governing bodies.

Professor Richard Florida, an expert in urbanisation based at the University of Toronto, argues that too much density can be as bad as too little. He says the 'skyscraper canyons' found in many Asian cities isolate and alienate people. Rather, the most innovative cities are home to the best kind of density – the 'downtown mix of towers, older low-rise industrial buildings and denser suburbs' found in places such as New York and San Francisco.[33]

Innovation hubs are beacons for economic activity, but this had led to geographic inequality. Florida describes this as 'winner-takes-all urbanism': 'The most important and innovative industries and the most talented, most ambitious and wealthiest people are converging as never before in a relative handful of leading superstar cities that are knowledge and tech hubs,' he writes. 'This small group of elite places forges ever forward, while most others struggle, stagnate, or fall behind.' This is 'the central contradiction of contemporary capitalism'. Clusters are drivers of both economic growth and inequality: 'The concentration of talent and economic activity in fewer and fewer places not only divides the world's cities into winners and losers, but ensures that the winner cities will become unaffordable for all but the wealthy.[34]

Just twenty years ago, economist Frances Cairncross was writing about the 'death of distance' – the idea that technology would 'tilt the balance between large and small, rich and poor'.[35] Yet, rather than telecommuting from small towns, knowledge workers are concentrating in dense downtown areas, fuelled by coffee and collaboration.

While it's undoubtedly true that wealth, talent and innovation have clustered in cities such as New York, San Francisco and Boston, Tom Osha thinks there are a number of countervailing forces that are supporting the rise of other cities. One is the cost of housing. In Silicon Valley, even tech workers on six-figure salaries can't afford to buy homes, and thousands are living in cars or trailers.[36] 'The price of housing is such that young people – whether they work for Google or Facebook or AstraZeneca or Genzyme – can't afford housing in Cambridge or San Francisco or Palo Alto,' Osha says. The price of a typical house in Silicon Valley would buy four houses in Phoenix.[37] Companies are increasingly looking to 'complementary cities' that 'have a better business climate, are more affordable, yet still have the intellectual capital coming out of a major university'.

And how do we make sure that innovative cities work for everyone, not just those poised to take advantage of the rivers of venture capital funds flowing into the city? Bruce Katz argues that the United States has 'lagged in building a workforce system that has kept pace with economic restructuring' but thinks that change is nevertheless achievable. 'Technology or innovation is not something that is owned by someone with a PhD from Stanford. It really permeates all occupations in the United States.' He believes that cities will soon 'crack the code' on how to upskill low- and moderate-income workers to participate in the innovation economy, giving them 'ladders of opportunity'. He sees a number of cities well down this path, including Philadelphia, where he is currently based. It has a booming innovation economy despite being the poorest big city in the country. The West Philadelphia Skills Initiative matches unemployed Philadelphians with employers seeking talent, and provides training and support to ensure people have a stable job with the opportunity for advancement.[38]

The World Economic Forum indicates that competitiveness and inequality are not tied, noting 'it is possible to be both pro-growth and "pro-equity"'. Germany, the Netherlands, Sweden and Denmark feature in the Global Competitiveness Index top ten and are among the most equitable countries in the world. So, 'more competitiveness seems neither to systematically reduce or increase inequality'.[39] But education is clearly key. Over the six years from 2012 to 2018, the United States added more than ten million jobs for college graduates and 1.6 million for high-school graduates. Yet for those who did not finish school, there were 200,000 *fewer* jobs in 2018 than in 2012. Across the country, the education levels of a zip code largely determine its income, poverty and mortality rate.[40]

Florida suggests the answer also lies in making it easier for those at the bottom of the economic ladder to benefit from the opportunities in newly thriving city centres. Inner cities need more housing, ideally located around public transport, to improve affordability and increase access. The status and productivity of service jobs needs to be increased too, turning them into middle-class occupations. Florida argues that raising the minimum wage is one way to do this.[41]

Another way of thinking about this divide may be something called 'distributed development', a concept currently being discussed in Europe. While it acknowledges the need for innovation to cluster in superstar cities and tech hubs, it focuses on working to 'stimulate economic activity in outlying places, by investing in skills and capabilities, strengthening connections between local universities and industries and connecting less-advantaged places with thriving ones'.[42] Rather than ignoring disadvantaged regions, or plying them with subsidies, this approach proposes the rather more challenging task of working with regions to strengthen their economies by developing areas in which they might specialise and even become globally competitive.

Addressing the distributional impact of city growth is clearly an enormous challenge. Yet it's important we work at it, as geographic inequality is a trend that is only getting worse. Left to proliferate unhindered, it risks driving an even larger wedge between inner-city elites and those in our suburbs and regions.

What the United States Can Teach the World

Not everything in the United States is to be emulated. It is one of the most unequal countries in the OECD, and it performs poorly in areas such as life expectancy and crime. Yet it dominates innovation and is the world's most competitive economy. On this front, there is a lot that other countries can gain from its experience.

Government Drives Innovation

Perhaps surprisingly for a country that prides itself on a limited role for government, the growth of innovation in the United States has been facilitated and encouraged by government. Innovation is not generated by market forces alone. The government's role – as funder of research, as a financer of commercial risk early in a company's journey, as customer and as partner in city development – is critical. National, state and local governments all play a role.

Without enormous government investment in research, it seems doubtful that the United States would be leading the world in innovation. This shows us that whether in defence, pharmaceuticals or energy, government funding builds the foundation for innovative industry. Without the new ideas generated through government-funded research, much of the world's commercial innovation would not be possible.

In the United States, government spending on research and development equates to 0.69 per cent of GDP, substantially above the OECD average of 0.63 per cent. The two other countries that the World Economic Forum identifies as 'statistical outliers' for innovation – Germany (0.84 per cent) and Switzerland (0.82 per cent) – also have large government-financed research and development programs.[43] Coincidence? Unlikely. In an analysis of economic growth in Europe between 1995 and 2013, Dr Irena Szarowská from Silesian University in the Czech Republic found that government expenditure on research and development was the main driver of economic growth. OECD figures show that direct government spending on research and development – for example, through grants to companies – results in significant additional investment by business. One dollar given to firms results in $1.70 spent on research in total.[44]

US government has also played a role in supporting innovation by providing regulatory certainty. Investors are spooked by uncertainty. Well-crafted regulation can give the market confidence. In many areas, US regulation creates the incentives that drive private sector innovation.

Creative Cities Need Curation

Cities, not nation-states, are now the primary units of the global economy. The United States shows that cities need to be curated to facilitate innovation. Governments, businesses, universities and community leaders need to work together to generate the right mix of density and amenity. They also need to attract, build and grow an innovation ecosystem, involving technology companies, startup incubators, accelerators and coworking spaces.

While this approach was pioneered in the United States, it is now being widely emulated. According to the Global Institute on Innovation Districts, there are now at least 100 innovation districts throughout the world. They can be found in the United Kingdom, Denmark, the Netherlands and elsewhere in Europe. They are also being pursued with vigour in Australia, Latin America, the Middle East and Asia. While innovation districts in the United States are dominated by civil society, other countries are learning to adapt the model to fit their local contexts. In Australia, Israel and the United Kingdom, for example, government is playing a much stronger leadership role.[45]

Skills-Based Learning Is Key

It's clear that the jobs of the future will require more education than ever. Governments play a critical role in providing an accessible, world-class education system. Education is the most important thing that can be done to reduce the inequality that intense innovation often brings. More and more students will need to complete further education or training post-school. As we saw in earlier chapters, the countries achieving the best education outcomes are building a foundation of quality early childhood education, they are supporting and investing in their teachers, and they are carefully tracking and refining the performance of their education system.

The types of learning we need are changing. While traditional education continues to be important, the World Economic Forum argues that 'as automation and work converge, skills gaps are set to change at a faster pace and at a greater volume – leading to both talent shortages and job redundancies'. It suggests that societies need to move in a 'skills-based' direction – to foster a 'system of lifelong learning infused with a shared set of skills-based indicators at its core'. The West Philadelphia Skills Initiative for jobseekers is a type of vocational program we need to see more of. There are many other examples of skills-based education initiatives. To take just one: in Chicago, community colleges are partnering with the Chicago Apprentice Network and with industry to build a 'college-to-career' pathway that involves skills targeted to roles in IT, insurance and cybersecurity.[46]

Second-Tier Is Not Second-Rate

While superstar cities dominate the discussion about innovation, other cities are increasingly learning to leverage their strengths, too. Many smaller cities are able to take advantage of their quality universities, affordable housing and engaged civic and business communities to develop their innovative capabilities in specific areas, to the extent that they are often able to compete with the world's best.

Tom Osha from Wexford Science and Technology says that it's all happening in Phoenix. A large foundation has agreed to fund a strategic plan for life sciences for the region. A new body, the Arizona BioIndustry Association, has formed to represent the 1310 bioscience businesses in the region. Entrepreneurs are choosing to start their businesses in Phoenix over Silicon Valley. 'We're really starting to see this dynamic shift to a more knowledge-led economy,' he says.

Christine MacKay emphasises that while once she would have to drag Silicon Valley–based venture capitalists 'kicking and screaming' to invest in a Phoenix-based company, 'they're now proactively reaching out to us and saying, "Let's talk about your list of companies that you have that need investment and which ones are out there."'

'Do we compete with Silicon Valley or New York or Boston?' MacKay asks. 'No. We're a completely different market. We're Phoenix.'

FIVE THINGS WE CAN DO NOW

1. **Invest in public research.** Research underlies the discoveries that lead to innovative products and services. Scientists and engineers trained in research settings also feed the workforce for knowledge-intensive industries.

2. **Incentivise private research and development.** Research and development has benefits that extend far beyond a single company, yet it is expensive and risky. With tax incentives and grants, companies invest in more research and development than they otherwise would, improving competition and fuelling innovation more broadly.

3. **Support startups.** New companies and startups are a major source of employment growth. Startups require mentorship, finance and collaborative partners. Government and business can support startups through incubators, accelerators and entrepreneurship programs, as well as seed funding to grow to the point where they become attractive to investors.

4. **Use government procurement to drive innovation.**
    All governments spend millions (or billions) on procuring
    technology and equipment in areas such as defence, transport
    and health. The US Small Business Innovation Research program
    provides startups and small businesses an opportunity to
    demonstrate that they can supply innovative products to meet
    government needs. Similar programs are run in Australia and
    several other countries. Such initiatives can fuel the creation of
    new businesses and industry sectors geared around supplying
    government.

5. **Develop innovation districts.** Innovative activity clusters in
    high-density urban precincts are increasingly where cutting-
    edge ideas are turned into new products. Local government,
    businesses, universities and philanthropic partners could work
    together to identify a city's or town's areas of economic strength,
    where businesses have the potential to grow into competitive
    clusters. Then, programs, initiatives and infrastructure to attract
    more like-minded businesses into this area could be developed.

10

FROM WARZONE TO WORLD'S HEALTHIEST NATION

How to Live Longer

What do you think of when you think about South Korea? If you're the average person from outside Asia, I suspect it's 'Gangnam Style' (which, for five whole years, held the record for the most-watched video on YouTube) or kimchi, the side dish of fermented cabbage that is a staple of the Korean diet. Or you might think of cars made by South Korean companies such as Kia and Hyundai.

Another thing that South Korea should be famous for is healthcare. The average life expectancy at birth in South Korea now exceeds that of every single English-speaking country, and will soon top the world.

Growth in life expectancy in Western countries is slowing or flatlining, due to the consumption of highly processed food, physical inactivity and rising obesity. In the United States, life expectancy has even started to decline. Largely preventable illnesses – heart disease, stroke and cancer – are now killing more people than any other conditions.

South Korea has had stellar economic growth, yet so far it has avoided the descent into chronic preventable illness. A traditional diet, a universal healthcare system and medical care that is among the world's best are the secrets. In a little over fifty years, South Korea has transformed from an impoverished, war-torn country to a nation with one of the best rates of longevity in the world. South Korea's residents are now significantly taller than a generation ago and can expect to stay healthy longer than people in almost any other country. By 2030, South Korean women will be the first group in the world to have an average life expectancy of greater than ninety. This chapter explores South Korea's story from war to wealth, walking frames and wizened old ladies.

During World War II, the former nation of Korea, located roughly halfway between Japan and China, was annexed by Japan. Thousands were conscripted into labour or the Japanese military; the Korean language and culture was suppressed. Between 1939 and 1945, 400,000 Korean labourers died due to famine and horrendous working conditions. Two hundred thousand women and girls were forced into sexual slavery.[1]

After Japan's surrender at the end of the war, the United Nations mandated – in a solution bound to lead to problems – that the Soviet Union would govern the Korean Peninsula north of the 38th parallel and the United States would govern the south. Cold War politics resulted in the establishment of two separate governments, each nation's boundaries partitioned along the 38th parallel.

In 1950, Soviet-backed North Korea invaded the South, starting the Korean War. Over three years of fighting, 1.2 million people were killed and most cities in the South were destroyed.[2] A 1953 armistice ended active fighting, but the two governments officially remain at war. Today, the nations are divided by a 4-kilometre-wide heavily fortified buffer zone, known as the demilitarised zone (DMZ), with thousands of pieces of artillery aimed across the border on each side. In the decades since the armistice, this border has been the site of intense propaganda campaigns, with loudspeakers blasting slogans and balloons carrying leaflets targeting the DMZ and beyond. Both sides assign physically imposing soldiers to patrol their side of the border.

In the aftermath of the war, life was hard, and food was sometimes difficult to come by. Kongdan Oh grew up in South Korea during this time. Today she has the title of Asian specialist at the Institute for Defense Analyses, a think tank based in Washington, DC. She recalls, 'In the springtime, after the autumn harvest had been eaten and before new crops could be gathered, poor people would scour the hills for edible herbs and plants ... Many schoolchildren depended on foreign food donations like powdered milk for their lunch.'[3] Children born during this period could expect to live until about fifty, around twenty years less than those born in Australia or the United States.

North Korea – officially known as the Democratic People's Republic of Korea – has remained a one-party state, with a centrally planned economy and a kooky but dangerously erratic leader in Kim Jong-un. US think tank Freedom House rates North Korea among the 'worst of the worst' for civil rights and political freedoms. Its economy is one of the poorest in the world, generating less economic output per person than Haiti or Afghanistan.[4]

By contrast, South Korea's economic recovery has been extraordinary. With a population of some 50 million people – slightly fewer than England – it is now the twelfth-largest economy in the world. The World Economic Forum's Global Competitiveness Index measures the conditions most likely to lead to sustained economic growth. It ranks South Korea the fifteenth-most competitive economy in the world, just behind Australia, and first in the world for adoption of digital technology.[5] The ordinary South Korean has an income comparable with residents of Italy or Japan – average annual incomes have increased from about US$100 per capita in 1960 to US$39,000 in 2017, the same as the European average.[6]

Alongside this, the improvement in citizens' wellbeing has been spectacular. Life expectancy at birth is a widely used standard for measuring the health of a population. In 1960, South Koreans had an average life expectancy at birth of fifty-three, fourteen years below the OECD average. It reached the OECD average in 2005, and is now eighty-three, just behind Japan and Switzerland (both eighty-four), and Hong Kong (eighty-five).[7] That's an extension of thirty years of life for the average citizen in less than sixty years!

There are many countries that currently have life expectancy rates similar to South Korea, including Spain, Italy, Israel, France and Norway. But most of these have not seen substantial *increases* in life expectancy in recent years, following the trend across much of the developed world. In some places, life expectancy is even declining. By 2030, for example,

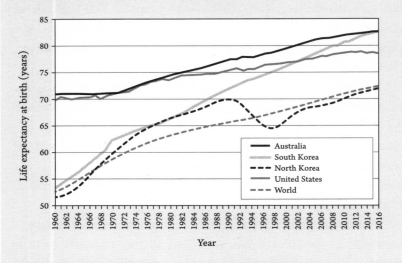

Life Expectancy in Selected Countries

Figure 26. Overall South Korean life expectancy is now at eighty-three, higher than in Australia (eighty-two) and the United States (seventy-nine). It is also increasing, whereas life expectancy in some developed countries is actually declining.

it seems likely that US women will have a life expectancy similar to women in Croatia or Mexico. This is due to greater obesity rates, deaths by homicide and lack of universal healthcare.[8]

As Figure 27 on the next page shows, the biggest success stories have been the emerging economies of East Asia. In countries such as South Korea, Hong Kong, Singapore and Macao, as well as Japan, life expectancy has increased by more than fifteen years over the past half-century. These countries have overtaken – or are fast on their way to overtaking – life expectancies in nations such as the United Kingdom and Australia. Since 1990, life expectancy for South Korean women has risen faster than anywhere else in the world: from seventy-six to eighty-six. Life expectancy for men has risen from sixty-eight to eighty over the same period.[9] A 2017 study from Imperial College London and the World Health Organization estimates that South Korean women will soon be the first in the world to live longer than ninety, on average. The study, which analysed

Life Expectancy Increase Across the World

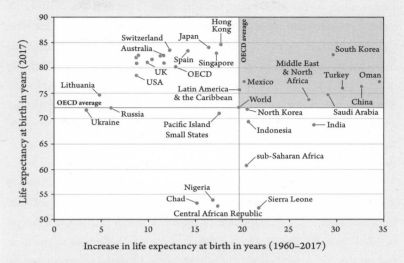

Figure 27. The top half of the figure features countries with long life expectancies; the bottom half features countries with short life expectancies. The left side shows countries with a relatively slow improvement in this rate, and the right shows countries with fast improvement.

lifespans in thirty-five industrialised countries, takes into account influencing factors such as smoking rates, medical advances and patterns of obesity. It also predicts that by 2030 South Korean men will live to eighty-four – to become the longest-living men in the world.[10]

Professor Danny Liew is passionate about population health, and with more than 300 academic publications under his belt, he knows what he's talking about. Relaxed and confident when we meet, wearing an open-necked shirt and an earring in his left ear, he seems younger than his résumé suggests. Liew heads up the clinical epidemiology division at Melbourne's Monash University, where his research and teaching focuses on how diseases occur in different populations and why. He also practises as a doctor at a leading Melbourne hospital. Liew tells me that while life expectancy is a good approximation of population health, 'the issue is not really to strive for longevity so much as to strive for maximum possible health while being alive'.

Accordingly, an alternative measure of population health is something called 'healthy life expectancy at birth'. It reflects the number of
years a newborn can expect to live without disabling injuries or illnesses.
On this measure, South Korea also performs well. With a healthy life
expectancy at birth of seventy-three years, South Korea is equal ninth
in the world, behind Singapore (76.2) and Japan (74.8), and level with
Australia. This figure is ahead of the United Kingdom (71.9), and four and
a half years better than the United States (68.5). South Korean women
can expect 74.8 years of healthy life, which is the fourth-highest rate in
the world, behind Singapore, Japan and Spain.[11]

Another of the world's leading experts points me to an additional
measure of population health. Professor Young-Ho Khang is a specialist
in health policy and management at Seoul National University College
of Medicine. He has written prolifically on South Korea's significant
increase in life expectancy. In slow, articulate English, he points me to
adult height as a measure of population health. Khang says that 'height
is associated with reduced mortality'. 'Taller people die later,' he says.
'Height is a marker of early childhood exposures and early childhood factors, because increase in height usually occurs in childhood. Childhood
infection, childhood nutrition and social factors in childhood are important predictors of height.'

In South Korea, gains in adult height have been the greatest in the
OECD, with young men 6 centimetres taller than their fathers' generation, and women 4 centimetres taller than their mothers'. This contrasts
with the poorest OECD performer, the United States, where there have
been no height increases over a generation.[12] Over a 100-year period,
South Korean women have become 20 centimetres taller, and South
Korean men 15 centimetres taller – an increase larger than in any other
country. Men in South Korea are now an average of 5 centimetres taller
than their cousins in North Korea, and women 2.5 centimetres taller.[13]

To unpack this last figure: the average citizen of North Korea will die
at seventy-two, eleven years earlier than their cousins in South Korea.[14]
This shows that 'political and social factors are important', says Khang, 'as
we share the same genetic backgrounds.' Khang points out that this gulf is
much greater than the one that existed between East and West Germany,

where the difference was only three and a half years for men and three years for women. The situation in North Korea is a 'constant humanitarian crisis'.[15] In a very visual reminder of the differences in health, North Korean children are on average 7 centimetres shorter than their cousins over the border. 'If in future unification is achieved between North and South Korea,' Khang says, 'we will be able to identify who is from the North or the South based just on height.'

There are two ways to increase life expectancy: stop people dying early, and keep them alive longer in old age.

Young-Ho Khang and his colleagues assessed South Korean life expectancy over the past few decades by examining the causes of death at each age. They concluded that a massive reduction in infant mortality, and far fewer injuries and accidents, had made the biggest impact in reducing premature deaths.[16]

In the 1960s, South Korea experienced sixty infant deaths for every 1000 live births. This was a much better rate than countries in sub-Saharan Africa, some of which experienced more than 200 infant deaths for every 1000 live births (about one in five), but it was about three times worse than the rate in Australia, the United Kingdom and the United States. Since then, it has reduced to just 2.8, which is among the lowest in the world. This is lower than Australia (3) and the United Kingdom (3.7), and less than half the rate of the United States (5.7).[17] Khang says these reductions in infant mortality were due to sanitation improvements and to the average South Korean woman having less children – down from more than five in the 1960s to just over one today.[18] Dozens of national programs established by the government to promote improved health in pregnant women, newborns and infants also helped. This involved measures such as screening for rare genetic conditions, and establishing nationwide neonatal intensive-care units and a reproductive health program, providing women with information on contraception, pregnancy, infant care and breastfeeding.[19] Reductions in infant mortality account for 17 to 18 per cent of the increase in Korean life expectancy since 1970, with most of this increase occurring before 1994.[20]

Similarly, because of far fewer injuries and accidents, most Koreans now live to old age. With improved transport infrastructure, better driver education and more stringent law enforcement, the annual road toll has plummeted in recent decades. The number of deaths has fallen from 278 per million inhabitants in 1996 to 81 per million in 2017, a result far better than that found in the United States (where there are 114 road deaths per million). Deaths from accidental falls and accidental poisonings have also more than halved over the past twenty years.[21]

A measure used to assess deaths before old age is 'premature years of life lost', which adds up the deaths that occur before the age of seventy. For every 100,000 Koreans, just 2593 years of life are lost prematurely. This is not far off the best in the OECD, and is a little over half the rate of the United States (4721).[22]

As almost all Koreans now live to seventy or over, the big gains to Korean life expectancy are now coming from keeping people healthy so that they live longer in old age. Reductions in heart disease and stroke, and lower rates of stomach cancer, liver disease and tuberculosis, mean that Koreans are staying alive longer in old age. Even since 2000, deaths from heart disease and stroke have declined by 41 per cent, while deaths from stomach cancer are down by 60 per cent.[23]

Khang says that early childhood health has a huge impact later in life. 'Stroke, stomach cancer, liver disease and tuberculosis are quite closely associated with early life exposures,' he says. Later-life stomach cancer often has its origins in an early childhood infection from a nasty bacterium called *helicobacter pylori*. Similarly, mother-to-child infections of Hepatitis B can cause liver diseases and liver cancer in later life. As risk factors for infection include poor living standards and limited education, South Korea's rapid economic and social development has reduced infection rates.[24] Furthermore, a comprehensive childhood vaccination program established in 1962 meant that by 1995, the prevalence of tuberculosis had declined by 77 per cent.[25]

South Korea has the lowest average blood pressure for both men and women, and it also has the lowest prevalence of raised blood pressure.[26] 'That's important because high blood pressure is quite closely associated with ischemic heart disease, haemorrhagic stroke and kidney disease,' says Khang. Ischemic heart disease, commonly called coronary heart disease, refers to heart problems caused by narrowed arteries that can ultimately lead to heart attack. Haemorrhagic stroke occurs when blood spills or leaks into the brain, causing swelling or pressure.

Blood pressure is influenced by lifestyle factors, such as lack of exercise, being overweight, and a diet high in salt and alcohol and low in fruit and vegetables. Appropriate early life nutrition is another factor that may influence blood pressure later in life.[27]

Khang and his colleagues also note that improvements in health are due to 'expanded access to primary and secondary healthcare' and 'the rapid scale-up of new medical technologies', which are on par with the best in the world. National health insurance has enabled improvements in stroke and hypertension treatments, which have led to reductions in cardiovascular diseases. Let's look at South Korea's approach in a bit more detail.

Sanitation and Urbanisation

In 1962, a tiny 18 per cent of South Koreans had a piped water connection, and there were no managed sewers. In 1971, an astonishing four out of every five Koreans were infected with parasitic worms – which cause malnutrition, anaemia and even death.[28]

Hygiene and sanitation are crucial in improving health outcomes because, as Young-Ho Khang notes, they reduce waterborne infection. In 1965, the government prioritised the provision of clean drinking water as a part of its overall strategy for economic development. At the same time, it pioneered the *Saemaul Undong*, or New Village Movement, which involved repairing rural sewerage systems and changing sanitation practices and behaviour on both a structural and an individual level – to ensure that, for example, human waste was cordoned from human contact, and villagers knew to wash their hands regularly with soap. This led to a dramatic decrease in the problem of intestinal parasites. The provision of clean drinking water and toilet facilities across the nation also led to a reduction in infectious and parasitic diseases, such as typhoid and cholera.[29] South Korea now has more or less universal water and wastewater services, and deaths due to waterborne diseases have been virtually eliminated.

Such giant leaps in health outcomes would not have been possible without South Korea's remarkable economic transition. One of the poorest countries on the globe in the 1950s, it is now one of the world's economic powerhouses. Since 1970, annual economic output per capita has increased by 11,000 per cent! Over the same period, average income per person has risen from just 6 per cent of the OECD average to 89 per cent. Rising incomes are a major factor in improved health outcomes, with a 10 per cent increase in per capita income associated with an increased life expectancy of 2.2 months.[30]

Some of this improvement in health is also due to South Korea's rapid urbanisation. People have flooded to the cities for jobs and other opportunities at a staggering pace. Today, with 82 per cent of its population living in cities, South Korea is one of the most urbanised countries in Asia, and twice as urbanised as it was in 1970, when only 41 per cent of residents lived in urban areas. This has facilitated improved access to healthcare and reduced exposure to waterborne infections.[31] Enormous progress has been made in rural areas too, where 98 per cent of people are now connected to public sewerage systems.[32]

With economic development came education. In the 1970s, high-school completion rates were as low as 40 per cent, as children in many low-income, rural families were encouraged to start working in agriculture as early as possible. Education placed an undue financial burden on the family. As South Korea's economy strengthened and the possibility of social mobility emerged, many parents chose to send their children to secondary school. In less than fifty years, South Korea has increased its secondary education completion rate to an incredible 100 per cent.[33] The country now ranks very highly in the OECD's Program for International Student Assessment (PISA), performing convincingly above the OECD average in science, reading and mathematics.

Like income levels, education is one of the most important factors contributing to better health outcomes. Across the OECD, people with a tertiary education live about six years longer than those with the lowest levels of education. One reason for this is that more-educated people are typically better informed about the risks and benefits of different behaviours, and are also more likely to act upon this information.

For example, people with lower education levels are more likely to smoke, be overweight, have poor diets and be less physically active.[34] Some of this is due to social environment and income levels – for example, fresh, high-quality produce is often more expensive than canned or packaged alternatives – but there is a clear link between education and a lack of understanding about health, or a low level of health literacy. Studies show that raising overall educational levels is one of the most important things a country can do to improve health outcomes.

Universal Healthcare

So, we know how the basics were improved and diseases endemic to the population all but eradicated. Next, how did South Korea go about keeping people in good health?

The introduction of universal healthcare between 1977 and 1989 was central to improving South Korea's health outcomes. Almost all OECD countries provide their populations with universal healthcare for a core set of services, such as doctor consultations and surgical procedures. The only exceptions are Chile, Greece, Mexico, Poland, the Slovak Republic and the United States.[35] In South Korea – as in Australia, New Zealand, Canada, Japan and most European countries – 100 per cent of the population is covered by public healthcare.

A recent study undertaken by experts at Yonsei University in South Korea found that around the world, access to universal healthcare is the single most important factor influencing life expectancy.[36] Danny Liew, our expert from Monash University, says that universal healthcare involves 'providing healthcare to all people, whether or not they can afford it'. It's key because it 'brings up the overall average health of the community'.

South Korea is a small-government country, meaning that government collects and spends relatively little tax revenue. Its comprehensive National Health Insurance Scheme is incredibly resource-efficient. South Korea spends just 8.1 per cent of gross domestic product on healthcare. This is substantially less than the amount spent by the English-speaking countries. For example, Australia spends 9.3 per cent of GDP; the United Kingdom, 9.8 per cent; and the United States, a whopping 16.9 per cent.[37]

Life Expectancy and Health Spending Per Capita

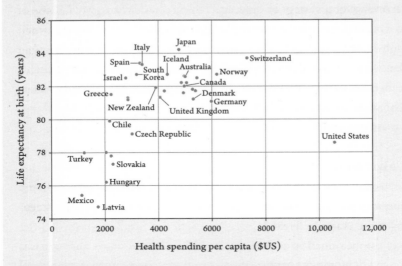

Figure 28. With the notable exception of the United States, countries with greater expenditure on healthcare generally have longer life expectancies.

As Figure 28 shows, countries with greater expenditure on healthcare generally have longer life expectancies, regardless of whether this invest-ment is from government or private spending. However, this effect is less pronounced beyond an annual spend of about US$4000 per capita. Spain, Italy, Japan and South Korea stand out as having relatively high life expectancy at birth given their level of health spending. At the other extreme, the United States has quite a low life expectancy given its sig-nificant spend on pharmaceuticals, doctors and diagnostic tests. Health outcomes in the United States are affected by high rates of poverty and income inequality, a significant portion of the population going unin-sured and poor health-related behaviours, such as greater obesity and a high homicide rate (murder is definitely not good for health!).[38]

South Koreans are provided with free regular health check-ups, with the nature and frequency of these check-ups dependent on a person's age. For example, Koreans over forty receive a free general medical check every two years that involves head and neck examinations, chest X-rays, blood tests, urine analyses and an oral examination. It also involves screening for a variety of cancers.[39] This preventative approach seems to work. For example, a 2017 study undertaken by researchers at Cornell University found that Koreans who were informed at a health screening that they were at high risk of developing complications from diabetes were more likely to take diabetes medication and lose weight than those who were not screened.[40]

An acquaintance of mine based in the Australian embassy in Seoul says that South Koreans are particularly health-conscious. 'People go to see doctors very often,' she says, because it's cheap and easy. 'People just go to clinics in the neighbourhood, and also you can easily go to a general hospital. So you can identify any possible disease at a very early stage.' With the National Health Insurance Scheme covering almost all the costs, only a small co-payment is required. The out-of-pocket expenses to see a doctor for a common illness are about 4000 won (US$3.50), and the cost to fill a prescription is the same. 'It's not a lot of money. It's really nothing. That's why people often go to see a doctor.'

This is evident in the data, with the average South Korean seeing a doctor sixteen times a year, by far the highest rate in the world. This is more than double the frequency of Australians (7.4) and quadruple the rate in the United States (4.0).[41]

Advanced Medicine

South Korea also provides its citizens with access to some of the most advanced medicine in the world. If you get sick in South Korea, you're in good hands. According to *Newsweek's* World's Best Hospitals list, based on data compiled by global market research company Statistica, ten of the world's top 100 hospitals are in Korea. Three in Seoul – the Asan Medical Center, the Samsung Medical Center and the Seoul National University Hospital – rate higher than any hospital in Australia or the United Kingdom.[42]

With treatment for most life-threatening conditions managed by some of the best doctors there are, survival rates are among the highest in the world. For example, South Korea has the highest five-year survival rate for rectal cancer and the second-highest five-year survival rate for colon cancer. In South Korea, your chances of surviving colon cancer are 19 per cent higher than in the United Kingdom and 10 per cent higher than in the United States. If you are admitted to hospital with a stroke, you're more likely to be alive after thirty days in South Korea than you are in any other place except Japan or Costa Rica.[43] (If it seems strange to see Costa Rica here, note that it has an average life expectancy of eighty – higher than the United States – and according to a World Health Organization report, it has the world's thirty-sixth best healthcare system.)[44]

Remember that Young-Ho Khang and his colleagues found that improvements in health were partly due to 'the rapid scale-up of new medical technologies'? Per person, South Koreans have access to more MRI units, which provide advanced medical imaging, than any country except Japan, the United States, Germany and Italy. South Korea also ranks sixth in the world for the number of CT scanners, which offer medical imaging used to screen for diseases, and has the second-highest number of mammography machines, used for early detection of breast cancer.[45]

One of the ways that South Korea ensures its residents have access to the best technology is by offering a fast-track evaluation process for innovative new medical equipment that incorporates robotics, artificial intelligence and implantable technology. This means that Korean technology companies get support to develop their products quickly so that they can be more globally competitive against companies from the United States and Europe. Fast-track evaluation is also available for technology that has the potential to treat cancer, heart disease, stroke, rare diseases and dementia, and to contribute to the rehabilitation of those with disabilities. While the normal approvals process for new technology can take many years, this fast-track system means that patients can benefit from the latest developments sooner and that technology developed in South Korea can leapfrog that of competitors from other countries.[46]

The Kimchi Diet?

South Korea has fewer deaths from cardiovascular disease – such as heart disease and stroke – than any other country in the world except France.[47] A Mediterranean diet and a relatively low obesity rate contribute to France's success. Similarly, South Korea's low death rate owes something to the traditional Korean diet, which is high in vegetables, low in red meat and free of dairy.

An impressive 98.9 per cent of South Koreans eat vegetables daily – the second-highest share in the OECD, just behind Australia (99.2 per cent). Although the obesity rate in South Korea has doubled since the 1990s, it is still extremely low. One in three South Koreans (33.7 per cent) are overweight or obese, the second-lowest figure in the OECD, behind Japan. By contrast, an astonishing 75 per cent of US adults are overweight or obese, as are 65 per cent in Australia and 64 per cent in the United Kingdom.[48]

'Even though there has been some increase in animal fat consumption in South Korea, the actual levels of fat consumption are still low,' says Young-Ho Khang. This is due to the low levels of meat consumed overall. 'The Korean government has been making efforts to sustain a traditional Korean diet.' To promote healthy eating and support childhood nutrition, the government provides free Korean meals in all primary schools, and has funded thousands of teachers to educate students about the Korean diet and opportunities for healthier eating.[49]

Koreans have a unique affinity for kimchi, which is high in probiotics and vitamins A and B, and some claim it is the reason for South Korean longevity. Yet that seems doubtful. 'Kimchi contains very high levels of salt,' Khang says. 'I don't believe it is beneficial. But the point is that by consuming kimchi, we adhere to our traditional diet.' If a little salty kimchi is used as an accompaniment to a bowl of bibimbap (a vegetable, egg and beef dish) or sundubu-jjigae (a spicy tofu stew), it shows South Koreans expressing their love for a national dish. And sometimes a bit of national pride swells the heart enough to offset the effect on the arteries. Or so it seems for South Koreans.

The health of humanity continues to improve. Over the past half-century, global life expectancy at birth has increased by 36 per cent, from fifty-three years in 1969 to seventy-two years in 2016.[50] What's caused this? According to Danny Liew, public health factors have played an important role in preventing people from getting sick in the first place. 'Sanitation, good quality of life, housing and education all help the population. All of those are critical. Maternal wellbeing, maternal mortality, infant mortality – these also contribute, as does vaccination.'

We have also become much better at managing health conditions once people do get sick. Liew says this ranges from identifying 'risk factor issues like blood pressure or cholesterol', right through to 'management of stroke, cancer, heart disease and heart failure'. 'Health systems have improved, so we are better at dealing with people presenting to hospital with an acute myocardial infarction [heart attack] or stroke, and rehabilitating them after they leave.'

It's not all good news. While global life expectancy has increased dramatically, significant disparities remain. Around the world, life expectancy at birth ranges from eighty-five years in Hong Kong down to fifty-two years in the Central African Republic.

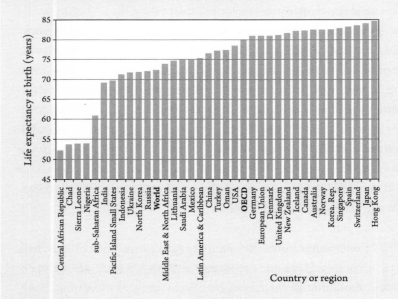

Life Expectancy in Selected Countries and Regions

Figure 29. According to the World Health Organization, countries in East Asia have the longest life expectancy, while sub-Saharan Africa lags behind the rest of the world.

Across the world, malnutrition and obesity both continue to rise, along with resistance to drugs such as antibiotics and antimalarials. Yet globally, the biggest causes of death are non-communicable diseases, such as heart disease, stroke and cancer. Across the OECD, more than one in three deaths is caused by heart disease, stroke or other circulatory diseases, and one in four deaths is from cancer.[51] Why have we made such poor progress – and in some countries, gone backwards – on this front?

There is now convincing evidence that income inequality adversely affects population health and wellbeing. In most countries, poorer people and those from marginalised communities are more likely to die from non-communicable diseases than the more affluent. This is because they tend to smoke more, develop higher blood pressure and have poorer access to healthcare and treatment options. The difference in health outcomes between rich and poor is known as health inequality.

It's not just that having less money leads to worse health outcomes. In a review of hundreds of studies, academics from the United Kingdom found that societies with large income disparities between rich and poor experience particularly damaging health consequences. This is because 'larger income differences increase social distances, accentuating social class or status differences'. In other words, in highly unequal societies the poorest people *feel* particularly poor. This leads, in turn, to an 'increasing frequency of most of the problems associated with low social status within societies'. These include infant mortality, violence, teen pregnancy, imprisonment, obesity, poor educational attainment, distrust of authority and lack of social mobility.[52]

South Korea is not immune to problems with health. While it is leading the way in many areas, it nevertheless faces a number of public health challenges.

For one, South Korea's suicide rate is the worst in the OECD, with 24.6 out of every 100,000 South Koreans committing suicide each year. This is about double the rate of Australia (11.9) and the United States (13.9), and more than triple the rate of the United Kingdom (7.3). Suicide is now South Korea's fourth most common cause of death. For young people (aged nine to twenty-four), suicide is the leading cause of death.[53]

South Korea is known for its high-stress educational and professional environments. It's customary for employees to work long hours, often into the night (South Korean working hours are the third-longest in the OECD),[54] and students face immense pressure to get into one of the top three universities. Coupled with this are cultural beliefs and a social stigma around seeking treatment for mental illness. While 90 per cent of those who commit suicide in South Korea have some form of mental illness, only about 15 per cent receive any form of treatment.[55] The emphasis on physical health, with South Koreans' propensity to visit the doctor for conditions large and small, has not been paralleled in mental health.

Suicide has traditionally been considered an individual problem in South Korea, not a community one, despite environmental, economic and social conditions influencing its rate. Prevention hasn't been a focus of South Korea's healthcare system. However, in 2018 the South Korean government began to develop a National Suicide Prevention Plan aimed at lowering the suicide rate. The government has said that the plan will involve tailored healthcare initiatives to support high-risk groups and those in need.[56]

While South Koreans are healthier and living longer than ever, life for elderly South Koreans is not necessarily great. Suicide rates are particularly high among this group too. There are some clear reasons for this.

One is poverty. Of those South Koreans aged over sixty-five, 44 per cent live in relative poverty (defined as earning less than half of the median household income). This is the highest rate in the OECD by a long way. It is almost twice the level of Australia and the United States (23 per cent), more than three times the level of the United Kingdom (14 per cent) and more than fourteen times the level of Northern European countries such as Iceland, Denmark and the Netherlands (3 per cent).[57]

Traditional Confucian ethics creates an expectation that children will look after elderly parents, but in recent decades this has become less prevalent, with a quarter of elderly South Koreans now living alone. The nation's age pension scheme was introduced relatively recently (in 1988), and government spends only a small amount on age pensions – public spending as a percentage of GDP is less than half the OECD average. The age pension amounts to just US$170 per month and is only available to those who have contributed to the scheme for at least ten years before retirement.[58] While there are various private pension schemes available, these often serve as short-term investment vehicles and are not commonly used as a form of long-term retirement savings.

The challenge of providing adequate income support to the elderly is only likely to be exacerbated in future, as South Korea's population is ageing faster than that of any other developed country. Between 2000 and 2050, the proportion of the population aged over sixty is likely to increase four-fold, placing enormous pressure on South Korea's welfare system.[59]

It is something of a paradox of South Korea that while the elderly have missed out on many of the benefits of the country's rapid economic development, the universal healthcare system has kept them healthy and alive for longer. The health of elderly South Koreans is also attributable to low levels of obesity and smoking, which contribute to low rates of heart disease and stroke.[60]

Speaking of smoking, it is a major risk factor not only for circulatory disease (such as heart disease and stroke) but also for cancer. While it is not common for South Korean women to smoke (just 4 per cent smoke daily), one in three men smoke every day. While this rate is far below other Asian countries such as China (48 per cent) and Indonesia (76 per cent), it is significantly above rates in the United States (13 per cent), Australia (14 per cent) and much of Europe. South Korea has recently introduced some tobacco control measures, but cigarette prices are still very low, tobacco advertising and sponsorship is only partially restricted, and only larger companies have smoke-free workplaces.[61] South Korea also continues to sustain a masculine smoking culture. This has its roots in the two-year compulsory military service for men – an environment in which there is social pressure to smoke.[62]

Lastly, as in many Asian countries, air pollution is a health concern. It poses a hazard particularly to the elderly and the young, as it can cause respiratory diseases such as pneumonia, asthma and lung cancer. Fine dust pollution – virtually unknown to those in Australia, Canada and New Zealand – involves particles in the air that penetrate deep into the lungs. Around the world, air pollution contributes to more than 4 million premature deaths each year, and the World Health Organization regards it as a more significant threat to public health than HIV or ebola.[63]

An average exposure of 10 micrograms of air pollution per cubic metre is generally regarded as the highest safe level. The figure in South Korea is 28.7, and it has increased over the past twenty-five years. This is nowhere near as bad as in China (58.4) or India (74.3), where air pollution accounts for 12.5 per cent of all deaths, but the trend is not promising.[64] In early 2019, the South Korean government introduced emergency measures to tackle what *The Guardian* termed a 'social disaster'. This included funds for mandatory high-capacity air purifiers in classrooms, and incentives for purchase of vehicles that run on liquid natural gas, which produces fewer emissions than petrol or diesel.[65] However, as at least half of the air pollution in South Korea originates in China, there does not appear to be an easy solution to this growing public health problem.

What South Korea Can Teach the World

Countries with high rates of infant mortality, such as some in sub-Saharan Africa or areas of Latin America, may see a way forward for their governments in South Korea's efforts to ensure clean drinking water and improve maternal and child health. There are also a range of measures that other nations can learn from South Korea.

Economic Growth Leads to Longevity

South Korea's trajectory over the past fifty years demonstrates that strong economic development and improved living standards make an enormous contribution to health and longevity. Around the world, richer countries tend to have a higher average life expectancy than poorer countries. Economic development also enables more money to be spent on healthcare, which in turn leads to better health outcomes.[66]

But the story does not stop there. Evidence from around the world shows that economic growth leads to the best health outcomes when the benefits are shared throughout society. High levels of inequality shape health outcomes, from child mortality to illness in old age. Reducing inequality will improve overall population health in the longer term.

As we saw with Norway, Iceland and Germany, reducing inequality can be achieved through a progressive taxation system, investing in education, increasing the power of employees in the labour market, assisting underrepresented groups to enter the labour market, and investing in health, housing and social welfare.

Ensuring access to education is particularly important, too. Better-educated people are healthier, regardless of their income level.[67] This is because more-educated people typically have better health literacy – an understanding of what they should or shouldn't do to strive towards better health. It is perhaps no coincidence that the East Asian economies leading the world in education (Singapore, Hong Kong, Japan and South Korea) also now have some of the longest life expectancies in the world.

Universal Healthcare Should Be Universal

When people can't afford healthcare, they avoid seeing the doctor, having tests or X-rays, and fail to purchase prescribed medicines. Universal healthcare is the single most important thing that can be done to improve health outcomes. It provides financial protection against the cost of illness and ensures that the whole population has access to care.

Almost every country in the OECD has universal or near-universal health coverage for a core set of services. Health outcomes in countries that have not yet achieved universal coverage are likely to fall further behind those countries that have. Poland and the United States have the highest rates of medical consultations skipped due to cost. The United States also has, by far, the highest rate of prescriptions not filled due to cost, and 43 per cent of low-income Americans report that they have care needs going unmet because they cannot afford treatment.[68] It's a dire situation for a country with such a high level of economic development.

A system of universal healthcare need not be expensive. South Koreans spend almost 80 per cent *less* per person on healthcare through government or compulsory health insurance than citizens of the United States (US$1908 versus US$8949).[69]

Universal healthcare systems around the world also vary in the extent of coverage they provide for different services and goods. Pharmaceuticals, dental care and eye care tend to require higher patient payments than do doctor consultations and hospital visits. Healthcare schemes in many European countries cover basic dental care. To improve overall health outcomes, countries with limited health coverage would do well to consider also expanding coverage into areas such as dental care.

Diet Is Destiny

We know that economic growth contributes to better population health and that in general, countries with higher incomes have better health outcomes. Wealthy countries have come pretty close to eliminating early childhood and other premature deaths. Almost everyone lives until retirement age.

However, in countries such as the United States, the United Kingdom and Australia, economic development has brought with it new challenges. The biggest causes of death now are largely preventable, a consequence of overconsumption. Heart disease, stroke and cancer are killing more than any other conditions, caused by obesity, diabetes and smoking.

Economic growth on its own will not deliver the best possible health outcomes. In addition to a well-educated population, a degree of equality and universal healthcare, a healthy lifestyle – with balanced diets, physical activity and low rates of smoking and alcohol consumption – is fundamental for improving health. The countries that can tick all of these boxes will be the ones leading the life expectancy tables in the future.

At present, those who most fit this bill are South Korea and the other East Asian powerhouse countries such as Japan, Hong Kong, Macao and Singapore. These countries have benefited and are continuing to benefit from enormous economic growth – but rather than descend headlong into hedonism and consumerism, they are using this opportunity to build world-class education and healthcare systems. At the same time, South Korea continues to maintain its traditional diet, and has so far avoided the worst excesses of Western capitalism: highly processed food, physical inactivity and obesity.

Nevertheless, there is an anxiety in South Korea that this is changing. Obesity, while still rare, is becoming more prevalent. With the nation's rapid economic growth, there is a sense among health professionals that

South Korea needs to act to ensure it doesn't adopt the unhealthy diets of other countries. 'Diet and smoking are really important,' Young-Ho Khang says, 'and if we do not regulate some of the energy-dense fast food and tobacco products, the speed of increase in our life expectancy will be reduced.'

Danny Liew says the focus for South Korea needs to be on keeping people healthy for longer. 'It's about health preservation,' he says. 'This is dealing with things that lead to very big outcomes, like controlling smoking, controlling lifestyle factors, obesity, diabetes. What strikes me, other than the commonness of these conditions and the burden they cause, is the preventability of them. But it is difficult to stop people from smoking and get them to exercise more.'

South Korea might just pull it off, though. My contact at the Australian embassy is optimistic. 'The male staff in our office who used to smoke, they all quit,' she says. Younger colleagues also prioritise health. 'They want to use their time after work for their own things, so they kind of avoid spending their precious after-hours drinking with work peers and things like that. They do a lot of exercise. They get together during lunchtime and exercise together.

'These kinds of attitude changes make me think that Korea can improve life expectancy even further.'

FIVE THINGS WE
CAN DO NOW

1. **Invest in maternal and child health programs.** Systematic
    support of maternal and child health plays a crucial role in
    improving the health and survival of mothers and newborns.
    Programs can be delivered before and after birth in hospitals,
    through home visits or in a community centre. The range of
    potential programs is enormous, but can include vaccinations,
    treatment of infections and illnesses, breastfeeding assistance,
    referrals for specialist treatment and guidance on diet and
    healthy lifestyle.

2. **Strengthen universal healthcare.** Ensuring that all people have
    access to appropriate healthcare is one of the best ways to
    improve population health. While most developed countries have
    universal healthcare for a core set of services, reducing out-of-
    pocket fees will further improve access to healthcare, as will
    extending full coverage to pharmaceuticals and dental services.

3. **Reduce smoking and alcohol consumption.** Smoking and
    drinking to excess are two of the major risk factors for non-
    communicable diseases. The most effective ways to reduce
    consumption are to raise taxes on cigarettes and alcohol,
    and to introduce regulatory measures such as advertising
    bans. Australia, for example, has successfully deployed these
    methods to halve the number of daily smokers, while Switzerland
    has achieved substantial reductions in the rate of alcohol
    consumption.

4. **Tackle obesity.** Over the past twenty years, obesity has risen enormously and has become an urgent priority for many Western nations. Like alcohol and smoking, obesity is a major risk factor for many of the most common causes of death, including heart disease, stroke and cancer. Obesity needs a comprehensive response, including health promotion, education, medical interventions, and broader regulatory and tax policy. There is substantial evidence that taxing junk and fast food – high in salt, fat and sugar – reduces their consumption. Several countries are adopting this approach, including Norway, France, South Africa and the United Kingdom.

5. **Increase efforts to address mental health.** Mental illness is a growing problem in many countries, and suicide remains a significant cause of death. Mental illness contributes to poorer educational outcomes, higher unemployment and decreased physical health. Most countries need to scale up their programs to address mental health, and to target their interventions to at-risk groups: the unemployed, youth and the elderly. Countries such as the United Kingdom have been at the forefront of mental health policy, responding to the huge economic cost of mild to moderate mental illness by encouraging 'talking therapies' rather than – or in addition to – medication, and establishing a payment system that rewards health providers for patient outcomes, not just for treatments provided.

11

ACHIEVING WORLD-BEST OUTCOMES
How Do We Get There?

Humanity has made extraordinary progress over the past century or two. As Johan Norberg points out in his book *Progress*, poverty, malnutrition, illiteracy, child labour and infant mortality 'are falling faster than at any other time in human history'.[1] Global life expectancy has doubled since 1900, and economic output per person is now at least ten times greater than it was in 1830.[2] These improvements began with the Enlightenment in the seventeenth and eighteenth centuries, when science and reason began to supersede tradition and superstition. They were accelerated further by the Industrial Revolution of the nineteenth century and by globalisation in the twentieth.

Silicon Valley entrepreneurs Peter Diamandis and Steven Kotler are optimistic this trend will continue. In their book *Abundance*, they suggest that science and technology will 'enable us to make greater gains in the next two hundred years' and that 'abundance for all is within our grasp'.[3]

Others, such as American economist Professor Robert Gordon, are more circumspect. They argue that while we have seen improvements in quality of life, the changes brought about by inventions such as electricity, the internal combustion engine and indoor plumbing were unique and 'one-off'. If that's the case, the impacts of technology are unlikely to be as significant in future, so there is no guarantee that economic growth will persist indefinitely.[4]

Technology and economic growth will no doubt drive massive change, and much of this change will be positive. However, there are challenges ahead for humanity that won't be solved by technology and economics alone. Global problems such as climate change, inequality and crime will require careful, active government stewardship. The countries achieving the best outcomes in these areas have both market economies and deeply engaged governments.

I've been surprised by much of what I have encountered in researching and writing this book. Like anyone who is not an expert on global development, I began with a number of preconceived ideas, and these were challenged along the way. While I was aware that East Asian countries topped the world education rankings, for example, I hadn't fully grasped just how dominant in education and research they are. In fact, most aspects of East Asia's economic rise have been downright incredible. Results from the United States, often considered the 'leader of the free world', disappointed me: the nation is underachieving on health, inequality and public safety, in particular. And many Nordic and Northern European countries are far more competitive economically than I had assumed.

A few overlapping ideas run through these chapters, and came to influence my thinking on the best way forward for humanity.

What Are World-Best Outcomes?

The stories in this book cover a diverse array of factors, all of which are important to leading a good life: economic development, democracy, inequality, health, education, crime and our impact on the environment. Governments may sometimes privilege one or two objectives above others – for example, economic development and education in Singapore. But we've seen that the most effective and enduring progress involves a comprehensive approach. There's enormous interrelationship between almost every aspect of policy: immigration, employment, childcare, welfare, climate change and renewables, education. Unless these elements come together, a country is holding itself back. Let's look at a few examples of world-best outcomes.

Strong Economic Development

Economic growth is the foundation that empowers countries to respond to social, political and environmental challenges. With economic development comes reduced poverty, more jobs, larger incomes and greater wealth. This leads to improved outcomes in a range of other areas. For example, a higher GDP per capita leads to longer life expectancies, as per capita GDP is associated with better sanitation, nutrition, education, vaccination rates and health technologies. It also leads to happier citizens, according to several studies.[5] More employment opportunities give parents an incentive to invest in the education of their children.

The importance of economic development can be seen across the world. In general, the countries with the strongest economies achieve the best outcomes in almost every area. In East Asia, enormous economic growth has been accompanied by large improvements in living standards. In this book, we've seen that economic growth has made possible South Korea's rapid improvements in health as well as the development of Singapore's world-leading education system.

But it's not just any economic growth that we should be striving for. If growth leads to substantial inequality, mistrust of government or environmental degradation, we'll fail to see its benefits. Growth is much more powerful – and sustainable – if the benefits are shared throughout society, and regulated with a focus on the long-term.

So, what can we do to grow the global economy in a positive way? Many economists and politicians used to think – and some still do – that all we need to do is reduce taxes, reduce costs and ensure that markets are functioning efficiently. Yet the key factor differentiating economies today is people. The world's most talented people are highly mobile, prepared to move city or country in search of an opportunity. The UN's International Labour Organization estimates that there are currently 164 million people worldwide who have moved country for work, a 9 per cent increase since 2003. Two-thirds of these have relocated to high-income countries.[6] Without a highly educated population, lower-income economies don't stand a chance.

In a connected global economy, all countries are competing with one another – for the most talented people, for exports and for investment dollars. If countries are to continue to grow and thrive in this context, remaining competitive is key. In its 'Global Competitiveness Report', the World Economic Forum argues that ensuring competition in an economy requires broad efforts across a society. It identifies twelve pillars of competitiveness:

- well-functioning formal and informal institutions (such as courts), transparent and efficient public sectors and strong corporate governance

- well-planned and -maintained infrastructure, such as transport and utilities

- the adoption of technology, including internet and mobile phone networks

- economic stability, including moderate inflation and sustainable government budgets

- healthy life expectancy (the number of years a newborn can expect to live in good health)

- strong skills (measured by education levels and ease of finding skilled labour)

- strong markets (competition in services and favourable trading conditions)

- a flexible labour market that protects workers' rights, including cooperation between unions and employers, female workforce participation and mobile labour

- a good financial system, including available venture capital and sound banks

- market size (the size of the economy)

- business dynamism (how easy it is to start and grow a business)

- innovation capability, including expenditure on research and development, and the growth of innovation clusters.

The Forum is adamant that 'in order to increase competitiveness, no area can be neglected.'[7] Success in one area is built on success in others. We have seen this in the countries featured in this book: Germany has grown its manufacturing sector by investing in vocational education, maintaining harmony between employers and workers, and supporting world-class industrial research. Norway has expanded its economy by encouraging workforce participation and investing in education. The United States has strengthened its economy over decades by spending massively on research and development and encouraging dense clusters of innovative activity in some of its cities.

The World Economic Forum's twelve pillars of competitiveness enable economies to expand through three different mechanisms: population growth, increases in the population share participating in the workforce and improvements to productivity.[8] The examples in this book offer a template for how countries might approach all three elements.

Population Growth

A larger population means more workers, as well as more consumers of goods and services. There are strategic benefits to a larger population, as bigger markets can enable greater economies of scale: things become cheaper when you make more of them. Larger populations also tend to foster more innovation, as there are more people to potentially use new products or services.

A nation's population increases naturally when there are more births than deaths. For this to happen, each woman needs to give birth to, on average, at least two babies over her lifetime (2.1, to be precise; this figure is slightly more than two to allow for deaths at various life stages). However, in many industrialised countries the fertility rate has dropped significantly below the replacement rate, leading to an ageing population. China, the world's most populous country, is experiencing no growth in the working-age population and a rising number of elderly, due to low birth rates and the effects of its one-child policy (implemented in 1979), and is projecting substantial population decline even though it has now relaxed this policy. Across the OECD, only Israel and Mexico have a fertility rate that is contributing to a natural population increase.[9]

The other way that a population can grow is through immigration. While many countries struggle with the challenges that immigration brings, Australia has demonstrated that a large migration program can be managed effectively. Yes, Australia is blessed with an enormous land-mass and a relatively small population – though it is worth noting that its population is heavily concentrated in a few urban centres. Australia's immigration program, with its focus on younger, skilled migrants, ensures the working-age population is kept replenished, even as the overall population ages. An economy is stronger when there are more people in the workforce and fewer dependents (those too young or too old to work). In countries with an ageing population, the increase in the share of dependents is significant. In Japan, for example, 28 per cent of the population is aged over sixty-five, and over the past decade its total population has been declining.[10] It would do well to learn from Australia's experience.

Above all, population growth needs to be sustainable. A larger population on its own does not lead to improved living standards. While continued population growth is usually accompanied by increases in the headline economic statistics, it really just leads to a bigger economy that is shared between more people. In many developing countries – particularly those in sub-Saharan Africa – population growth is outpacing economic development. With young dependents comprising a disproportionate amount of the population, these countries struggle to invest in the education, employment and health services their citizens need.[11] Rapid population growth can also put extreme pressure on land and natural resources. Quality of life can suffer if growth is not managed with care.

High Workforce Participation and Productivity

An economy grows when there are more people in the workforce and each employee's productivity is high. One way to increase the share of the population in paid employment is by supporting women to participate in the workforce.

Due to a range of historical factors and structural barriers, women typically engage in paid work at a lower rate than men. In the last few decades, an enormous proportion of economic growth has come from an increase in the number of women working, and there are ample opportunities to improve this further. Improving female workforce participation means not just getting women into jobs, but assisting them to work more than they might otherwise. While this helps individual women and families to improve their economic circumstances, it also benefits a country's economy by allowing it to draw on the capacity and talents of more of its citizens.

With structural measures such as paid paternity leave, well-funded childcare and robust equal pay legislation, Iceland shows us that increased female workforce participation is possible. Seventy-two per cent of Icelandic women are now in the workforce – the highest figure in the OECD.[12]

Another way of increasing the share of those participating in the workforce is by assisting refugees, people with disabilities and other marginalised groups to find work. Norway's labour market programs show how this can be done. They involve training schemes to help people improve their employability, tailored services to assist in job-seeking and temporary wage subsidies that allow the unemployed to build up experience in the workplace while they seek a permanent position.[13]

Underpinning these efforts is a strong cultural emphasis on the importance of work and the contribution that employment makes to the nation. In Norway, paid work is seen as the main way to contribute to society for both old and young. Similarly, in Germany the curriculum focuses on preparing students for the workforce by tailoring their education – academic or vocational – to employment skills. In Singapore, teaching is viewed as a national mission, and education the main lever in facilitating economic growth.

But while there is an inbuilt cap on workforce participation (it's impossible to increase participation beyond 100 per cent of those of working age), there is no limit on productivity increases. Labour productivity is the number of goods and services generated by workers in a given period of time. It is influenced by three main things: investment, use of technology and workers' skill levels.

In developed economies, the fastest-growing category of jobs are those that are non-routine, involving complex decision-making and independent thought (such as in the fields of management, computer science and architecture).[14] They require high levels of education and skill. New technology is increasingly coming from cities, which are hotbeds of research, entrepreneurialism and collaboration. The United States shows how leveraging government support for research and development can create the perfect conditions to nurture new technologies. This involves building strong links between industries and universities, supporting start-ups and facilitating industry-based collaborations.

There are less obvious ways to improve labour productivity, too. Productivity is highest when people are not overworked, as stress, fatigue and sleep deprivation make employees substantially less productive. Norway – with the highest labour productivity rate in the world – shows that a model of shorter hours works. Shorter hours have the added benefit of making it easier to balance a job with family, facilitating greater female workforce participation.

Minimal Inequality

Global evidence is overwhelming: reducing inequality makes sense. Apart from the moral argument for doing so, greater equality leads to better health and education outcomes, less crime, stronger democracies and faster economic growth. In fact, there is now virtually consensus among economists and global financial institutions – including the World Bank and the International Monetary Fund – that too much inequality reduces economic growth.

Countries with low inequality, such as Sweden, Norway, Denmark, Iceland and Finland, lead the world, with the strongest democracies, the greatest productivity rates, the highest median incomes, the highest levels of happiness and low carbon emissions. GDP growth in these countries has exceeded that of the English-speaking countries, which have much greater inequality. The Nordic countries have unique attributes – Norway, for instance, has had an undeniable economic boost due to its oil reserves, and Iceland, too, has profited from geothermal energy – but others can still learn from them and employ some of their methods.

Universal access to services – including education, healthcare, child-care and aged care – goes a long way to ensuring that everyone, regardless of their income, can participate fully in society. While most industrialised countries have free primary and secondary education, university tuition in the United States, Japan and South Korea requires a significant private contribution and can lead to crippling levels of personal debt. Similarly, in the United Kingdom, the United States and New Zealand, working parents are forced to spend a large portion of their income on childcare.[15] These nations could do well to look to the Nordic countries for inspiration on how to make the system fairer.

A strong welfare system is another important means of ensuring that inequality stays low. Welfare involves supporting society's vulnerable, such as those who are sick, disabled or unemployed. It can mean cash benefits, direct provision of goods or services, or tax breaks that have a similar effect. Across the OECD, countries spend an average amount equivalent to 20 per cent of GDP on welfare, while in Northern European nations such as France, Belgium and Finland, this is closer to 30 per cent. However, welfare systems in countries such as Mexico, Chile and South Korea are much smaller, amounting to only about 10 per cent of GDP.[16]

Higher Tax Rates

Tax, coupled with a strong welfare system, plays an important role in transferring income from the richest to the poorest in society. Australia, the United Kingdom, the United States, New Zealand and South Korea redistribute less than the OECD average through the tax and transfer system.[17] They could make huge inroads into alleviating inequality by increasing tax revenue by only a couple of percentage points, if the political will was there.

In many parts of the world, low taxes have been the accepted wisdom for decades. Yet there is reason to reconsider. Now we know that equality charges economic growth, there is a strong basis to revisit tax revenue and models of taxation.

Evidence is ample that increasing the tax take won't hurt economic growth. The Nordic and Northern European countries generate an annual tax revenue equivalent to 42 per cent of their GDP. This is significantly higher than the 27 per cent generated in the English-speaking

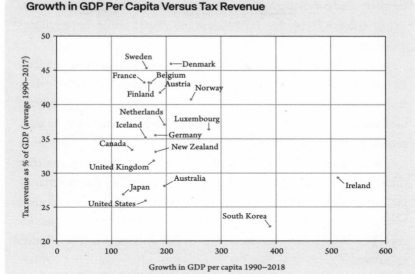

Growth in GDP Per Capita Versus Tax Revenue

Figure 30. Since 1990, countries with lower overall tax takes have not grown any faster than those with higher tax takes.

countries. Of the fifteen countries with the highest median incomes, eleven have tax rates higher than the OECD average. The International Monetary Fund now argues that higher tax rates for top income earners is good national policy.[18]

Countries with lower overall tax takes don't necessarily grow faster. As Figure 30 shows, since 1990 the United States, Canada, New Zealand and the United Kingdom have experienced less growth in GDP per capita than Luxembourg, Norway, Denmark, the Netherlands and Austria, all of which have much greater tax takes.

Increased tax revenue provides government with more money to fund services such as healthcare, education, childcare and aged care, leading to longer life expectancies. And, as we've read, public spending on services such as health and education also underpins economic growth.[19]

While the size of the tax take is important, more so is the design of the tax system. For example, there is merit in shifting away from income tax, which is imposed on a relatively mobile base, towards taxes on property and on consumption, which are more stable and lend themselves to fewer loopholes. Increases in these taxes could, in turn, fund reductions in income tax.

Consumption taxes are levied on the sale of goods and services. Examples include sales taxes and value-added taxes (known as goods and services taxes in some countries). Alone, they are likely to increase inequality, since the rich spend a smaller portion of their income than others. However, if consumption taxes are introduced along with other measures, it's possible to offset any negative impact and ensure that the overall package reduces inequality. For example, the removal of tax expenditures that disproportionately benefit high-income earners, such as concessional tax rates and tax exemptions, could be considered. Environmental taxes, including on carbon, could also be applied to business.[20]

This is not to be naive. Generating new forms of tax revenue is never easy. In Australia, efforts to introduce a carbon tax and to remove tax concessions for wealthy retirees have failed. This was partly due to political leaders' inability to adequately explain the benefits of such reforms. But there is precedent. Despite their high overall tax takes, Nordic and Northern European countries don't rely on personal income tax anywhere near as much as the English-speaking countries – they generate less than a quarter (24.7 per cent) of their tax revenue from personal income tax, whereas the English-speaking countries rely on it for more than a third (36.8 per cent).[21] Instead, they have substantial goods and services taxes. Denmark, Norway and Sweden, for example, all apply a value-added tax of 25 per cent to the sale of most goods and services.

Lots of Education

Education is a key to a sunnier life for both individuals and societies. Improving education levels is likely to lead to better health, an improved democracy, a stronger economy and reduced inequality.

Education contributes in all sorts of ways to better health: it improves maternal and child health, and so reduces child mortality, and it enhances health literacy, leading to positive behaviours such as giving up smoking and taking up exercise.

More education also contributes to stronger democracies, as it typically emphasises the benefits of civic participation. The effect of education on democracy is strongest in less-developed countries – places such as Afghanistan, Bangladesh, Haiti, Nepal and most of sub-Saharan Africa.[22] The enormous improvement in global educational outcomes over the last few decades bode well for democracy.

Knowledge has become the key driver of economic development, and a country's economic potential is now tied inextricably to the education of its people. The economic benefits of education will be felt most acutely when efforts are aimed at those from disadvantaged backgrounds. Targeted interventions can unlock the potential of those who would not otherwise have the capacity to invest in their education. This has the dual benefit of reducing inequality and raising the productive potential of the economy. The OECD reports that countries such as Canada, Norway, Estonia, Hong Kong and Macao, which employ this model, are achieving high levels of student performance as well as equity in educational outcomes.[23]

Investing in early childhood education is also one of the most effective moves governments can make. There's now a huge body of evidence suggesting that it leads to better academic achievement at school and improved outcomes later in life, including reduced criminality, less welfare dependence and higher incomes. Sweden's early childhood system – with its nationwide network of subsidised preschools that provide education and childcare from the age of one – is often cited as the global gold standard.[24] Countries such as Singapore are already looking towards it, and others should too.

Lots of Democracy

A democratic political system is associated with a host of things: higher incomes, less poverty, better health, more innovation and greater life satisfaction. While it's not clear that democracy *causes* these things, the weight of recent evidence does seem to suggest that democracy is positive for economic growth. Democracy also has value in its own right, as it enshrines principles such as freedom of speech, freedom of the press and freedom of association, which I think we can all agree make for healthy societies.

It seems that if we want better democracies, education and greater equality will help get us there. As we've seen, countries with more educated citizens generally have stronger democracies. Similarly, studies have shown that more equality leads to increased support for democracy. Financial inequality has all sorts of adverse impacts on democracy, as it undermines social trust and belief in institutions, and leads to reduced civic participation.[25]

Countries can strengthen democratic freedoms by enhancing anti-corruption and democratic oversight mechanisms. Australia, for example, does not yet have an independent national anti-corruption agency to investigate elected representatives – recently, instances of unethical political behaviour have come to light after occurring for far too long, and this has strengthened calls for an institutional safeguard.

Urbanisation

Around the world, more and more people are moving to cities. This is bringing challenges, including air pollution, crowded neighbourhoods, overburdened public services and congested traffic. But on the whole, urbanisation is leading to better societies, providing people with more highly paid jobs and access to services. Students who attend urban schools achieve better educational outcomes than those in rural areas, and although it's still more dangerous to live in a city than in a remote or rural community, crime has been falling faster in big cities than elsewhere. People living in cities also have better health – we've seen that an increase in the proportion of South Koreans living in cities has been accompanied by a rapid increase in life expectancy.[26] Finally, cities are the source of most of the world's innovation.

As humanity moves towards greater urbanisation, how well we organise our cities – to minimise the downsides and maximise the benefits – is critically important. City governments, working in partnership with businesses and local organisations, can improve transport systems, building regulations and urban planning to develop attractive, liveable and sustainable cities. Copenhagen is well on its way to becoming carbon neutral by 2025. It can be done.

Local Solutions

Many of the stories in this book show that, often, the most effective response to a big problem is developed with – or by – the communities it affects. Most seemingly intractable issues are complex, with many strands and players. Consequently, the solutions need to be nuanced and multifaceted too, and it is easiest to achieve this on a local level. For example, lower greenhouse gas emissions on Denmark's Samsø Island could only be achieved by strengthening the local farming community and providing a viable financial alternative to crops and livestock. In Phoenix, Arizona, creating an environment for more innovation meant leveraging the city's unique research capabilities as well as its affordable housing.

While national policy frameworks are important, individuals and local community groups can play a huge role in achieving change. National and even international change can begin with action at the local level. So, while we may sometimes feel powerless to address global challenges, there are practical actions we can take to make a significant difference.

Which Countries Are Getting It Right?

Most of the countries in this book can be broadly grouped into one of three categories: the English-speaking countries, the Nordic and Northern European countries and the East Asian countries.

The English-speaking countries include Australia, Canada, Ireland, New Zealand, the United Kingdom and the United States. These are, of course, not the only countries in which English is widely spoken, but they are the main ones, considered to constitute the Anglosphere. These countries have tax rates far below the OECD average and generally have smaller governments. Tax revenue across these six English-speaking countries ranges from a low of 22 per cent in Ireland to a high of 34 per cent in the United Kingdom. Tax revenue enables the funding of services such as welfare, health, education and defence, with these governments spending an amount equivalent to 35 per cent of GDP. This is far less than the Nordic and Northern European countries.

Nordic countries (Denmark, Finland, Iceland, Norway and Sweden) and Northern European countries (Austria, Belgium, France, Germany,

Luxembourg and the Netherlands) generally generate more tax revenue. With substantial welfare systems, their governments spend more than either the English-speaking countries or the East Asian countries. On average, government spending is equivalent to about 49 per cent of GDP, and ranges from 42 per cent in the Netherlands through to 56 per cent in France.

The four 'Asian tiger' countries of East Asia (Hong Kong, Singapore, South Korea and Taiwan) underwent rapid industrialisation and maintained a high rate of economic growth between the 1960s and 1990s. They are generally low-taxing, but are characterised by state-sponsored capitalism, which has seen substantial government investment in certain sectors of the economy to stimulate growth. The economic performance of these countries now rivals, and sometimes exceeds, that of Nordic and Northern European countries, as well as the English-speaking countries.

These are not the only country groups in the world, of course. There are many others, including among the industrialised nations of the OECD, such as Latin America and Southern Europe. There are also single nations, such as China and India, that are large enough to be considered separately in their own right. But these three groups of countries can all make claims to achieving the world's best outcomes in a range of areas. I was curious to see how they compare.

Patterns at a Glance

Let's look at how these groups stack up in areas such as the economy, education, inequality, health, crime, carbon emissions, life satisfaction and democracy. I've based my conclusions on a weighted average, which means that countries with larger populations influence the results more than smaller countries. For example, New Zealand has less than five million residents, and if we are trying to form an overall picture, it makes sense that its results carry less weight than the United States, which has seventy times more people.

I've relied on all available data, but there are some unavoidable gaps and omissions. Data for Taiwan and Hong Kong is not always available, as they are sometimes counted as part of the overall data for China. But despite this, I think the patterns reveal themselves clearly.

The English-Speaking Countries

Strengths	
Strong economic output	GDP per capita is US$58,159: 21 per cent higher than Northern European (US$48,200) and 60 per cent higher than East Asian countries (US$36,324).
High incomes	The average income per person is US$47,057: 25 per cent higher than in Northern Europe (US$37,683) and 79 per cent higher than East Asia (US$26,345).
Competitive economies	The average score in the Global Competitive Index is 82.6, compared to 80.4 for East Asia and 80.2 for Northern European and Nordic countries. The average score in the Global Innovation Index is 60.4, compared to 56.6 for Northern Europe and East Asia.
High rates of immigration	A huge 15.7 per cent of the population were born overseas, compared to 13.5 in Northern Europe and 10.6 per cent in East Asia (although the share in Hong Kong and Singapore is much higher).

Weaknesses	
Economic deficits	A current account balance is the difference between a country's exports and imports. English-speaking countries run a current account deficit equivalent to 3.2 per cent of GDP (meaning they import more than they export), while East Asia has a current account surplus of 5.8 per cent, and Northern Europe, a surplus of 3.9 per cent.
	A government deficit means a government spends more than it makes. English-speaking countries run a government deficit equal to 3.2 per cent of GDP, while Northern Europe runs a government surplus of 0.2 per cent of GDP.
Slow economic growth	GDP per capita grew 168 per cent between 1990 and 2018, but 177 per cent in Northern Europe and 270 per cent in East Asia.
Poorer education outcomes	Reading performance of fifteen-year-olds lags behind East Asia. The PISA score is 506, compared to 495 in Northern Europe and 514 in East Asia.
	Maths performance of fifteen-year-olds is a year and a half behind East Asia. The PISA score is 485, compared to 501 in Northern Europe and 532 in East Asia.
High rates of inequality and poverty	A lower gini coefficient score means less inequality. The gini coefficient for net income is 0.362, compared to 0.316 in East Asia and 0.284 in Northern Europe.
	The poverty rate is 0.16, compared to 0.09 in Northern Europe.
Less longevity	Life expectancy at birth is 79.5 years, more than three years shorter than in East Asia (82.9 years) and two years shorter than in Northern Europe (81.7 years).
	Infant mortality is almost double the rate in East Asia: 5.1 deaths per 1000 live births in the English-speaking countries, 3.1 in Northern Europe and 2.7 in East Asia.
High murder rates	The homicide rate, skewed by a high rate in the United States, is eight times higher than in East Asia and four times higher than in Northern Europe: 4.1 homicides per 100,000 people, compared to 1.1 in Northern Europe and 0.5 in East Asia.
Sky-high carbon emissions	Carbon emissions per capita are almost double those in Northern Europe: 13.5 tonnes, compared to 10.7 tonnes in East Asia and 7.1 tonnes in Northern Europe.

*All averages are weighted by population.

Nordic and Northern European Countries

Strengths	
Strong democracies and democratic freedoms	The average score on the EIU Democracy Index is 8.45 (out of 10), compared to 8.22 in English-speaking countries and 7.67 in East Asia.
	The average score on the Freedom in the World Index is 93.9 (out of 100), compared to 88.9 in English-speaking countries and 81.6 in East Asia.
	The average score on the Corruption Perceptions Index is 77.9 (out of 100), compared to 73.6 in English-speaking countries and 62.0 in East Asia.
High productivity	In Northern Europe, workers generate US$61.70 in GDP for every hour worked. In English-speaking countries, the figure is US$60.75.
Shorter working hours	The average worker spends 293 hours (about 7.5 weeks) less at work each year than those in the English-speaking countries.
Low rates of inequality and poverty	The gini coefficient for net income is 0.284, compared to 0.316 in East Asia and 0.362 in the English-speaking countries.
	The poverty rate in Northern Europe is 0.09, compared to 0.16 across the English-speaking countries.
	The 'Global Gender Gap Report 2020' indicates that Northern European countries have closed 78.1 per cent of the gap, while English-speaking countries have closed 73.6 per cent and East Asia 67.7 per cent.
Economic surpluses	Northern Europe runs a current account surplus equivalent to 3.9 per cent of GDP. The English-speaking countries run a current account deficit equivalent to 2.7 per cent of GDP.
	Northern Europe runs a government surplus of 0.2 per cent of GDP. The English-speaking countries run a government deficit equal to 3.2 per cent of GDP.
Low carbon emissions	Carbon emissions per capita in Northern Europe are about half those in the English-speaking countries: 7.1 tonnes, compared to 10.7 tonnes in East Asia and 13.5 tonnes in the English-speaking countries.

Weaknesses	
Less-competitive economies	The average score for Northern Europe and Nordic countries in the Global Competitiveness Index is 80.2, compared to 82.6 for the English-speaking countries and 80.4 for East Asia.
	The average score for the Northern European and Nordic countries in the Global Innovation Index is 56.6, behind the English-speaking countries (60.3) and level with East Asia (56.6).

*All averages are weighted by population.

East Asian Countries

Strengths	
Stellar education outcomes	Reading performance of fifteen-year-olds is more than six months ahead of the Northern European countries. The PISA score is 514, compared to 495 in Northern Europe and 506 in the English-speaking countries. Maths performance of fifteen-year-olds is nearly two years ahead of English-speaking countries. The PISA score is 532, compared to 501 in Northern Europe and 485 for English-speaking countries.
Longevity	Life expectancy at birth is 82.9 years, more than three years longer than in the English-speaking countries (79.5 years) and more than a year longer than in Northern Europe (81.7 years). Infant mortality is almost half the rate of the English-speaking countries: 2.7 deaths per 1000 live births, compared to 3.1 in Northern Europe and 5.1 in the English-speaking countries.
Strong economic growth	GDP per capita grew by 270 per cent between 1990 and 2018, vastly topping the 177 per cent in Northern Europe and 168 per cent in the English-speaking countries.
Current account surplus	East Asia runs a current account surplus of 5.8 per cent of GDP. Northern Europe also runs a surplus, equivalent to a lesser 3.9 per cent of GDP, while the English-speaking countries run a current account deficit equivalent to 2.7 per cent of GDP.
Spending on research and development	East Asian countries spend an amount equivalent to 3.91 per cent of GDP on research and development, compared to only 2.65 per cent in Northern Europe and 2.47 per cent in English-speaking countries.
Low murder rates	The homicide rate in East Asia is 88 per cent lower than in the English-speaking countries and 55 per cent lower than in Northern Europe: 0.5 homicides per 100,000 people, compared to 1.1 in Northern Europe and 4.1 in the English-speaking countries.

Weaknesses	
Weak economic output	GDP per capita is US$36,324: 38 per cent less than in English-speaking countries (US$58,159,) and 25 per cent less than in Northern Europe (US$48,200).
Low incomes	The average annual income per person is US$26,345: 30 per cent less than in Northern Europe (US$37,683) and 44 per cent less than in English-speaking countries (US$47,057).
Low rates of immigration	Only 10.6 per cent of the population was born overseas (although the share in Hong Kong and Singapore is much higher). In the English-speaking countries and Northern Europe, the figures are 15.7 per cent and 13.5 per cent respectively.
More unhappiness	The average happiness score in the 'World Happiness Report 2019' is 6.0 out of 10. In the English-speaking countries and Northern Europe, the average score is 7.0.
High gender gap	The 'Global Gender Gap Report 2020' indicates that East Asian countries have closed only 67.7 per cent of the gender gap, compared to 73.6 in the English-speaking countries and 78.1 in Northern Europe and Nordic countries.
Weak democracies and high levels of corruption	The average score on the EIU Democracy Index is 7.67 (out of 10), compared to 8.22 in the English-speaking countries and 8.45 in Northern Europe.
	The average score on the Freedom in the World Index is 81.6 (out of 100), compared to 88.9 in the English-speaking countries and 93.9 in Northern Europe.
	The average score on the Corruption Perceptions Index is 62 (out of 100), compared to 73.6 in the English-speaking countries and 77.9 in Northern Europe.

* Data for East Asia includes South Korea, Singapore and Hong Kong and Taiwan where available. All averages are weighted by population.[27]

We can see that the English-speaking countries have strong economies, generating more output per capita than Nordic and Northern European countries and those in East Asia. They are also more competitive and innovative, ranking highest in the Global Competitiveness Index and the Global Innovation Index. The English-speaking countries are absorbing substantial immigrant populations, particularly skilled migrants, which is addressing labour shortages.

Yet in most areas, the English-speaking countries are underperforming. Economic growth has been materially slower than in both Northern Europe and East Asia. GDP per capita in the United States grew more slowly than in every Nordic and Northern European country except France (which has struggled to recover following the 2008 global financial crisis). Even Australia, the only developed country to avoid recession in the financial crisis, has been outperformed by Denmark, Norway and Luxembourg.[28]

The English-speaking countries are running huge government deficits. General government debt across the English-speaking countries now averages 127 per cent of GDP, far higher than the 87 per cent found in Nordic and Northern European countries.[29] This government debt will eventually need to be repaid, and it effectively amounts to borrowing against future generations. For example, if the United States wanted to pay off its debt, every person in the country would owe US$61,539.[30]

The English-speaking countries are not even close to world-best educational outcomes, with their students months and sometimes even years behind those in the East Asian countries. Inequality is also far worse than in Northern Europe. It's worse than in South Korea too (but better than in Singapore).[31] The relative poverty rate in the English-speaking countries is almost double that of Northern European and Nordic countries.

Life expectancy at birth is flatlining across most of the English-speaking countries, and in the United States it has even declined. A baby born in Hong Kong today can expect to live six years longer than one born in the land of the free. Infant mortality in the English-speaking countries is almost twice as high as the rate in East Asia. The homicide rate in the United States is also fifteen times worse than in East Asia and twelve times worse than the average across Nordic and Northern European countries.[32]

Finally, as most of us know, the English-speaking countries continue to be a long way behind others when it comes to reducing carbon emissions, with per capita emissions roughly double those of Nordic and Northern European countries and 26 per cent higher than those in East Asia.[33] While the United Kingdom, the United States and Ireland have reduced their emissions, the other English-speaking countries have failed to achieve any improvements in nearly thirty years.

With these outcomes, it seems difficult to sustain an argument that the low-taxing, small-government approach of the English-speaking countries is the most effective global model.

The Nordic and Northern European countries earn a gold star for leading the world in most areas. They are ranked as the most democratic, and their governments as among the least corrupt. People in Nordic and Northern European countries work far fewer hours than those in the English-speaking countries or East Asia, yet they are the most productive. They rate highly on the 2019 World Happiness Report, with the top five happiest countries in the world from this region.[34] While they have high taxes, unlike the English-speaking countries their governments are running budget surpluses. These nations are globally competitive too, exporting far more goods and services than they import. As a group, they are marginally behind the English-speaking countries in innovation and economic competitiveness, yet Germany, the Netherlands, Sweden and Denmark rank in the top ten in the Global Competitiveness Index, ahead of Canada, Australia, New Zealand and Ireland. Finland, Norway, France and Luxembourg are not far behind.

The Nordic and Northern European countries have the lowest poverty rate and the smallest gender gap of our three country groupings. Finally, they show us that strong economic growth does not require large carbon emissions. Denmark has almost halved its per capita emissions since 1990, at the same time as its economy grew substantially faster than the United States, Australia, Canada, New Zealand and the United Kingdom.

Governments in East Asia have adopted a low-tax model, with minimum provision of welfare services, much like many English-speaking countries. The economic development model for the Asian tiger countries was based on building a manufacturing industry that could deliver cheap exports, leveraging low wages and low costs.

Yet don't think for a second that East Asian countries have weak governments. Governments in East Asia play a strong role in the economy and in society more generally. As we've seen, more than 80 per cent of residents in Singapore live in government housing, and the public sector is a massive investor in 'government-linked' corporations, driving economic development. The East Asian countries are convincingly outperforming the rest of the world on health and education, and have aspirations for world-best outcomes in other areas, too. They look likely to succeed. According to the World Economic Forum, Singapore and Hong Kong are among the top ten most competitive countries in the world, ahead of the United Kingdom, Canada and Australia. South Korea and Taiwan are not far behind. Singapore's GDP per capita is now greater than Australia's, and Hong Kong's is higher than the United Kingdom's.[35] Given the rapid progress being made in East Asia, countries elsewhere in the world exhibiting any degree of complacency risk being outperformed in the near future.

Yet the East Asian countries remain behind in many areas. Their governments are the least democratic, and score highest on the corruption perceptions index. Singapore and Hong Kong cannot be considered full democracies. Residents of East Asia are also relatively unhappy, scoring quite a bit lower than those in our other two country groupings in the 2019 World Happiness Report.[36] Given that freedom from corruption is a big factor in overall social happiness, this is perhaps not a surprise.

While Singapore and Hong Kong have large overseas-born populations, South Korea has not embraced immigration, despite a fast-ageing population. Less than 3 per cent of its population was born overseas. Nor have East Asian countries embraced other means of growing the workforce. For example, women's workforce participation is significantly lower than men's. Having closed just 68 per cent of the gender gap, East Asian countries have a long way to go. For example, women in South Korea spend nearly five times as much time on unpaid household tasks as men.[37]

I've focused on the four Asian tigers, which commenced their development phase in the 1960s, because the patterns here are clearest due to the length of time over which we can measure. But we shouldn't forget that other countries in Asia are developing rapidly, too. The 'tiger cub' economies of South-East Asia (Indonesia, Malaysia, the Philippines, Thailand and Vietnam) are attempting to follow the same development trajectory. A similar model has also fuelled China's growth. In future, we can expect to see a number of other Asian countries join Singapore, Hong Kong, South Korea and Taiwan with levels of wealth and economic power that rival the English-speaking, as well as Nordic and Northern European, countries. It's a fascinating world that our children will live in as we move through what is now undeniably the Asian century.

This chapter sketched the key areas of economic, political and social policy emerging from the stories in this book, and examined who is performing best on which measures. In the next chapter, we'll consider what things they – and we – we might do to bring about change.

12

TOOLS FOR THE FUTURE
What to Do Next

So, we've seen that countries on the other side of the world are achieving exceptional things. Could these ideas and strategies really work in your country? I think they could.

Of course, every country has its own history, institutions, politics and culture. It's unreasonable to expect that what works in one country will have the same impact globally. Countries with similar resources and societies are likely have more to offer one another than those that are radically different. The bright examples in this book won't apply to every nation in the same form. Even so, there are significant lessons we can learn from international experience. The challenge is to take inspiration from overseas and adapt relevant ideas to apply in our own local, regional or national context.

Why look to others for solutions to our issues? Domestic problems that have been simmering for a long time – those sometimes referred to as 'intractable' – are the most likely to lend themselves to injections of outside wisdom. As long-standing challenges are particularly difficult to address, the value of seeing how other countries have tackled them is greater, too. Together, we really can work towards solving the world's problems.

The results the countries in this book have achieved provide enormous grounds for optimism, showing just what is possible. You may read about your own nation and cheer. Yet, for many of us, these stories also serve as a reminder that our country simply isn't doing well enough.

For every nation muddling along, trading on past successes, there's another racing to catch up. If this isn't abundantly clear, take another look at the chapter profiling Singapore's education system, or the one exploring healthcare in South Korea. They make for salutary reading.

While your country's context is unique, there's no reason why it can't halve greenhouse gas emissions like Denmark. Change may take time, but your nation can reach the educational outcomes Singapore has, achieve life expectancies comparable with South Korea and pursue greater social equality like Norway. Why not? Why can't your country welcome immigrants like Australia does, develop cities as innovative as those in parts of the United States and aim for the paid parental leave that Iceland enjoys?

We live in a hyper-connected world. Information flows instantly between people, nations and regions. Witnessing what other countries are up to just requires turning on the news, picking up the financial pages of a daily paper, listening to those who have travelled and worked overseas. Your political leaders, policy strategists and senior public servants are members of a global as well as a local community. They can see and hear what other countries are achieving. They know that it can be done. And now we do too.

What Can Governments Do?

One thing this book shows us is that governments are crucial to change. They play a critical role in every aspect of our lives, through their actions or their absence. They enable and constrain us through regulation and legislation, they tax us and spend the proceeds on programs (hopefully) in the public interest and they help us to steer a course to the future. What governments do impacts on our prosperity, our safety, our health and our environment.

Let's look at our three groups of countries again.

The English-Speaking Countries

While the English-speaking countries are the wealthiest and most competitive in the world, here are some actions they might consider to maintain their position as global leaders.

- **Redesign the tax system.** The average tax revenue of the English-speaking countries is, at 29 per cent of GDP, at the low end of the OECD. There is scope to go up a couple of percentage points without hurting economic growth. With well-applied measures – such as taxes on goods and services, property or carbon, and removal of tax incentives aimed at the rich – an increase in tax revenue won't hurt competitiveness. It will, however, provide extra funds to invest in education, childcare and healthcare, and could also help address large budget deficits.

- **Reduce working hours.** Employees in the English-speaking countries work 1733 hours a year. This is 287 hours, or seven and a half weeks, more than the average worker in a Nordic or Northern European country, where there are more leave provisions and limits on overtime. The United States could introduce an annual leave and maternity leave entitlement, while other countries could legislate paid paternity leave and trial a shorter working week. Who knows? Working less might even enable people to exercise more, alleviating the skyrocketing level of obesity and its impact on the health system!

- **Improve healthcare.** The United States should look to joining the rest of the OECD by introducing universal healthcare for a core set of services. For the other English-speaking countries, whose residents already enjoy this, reducing out-of-pocket fees will further improve access to treatment, as will extending full coverage to pharmaceuticals and dental services.[1] There is also scope to improve access to maternal and child health services, mental-health services, and aged care.

- **Tackle carbon emissions (really).** Making a determined effort to move to renewable sources of electricity generation is an obvious next step for many English-speaking countries. The technology exists, and places such as Denmark have demonstrated that, with smart planning, the transition can be done at little or no cost to the economy. The United Kingdom has managed to reduce per capita emissions by more than 40 per cent since 1990, as it has transitioned away from coal in favour of gas and renewables. What's required now for countries such as New Zealand, Australia and Canada, which have made no progress over the same period, are government policy frameworks that support investment, such as renewable energy targets or emissions trading schemes.

- **Reduce inequality.** Redistributing tax revenue through targeted welfare payments is one of the best ways of reducing inequality. Tailored employment services can help immigrants, especially those from non-English-speaking backgrounds, to find jobs more quickly, and well-funded, affordable childcare can help more women return to work. Reducing inequality will improve lagging economic growth and contribute to better educational outcomes in these English-speaking countries.

- **Invest in schools and teachers.** To avoid the risk of falling further behind East Asian countries, and to ensure that they are well positioned to thrive in an increasingly knowledge-oriented economy, the English-speaking countries will need to invest more in education, and take a systematic approach to improving outcomes through teacher training, school leadership and government policy.

- **Encourage healthier living.** Life expectancy rates are halting, and in some places even falling, due to preventable diseases caused by smoking, alcohol consumption, poor diet and obesity. It is remarkable: many English-speaking nations have worked hard over centuries to increase quality of life, only to see its actual length decline today due to overconsumption. A serious effort to address these health problems could involve taxes on sugar, junk food, alcohol and cigarettes, or regulation around the advertising of harmful products.

- **Double down on innovation.** The greatest strength of the English-speaking countries is economic competitiveness. Continued effort is needed to maintain this lead. Governments in English-speaking countries should increase their investments in research and innovation. One approach is to develop clusters of innovation activity in cities to attract the world's best talent, and to ensure that finance is available for new technology and industries, such as robotics and artificial intelligence.

Nordic and Northern European Countries

Nordic and Northern European countries are the highest-taxing in the world, and are sometimes criticised for it. But the high-taxing model doesn't seem to have led to adverse outcomes, and in fact these countries perform well on a vast number of political, social and economic measures. They are leading the world in almost every area.

Yet there is always room for improvement. Here are some ideas for these countries to consider.

- **Become more entrepreneurial.** Germany, the Netherlands, Sweden and Denmark are already highly competitive. Yet others in this region – such as Austria, Belgium and Iceland – are a little off the pace, and will need to develop more entrepreneurial cultures that welcome disruptive thinking and are more tolerant of failure.

- **Invest in education.** While Nordic and Northern European countries are achieving better educational outcomes than the English-speaking countries in some areas, they are still a long way behind the East Asian tigers. Finland, which once topped the global rankings, now sits well outside the top ten in maths. Nordic and Northern European countries will need to keep investing in and improving their public education systems if they are to reach the heights of Singapore.

- **Reduce carbon emissions.** While Nordic and Northern European countries have relatively low per capita emissions (roughly half those of the English-speaking countries), collectively they have only managed to reduce emissions by 22 per cent since 1990. Denmark has been enormously successful in reducing its emissions, but countries such as Norway, Austria and the Netherlands have made far less progress. They need to accelerate the transition to low-emission energy sources. To demonstrate global leadership, Norway, which relies heavily on oil and gas exports, should consider an orderly phasing out of fossil-fuel production.

East Asian Countries

While the East Asian countries are leading the world in economic growth, education and health outcomes, here are some ideas to enhance their overall performance.

- **Collect more tax.** East Asian tax revenue is low. This was a deliberate – and successful – strategy for many East Asian governments during the first stages of economic development. However, as these economies mature, increasing the tax take by a couple of percentage points will enable East Asian governments to provide the services their growing and ageing populations require. Singapore has already announced moves to increase its sales tax to address the health and welfare costs associated with its ageing population.[2] In addition, inequality in East Asia is high – there are disparities between urban and rural areas especially. More progressive taxation can be used to alleviate inequality, with the revenue used to improve social services.

- **Welcome more migrants.** A rapidly ageing population is an enormous challenge on the horizon for the countries of East Asia. Immigration is the fastest way to slow down this trend. Singapore and Hong Kong have been magnets for migrants, with a higher share of residents born overseas than Australia.

However, to stimulate their economies and address ageing demographics, South Korea, Taiwan and other East Asian countries such as Japan need to open their doors to immigrants and do more to attract global talent.[3]

- **Get serious about gender equality.** Women in East Asian countries are now graduating from university at nearly the same rate as men, and it makes sense to take advantage of this talent. Increasing women's workforce participation will demand a significant shift in cultural norms, and may require quotas in the workplace and in politics.

- **Strengthen democratic freedoms.** East Asian countries have much scope to improve their democratic systems. Singapore and Hong Kong are only partial democracies. Perhaps as a result, happiness and life satisfaction in these places lags a long way behind the English-speaking and Northern European countries. Increasing the quality of the political system, elections and democratic freedoms is an important longer-term step these countries can take to improve the lives of their citizens.

- **Reduce carbon emissions.** Per capita carbon emissions in East Asia have increased by a whopping 89 per cent since 1990, and are now higher than in Northern Europe. While East Asian economies are growing fast, Denmark shows that economic growth does not have to be accompanied by increased greenhouse gas emissions. Technology will very soon reach the point where zero-emission electricity is cheaper to produce than electricity generated from fossil fuels. With the right policy leadership, East Asian countries have an opportunity to take advantage of these developments, and to grow their economies without an accompanying rise in emissions.

What Can You Do?

The ideas above are big, and rely on high-level involvement. Government needs to lead and support any widespread program or policy for structural change. Some governments – local, state or national – are likely to be open to these ideas, and are perhaps already working towards them. However, others may be less amenable to innovative policy – even when there is significant community support for it.

If your government seems less than motivated, don't despair. Insipid leadership need not mean that all is hopeless. Often, change starts small. Local activism can lead to differences on a community level, alert others to the potential of world-best ideas and, in time, shape the wider political context.

American political scientist Richard Rose argues that while policy analysis is about 'the careful linkage of cause and effect', political rhetoric is about 'the convincing association of ideas and symbols'.[4] The task is to tell the facts as compelling stories, building a case for change. The goal for each of us – as individuals, as members of a community and as citizens of a nation – is to take the lessons this book reveals, speak about them, apply them to our own local contexts and demand more of our governments when it comes to leading our communities into the future.

If you are a government minister, a politician or a local mayor reading this book and you've been persuaded by these arguments, your job is simple – you can agitate to adopt these policy directions in your country or community. You may have to put in the time and effort to build the case for change, and you may have to expend some political capital, but you have more levers at your disposal than most.

Similarly, if you're an elected representative or a community leader, you can work with government to ensure it is drawing on research and evidence from around the world. If you're a public servant, you can provide informed advice to the government you work for, drawing on the best available evidence (much of which is found in this book!).

But you don't need a policy role in government to take action. If you're a school principal or teacher, you can draw on best educational practice from Singapore and other East Asian countries and implement changes in your school or classroom. If you're a police officer, you can talk with your colleagues about the United Kingdom's focus on partnership-based approaches to policing and explore the potential to bring more of this into your local area. If you're a nurse or a doctor, you can think about how your workplace can improve health literacy, or collaborate with police to reduce community-based violence.

If you're a working mother, you can talk to your employer about introducing greater transparency for the gender pay gap. If you're a working father, you can lobby your workplace for greater flexibility in working hours. If you're a migrant who has navigated your way through a minefield of confusing job-seeking services, you can volunteer at a community organisation to advocate for tailored employment programs or share your experiences with recent arrivals to help keep them from falling into the same holes. If you're a parent or a childcare teacher, you can skill up in educational games and activities that best support imaginative thinking and learning, and share this knowledge with other parents.

National governments have significant powers that enable change at a broader scale. They take the lead on federal regulation, are key to climate policy, control the country's borders and determine many of the nation's tax and welfare policy settings, including parental leave, childcare and healthcare.

If your national government seems unlikely to change its attitude any time soon, seek action at a local level. State or provincial governments have an important role in service delivery, and are often open to leading when federal governments are not. Sometimes, enough momentum can be generated at the state or province level so that national change follows. For example, the Australian state of Victoria played a major role in reforms to early childhood education, which ultimately led to national initiatives, including substantial funding support for kindergartens.[5] California has some of the most aggressive renewable energy targets in the United States, and we can only hope that its leadership will inspire national change.

Local or city governments are great partners in community initiatives, and as we've seen, locally developed solutions are often the most effective. You could consider working with your local government on a community renewable energy project, for example, as residents on Samsø Island did, or on a neighbourhood-based initiative to reduce crime rates.

Local government also has a lead role in city planning and development. As in Copenhagen, city governments can work towards cities becoming carbon neutral with better planning of buildings, transport and infrastructure. Along with state governments, city governments are likely to be key partners in the development of innovation districts, such as those we read about in Phoenix and Boston. If you work for a local university, institution or company, you can help your organisation explore the contribution it can make here. By working in conjunction with local or state governments, such organisations can help to create innovation districts, or support start-ups, contributing to economic development in your city. Similarly, collaboration between institutions, companies and training organisations can help build the workforce that enables industry to thrive.

Don't believe that change is possible? While it may stretch credibility for some to imagine the little guy taking on city hall and winning, when individuals work together as part of a movement it can be done. Iceland's impressive efforts to tackle gender inequality began with a community protest, and the issue remains on the national agenda due to assertive, activist-led campaigns. In Indonesia, the transition to democracy was mobilised by mass demonstrations. In Norway, widespread trade union membership has shaped the policy framework that has enabled the country to be both productive and more equal, and unions in Germany have contributed to higher wages and greater productivity.

So, take part in a campaign. Join a political party. Write to your local, state or national representative. Governments are not immovable. They do respond to community pressure.

And vote. Absolutely every vote counts. In 2000, American president George W. Bush won office after winning in Florida by just 537 votes.[6] In 2016, Australian prime minister Malcolm Turnbull was re-elected with a one-seat majority, which included a seat won by just 1000 votes.[7] A small number of votes in the right places can determine which party forms government.

It's easy to feel overwhelmed, and disengaged from the political process. But joining together, as part of a community group, a campaign or a wider movement, is a way to connect with others, and to remind yourself that people together can change the world.

The stories in this book point to positive things we can do in our everyday lives. We can join a union, which, as we've seen in Norway, increases the power of employees in the labour market and can contribute to greater equality. We can participate in a local community group – a climate-action group, a tree-planting group, a support group for working women. We can welcome migrants into our communities, perhaps inviting them to share a meal. In our own households, we can divide the domestic and paid workload more fairly, serving as role models to our children.

The journey I took to write this book has reassured me that we *can* successfully tackle the big problems, and that others elsewhere in the world are already doing it. Imagine if we could take some of the methods and ideas in this book and put them into practice in ten or twenty countries – or even more! Knowledge is power, and the knowledge of what others are doing to address seemingly intractable problems can transform our own views, and eventually the globe.

More than ever, we are connected globally – through migration, travel, trade and information. This global connectedness can empower us to draw on the world's most effective policy responses and adopt – or adapt – them in our home countries.

Good government is a core part of the solution. Good government requires robust institutions, political leadership and competent public servants. But fundamentally, it requires an informed, empowered and mobilised citizenry – change rarely comes about without it. My hope is that this book will equip citizens around the world with the arguments – and the optimism – to demand more of their governments. It's vital that we do, because good government is the best hope we have. The future of the planet depends on it.

Philosopher Joseph de Maistre famously said, 'every nation gets the government it deserves'.[8] My view is that we deserve nothing less than the very best. We need to insist upon governments that will tackle the great challenges of our time with passion and purpose. And with this, change *is* possible.

ACKNOWLEDGEMENTS

Whether I've been writing at five in the morning or ten in the evening, this book has not felt at all like work. With a compulsion driving me, I didn't need any convincing to allocate time to researching or writing. Yet this project wasn't mine alone. I'm grateful for the assistance of many others, who, despite having their own priorities, generously contributed their time and insights.

Speaking with – and learning from – an impressive array of people from around the world has been one of the real pleasures of this project. Thank you to the following individuals for agreeing to be interviewed: Chirag Agarwal, Hazem Ali, Sigurður Bragason, Stefan Brück, Salvatore Fratantonio, Gunnar Garfors, Professor Saravanan Gopinathan, Professor Vedi Hadiz, Dr Kristian Heggebø, Søren Hermansen, Julian Hill MP, Professor David Hogan, Hutch Hussein, Professor Bruce Katz, Dr Nicole Keller, Professor Young-Ho Khang, Professor Danny Liew, Travis McCready, Christine MacKay, Finn Mortensen, Dr Peter Neyroud, Associate Professor Ng Pak Tee, Thomas Osha, Esther Rajadurai, Anne Sigrid I. Refsum, Abul Rizvi, Dr Nathkai Safi, Dr Ken Setiawan, Emeritus Professor Jonathan Shepherd, Rut Ríkey Tryggvadóttir, Fríða Rós Valdimarsdóttir, Julie Wagner, Claudia Whitehead and Dr Jeromin Zettelmeyer.

At various points in the life of this book, I have also been fortunate to draw on input from a number of friends and acquaintances, who have been willing to go out of their way to assist. Their contributions made the book better than it would have been otherwise. The following people generously provided reflections on structure, reviewed draft chapters, made introductions or provided encouragement: Professor David Adams, Mike Allen, Van Badham, Anna Burgess, Rod Commerford, Tim Delany, Stephen Fraser, Andrew Giles MP, Owen Gill, Tom Gorman,

Toby Hemming, Bradley Huestis, Rebecca Huntley, David Imber, Maria Katsonis, Robert Larocca, Professor Tim Lindsey, Julian Littler, Jeff Lynn, Eamon O'Hearn Large, David Paroissien, Laks Prabhala, Simone Quinn, Nicole Rees, Dr Tania Strahan, Dr Vincent Versace, Eleanor Williams, Tony Wilson and Dr Michael Zettinig. If I've overlooked anyone, please forgive me.

Jeanne Ryckmans was the agent who took a chance and who has supported me throughout this journey. Sophy Williams at Black Inc. believed in this project from the beginning, and made an enormous contribution shaping its direction. Julia Carlomagno has been amazing to work with; she managed to extract more from me than I ever thought possible. Without her editing and superb judgement, this would be a far lesser book. Thanks also to the rest of the team at Black Inc.

Finally, this project was only achievable with the support, patience and forbearance of my family. My wife, Claire, was the catalyst who enabled this book to move beyond an idea to become an actual project. As well as reading and providing feedback on every chapter, Claire shared the vision for this book and provided the fortitude that ensured it was completed. Sophie, Genevieve, Charlotte and Alice offered encouragement and all the motivation I needed to search for solutions to the world's problems. My mother-in-law, Colleen, regularly – and generously – hosted the family while the book was written. And as deadlines loomed, my mum and dad, Jan and David, fed me and provided a quiet house to write in. More importantly, they endowed me with an incredible start in life, without which I doubt this book would have been possible.

LIST OF FIGURES

Figure 1: 'Air and GHG Emissions: Carbon Dioxide (CO_2), Tonnes/Capita, 1992–2016', IEA CO_2 Emissions from Fuel Combustion Statistics: Indicators for CO_2 Emissions, OECD, Paris, 2018.

Figure 2: 'Energy Statistics 2017', The Danish Energy Agency, Copenhagen, April 2019. Note, this graph assesses Danish GDP using 'constant 2010 prices', which means it is adjusted for inflation.

Figure 3: 'PISA 2015: Results in Focus', OECD, Paris, 2016, p. 5.

Figure 4: 'PISA 2009 Results: What Makes a School Successful?', vol. IV, OECD, Paris, 2011, p. 224, Table IV 3.9.

Figure 5: 'GDP Per Capita, Constant 2010 US$', World Bank, Washington, DC, 2017.

Figures 6 and 7: 'Health Status: Causes of Mortality – Assault, Deaths Per 100,000 Population (Standardised Rates), 2017 or Latest Available', OECD, Paris, 2018. In the ICD-10 – the tenth revision of the *International Statistical Classification of Diseases and Related Health Problems*, a medical classification list developed by the World Health Organization – death by assault is defined as 'homicide; injuries inflicted by another person with intent to injure or kill, by any means'.

Figure 8: 'Crime in England and Wales: Appendix Tables – Year Ending March 2019', Office for National Statistics, UK Statistics Authority, UK Government, London, 18 July 2019.

Figure 9: 'Global Firearms Holdings', Small Arms Survey 2017, Graduate Institute of International and Development Studies, Geneva and Washington, DC, 2017.

Figure 10: Klaus Schwab et al., 'The Global Gender Gap Report 2018', World Economic Forum, Geneva, 2018, p. 10.

Figure 11: Gender equality figures from 'Global Gender Gap Report 2020', and democracy figures from 'Democracy Index 2018: Me Too? Political Participation, Protest and Democracy', The Economist Intelligence Unit, London, 2019.

Figures 12 and 14: Janet Phillips and Joanne Simon-Davies, 'Migration to Australia: A Quick Guide to the Statistics', Parliament of Australia, Canberra, 18 January 2017.

Figure 13: 'Settling In 2018: Main Indicators of Immigrant Integration', OECD and European Union, Brussels, 2018, p. 19.

Figure 15: Net income gini and median income from 'The Inclusive Development Index 2018: Summary and Data Highlights', World Economic Forum, Geneva, 2018, pp. 18–20.

Figure 16: 'Hours Worked, Total, Hours/Worker, 2018 or Latest Available' and 'GDP Per Hour Worked, Total, US Dollars, 2018 or Latest Available', OECD, Paris, 2018.

Figure 17: 'Focus on Inequality and Growth', OECD, Paris, December 2014.

NOTES

Introduction

1   Steven Woolf, 'Failing Health of the United States', *British Medical Journal*, no. 360, 2018 and Ben Tinker, 'US Life Expectancy Drops for Second Year in a Row', *CNN*, 22 December 2017.

2   'Life Expectancy at Birth, Total (Years)', World Bank, Washington, DC, 2019.

3   Seungmi Yang et al., 'Understanding the Rapid Increase in Life Expectancy in Korea', *American Journal of Public Health,* vol. 100, no. 5, 2010, pp. 896–903.

4   Vasilis Kontis et al., 'Future Life Expectancy in 35 Industrialised Countries: Projections with a Bayesian Model Ensemble', *The Lancet*, vol. 389, no. 10076, 2017, pp. 1323–35.

5   'Air and Greenhouse Gas Emissions: Carbon Dioxide (CO_2), Tonnes/Capita, 1992–2016', *IEA CO_2 Emissions from Fuel Combustion Statistics: Indicators for CO_2 Emissions*, OECD, Paris, 2018.

6   'Air and Greenhouse Gas Emissions: Carbon Dioxide (CO_2), Tonnes/Capita, 1998–2018', OECD, Paris, 2019.

7   'Reading Performance (PISA), Total, Mean Score, 2000–2018' and 'Mathematics Performance (PISA), Total, Mean Score, 2018 or Latest Available', both OECD, Paris, 2017.

8   For further analysis, see Uri Friedman, 'Trust in Government is Collapsing Around the World', *The Atlantic*, 1 July 2016.

9   Hong Kong: 'Life Expectancy at Birth, Total (Years)', World Bank. Sweden: 'Air and Greenhouse Gas Emissions', OECD. Singapore: 'Reading Performance, PISA, Total, Mean Score, 2015', OECD, Paris, 2017. The OECD PISA assessment measures the reading skills of fifteen-year-olds around the world. Thirty scored points equates to one year of schooling. Singapore scored 535 and Mexico scored 423.

10 See for example David Colander et al., 'The Financial Crisis and the Systemic Failure by Academic Economics', Economics Discussion Paper No. 09–01, Middlebury College, Vermont, March 2009.

11 See Noah Smith, 'How Economics Went From Philosophy to Science', *Bloomberg*, 2 August 2018.

12 David McKenzie, John Gibson and Steven Stillman, 'How Important is Selection? Experimental vs Non-Experimental Measures of the Income Gains From Migration', *Journal of the European Economic Association*, vol. 8, no. 4, 2010, pp. 913–45 and Shannen Vallesi et al., 'A Mixed Methods Randomised Control Trial to Evaluate the Effectiveness of the Journey to Social Inclusion – Phase 2 Intervention for Chronically Homeless Adults: Study Protocol', *BMC Public Health*, vol. 19, no. 1, 2019, p. 334.

1:   Gone With the Wind

1   'Transition', Samsø Energy Academy, Samsø, 2019.

2   Jan Burck et al., 'The Climate Change Performance Index', Germanwatch, New Climate Institute and Climate Action Network Europe, 2019, p. 9 and Anne Vestergaard Andersen, 'Denmark Still Best at Fighting Climate Change', *State of Green*, 15 December 2015.

3   Denmark's carbon emissions have declined from 11.7 tonnes per capita in 1997 to 5.8 tonnes per capita in 2016. 'Air and Greenhouse Gas Emissions', OECD, Paris, 2018.

4   'Renewable Energy Island', *Visit Samsø*, 2019.

5   'Wind Power Capacity Worldwide Reaches 597 GW, 50.1 GW Added in 2018', World Wind Energy Association, Bonn, 4 June 2019.

6   'Climate Change 2014 Synthesis Report – Summary for Policymakers', Intergovernmental Panel on Climate Change (IPCC), Geneva, 2015, p. 20.

7   Sea level rise 0.45–0.82 m under scenario RCP8.5 (baseline scenario) (p. 13); species extinction and Artic ice (p. 12); extreme weather events (p. 72), all in ibid.

8   ibid., p. 2.

9   ibid., p. 51.

10 ibid., p. 16.

11 'Challenge One: Sustainable Development and Climate Change', Global Futures Intelligence System, The Millennium Project, Washington, DC, 2017.

12 Curt Storlazzi et al., 'Most Atolls Will Be Uninhabitable by the Mid-21st Century Because of Sea Level Rise Exacerbating Wave-Driven Flooding', *Science Advances* vol. 4, no. 4, 2018, abstract, and Richard Curtain and Matthew Dornan, 'Climate Change and Migration in Kiribati, Tuvalu and Nauru', *DevPolicyBlog*, 15 February 2019.

13 'Electricity Production from Oil, Gas and Coal Sources', World Bank, Washington, DC, 2015.

14 'Daily CO_2: Mauna Loa Observatory, Atmospheric CO_2 Concentrations', *CO_2.Earth*, May 2019.

15 Roddy Scheer and Doug Moss, 'Is it Too Late to Avoid the Worst Impacts of Climate Change?', *Scientific American*, 19 August 2012.

16 United Nations Framework Convention on Climate Change, 'What is the Paris Agreement?', United Nations Climate Change, Geneva, 2019.

17 'Investing in Climate, Investing in Growth', OECD, Paris, 2017, p. 137.

18 'Taking Action on Climate Change Will Boost Economic Growth', OECD, Paris, 23 May 2017.

19 Denmark had a happiness score of 7.6 between 2016 and 2018, behind Finland, with a happiness score of 7.769. John Helliwell et al., 'World Happiness Report 2019', Sustainable Development Solutions Network, New York, 2019, p. 25.

20 Mark Jacobson et al., '100% Clean and Renewable Wind, Water and Sunlight All-Sector Energy Roadmaps for 139 Countries of the World', *Joule*, vol. 1, no. 1, 2017, pp. 108–21.

21 Jim Malewitz, '1 Energy Crisis, 2 Futures: How Denmark and Texas Answered a Challenge', *The Texas Tribune*, 21 November 2016.

22 'Text of Fact Sheet on the President's Program Issued by White House Energy Staff', *The New York Times*, 21 April 1977.

23 Anders Heine Jensen, 'BWSC Lands Biomass Order in Northern Ireland', *State of Green*, 2 August 2013 and 'Danish-Vietnamese Partnership Reveals an Affordable Route to Saving Water and Energy in Vietnam', *State of Green*, 8 May 2019.

24 'About Us', Vestas, Copenhagen, 2019.

25 At the end of 2017, there were 6157 operational turbines.

26 Akshat Rathi, 'The World's Largest Wind Turbine Can Power 8000 Homes on Its Own', *QZ*, 14 June 2017.

27 It's worth noting that wind power does not operate at peak capacity all the time. For example, offshore wind has a 'capacity factor' of 41.7 per cent in Denmark. See 'Capacity Factors at Danish Offshore Wind Farms', *Energy Numbers*, 1 March 2019. However, coal and other conventional energy generation sources don't run at full capacity either. In the United Kingdom in 2015, coal-fired power plants had a capacity factor of 39.1 per cent, and combined-cycle gas turbines had a capacity factor of 31.7 per cent. See 'Digest of United Kingdom Energy Statistics 2015', Department of Energy and Climate Change, UK Government, London, 2015.

28 David Weston, 'Dong and EnBW Win German Auction with Zero Subsidy Bids', *Wind Power Offshore*, 18 April 2017.

29 This does not apply to turbines less than 25 metres high.

30 Dan Haugen, 'How Denmark Turned an Efficiency Obligation Into Opportunity', *Midwest Energy News*, 8 October 2013.

31 Adam Vaughan, 'EU Raises Renewable Energy Targets to 32% by 2030', *The Guardian*, 14 June 2018; 'Victoria's Renewable Energy Targets', *Renewable Energy*, Department of Environment, Land,

Water and Planning, Victorian Government, Melbourne, 27 August 2019; Katy Steinmetz, 'California Pledges 100% Clean Electricity by 2045', *Time*, 10 September 2018.

32 Seventy-five per cent of Danes report having trust in others. Fifty-two per cent of Danes report having confidence in national government. The OECD average is 42.3 per cent. See 'Society at a Glance 2016', OECD, Paris, 2016, p. 129.

33 'Fact Sheet: News Media and Political Attitudes in Denmark', Pew Research Center, Washington, DC, 17 May 2018.

34 For more on this, see Mohamed El-Erian, 'How Political Polarisation is Crippling Western Democracies', World Economic Forum, Geneva, 12 May 2015.

35 'Energy Statistics 2017', The Danish Energy Agency, Copenhagen, April 2019.

36 Arthur Nelson, 'Wind Power Generates 140 Per Cent of Denmark's Electricity Demand', *The Guardian*, 10 July 2015.

37 Rafael Tablado, 'Wind Energy Cheapest Form of Power, According to Denmark', *Energy Digital*, 22 July 2014.

38 Senator the Hon. Matt Canavan quoted in Ben Packham, 'Dual Blackouts Put New Generation on Notice to Act Fast', *The Australian*, 27 August 2018. See also Benjamin Zycher, 'The High Cost of Unreliable Power', *The Washington Times*, 7 August 2017.

39 'CEER Benchmarking Report 6.1 on the Continuity of Electricity and Gas Supply: Data Update 2015/16', Council of European Energy Regulators, Brussels, 2018.

40 'Denmark's Electricity Grid Leading in Europe', Ministry of Foreign Affairs, Government of Denmark, 14 February 2017.

41 Silvio Marcacci, 'Denmark May Hold the Key to Integrating Large Amounts of Intermittent Renewables', *Green Tech Media*, 27 July 2016.

42 Nick Rosen, 'Off-Grid Living: It's Time to Take Back the Power from the Energy Companies', *The Guardian*, 11 April 2014.

43 'Copenhagen, City of Cyclists: Facts and Figures 2017', Cycling Embassy of Denmark, Copenhagen, 2017.

44 John Berger, 'Copenhagen, Striving to Be Carbon-Neutral: Part 1, The Economic Payoffs', *Huffington Post*, 13 March 2017 and William Steele, 'State-of-the-Art Biomass Plant for Copenhagen', *Renewable Energy World*, 24 October 2016.

45 'Ecological Footprint of Countries 2016, Denmark', Global Footprint Network, California, 2016.

46 Gitte Seeberg quoted in 'Denmark's Ecological Footprint is Fourth Largest', *The Local*, 30 September 2014.

47 Keane Gruending, 'Denmark's Race to Renewable Electricity: How Costly? How Effective?', Keane. Gruending.com, 21 March 2016.

48 'Pull the Plug! Danes Pay EU's Highest Electricity Prices', *The Local*, 1 March 2016.

49 John Barwise, 'ETS Emissions Decline Sharply', *Institute of Environmental Management and Assessment*, Lincoln, 7 April 2015.

50 'Registration Tax', Government of Denmark, Copenhagen, 2019.

51 Nick Rigillo, 'Denmark Does U-Turn on Electric Cars to Reach Fossil-Free Future', *Bloomberg*, 9 October 2018.

52 Leo Mirani, 'Why Tesla is Focused on Oil-Rich Norway As It Expands Beyond the US', *Quartz*, 30 August 2013.

53 'OECD Work on Climate Change 2013–14', OECD, Paris, 2014, pp. 14–15.

54 Timna Jacks and Clay Lucas, 'Parking Spaces to Go for Bike Lanes on Busy CBD Streets', *The Age*, 7 May 2019; 'Kicking off a New Bicycle Network Plan in Shymkent, Kazakhstan', *Copenhagenize*, 2 April 2019; Charlotte Gjedde, 'Copenhagen's Climate Adapted Neighbourhood Inspires New York', *State of Green*, 17 March 2016.

55 'The Social Dimensions of Climate Change: Discussion Draft', United Nations, Geneva, 2011, p. 5.

56 Joel Goodstein, 'First Danish Ferry Powered by LNG', *Maskinmesteren*, August 2015, p. 3.

2: Education Nation

1   'GDP Per Capita (Current US$) – Singapore', World Bank, Washington, DC, 2018 and 'Strong Performers and Successful Reformers in Education: Lessons from PISA for the United States', OECD, Paris, 2011, p. 160.

2   C.B. Goh and S. Gopinathan, 'The Development of Education in Singapore Since 1965' in S.K. Lee, C.B. Goh, B. Fredriksen & J.P. Tan (eds), *Toward a Better Future: Education and Training for Economic Development in Singapore Since 1965*, World Bank, Washington, DC, 2008, p. 14.

3   'Population in Brief 2019', Singapore Department of Statistics, Singapore, 2019, p. 20.

4   'General Household Survey 2015', Statistics Singapore, Singapore City, p. vii.

5   Article 153, Federal Constitution of Malaysia, as at 1 November 2010.

6   'PISA 2018 Results: Combined Executive Summaries, Volume I, II & III', 2019, pp. 17–18 and 'PISA 2015: Results in Focus', 2018, p. 24, both OECD, Paris.

7   Highest GDP per capita: this is the case regardless of whether GDP is measured in US dollars or adjusted for purchasing power parity; see 'GDP Per Capita, PPP (Current International $)', World Bank, Washington, DC, 2018. Most competitive country: Klaus Schwab, 'The Global Competitiveness Report 2019', World Economic Forum, Geneva, 2019.

8   '2019 Index of Economic Freedom', Heritage Foundation, 2019; 'Corruption Perceptions Index 2018', Transparency International, 2018; 'Ease of Doing Business Rankings', *Doing Business: Measuring Business Regulations*, World Bank, Washington, DC, 2019.

9   'Global Revenue Statistics Database – Tax Revenue as % of GDP' and 'Government at a Glance – SEA Countries: Public Finance and Economics, General Government Revenue as a Percentage of GDP', both OECD, Paris, 2019.

10 Singapore generates $22,185 in revenue to Australia's $17,005. See 'Government at a Glance – SEA Countries'.

11 Alastair King, 'Investigating the Scale of State-Owned Business in Singapore', *Bureau Van Dijk*, 29 November 2017.

12 'Why 80% of Singaporeans Live in Government-Built Flats', *The Economist*, 6 July 2017.

13 'Democracy Index 2018: Me Too? Political Participation, Protest and Democracy', The Economist Intelligence Unit, London, 2019, p. 37.

14 'PISA 2018 Results: Volume II', Table B3.1.1

15 For further discussion, see Michael McGowan and Nick Evershed, '"Warped and Elitist": Are Australia's Selective Schools Failing the Fairness Test?', *The Guardian*, 20 May 2018.

16 'Setting or Streaming', Education Endowment Foundation, London, 2019.

17 'PISA 2018 Results: Combined Executive Summaries, Volume I, II & III', pp. 17–18.

18 Top performers are those students at Level 5 or Level 6 standard, which means they have a PISA score of 633 or above. 'PISA 2018 Results, Volume I', pp. 17–18.

19 'Equity in Education: Breaking Down Barriers to Social Mobility', OECD, Paris, 2018, p. 35.

20 'PISA 2015', p. 25.

21 Louisa Tang, 'Singapore Students Emerge Tops in Collaborative Problem Solving', *Today*, 21 November 2017.

22 'Private Schools. Who Benefits?', *PISA in Focus*, 2011/7 (August), OECD, Paris, 2011.

23 ibid.

24 'The OECD Teaching and Learning International Survey (TALIS) 2013 Results – Excel Figures and Tables', OECD, Paris, 2019, Table 2.18.

25 Ng Pak Tee, *Learning from Singapore: The Power of Paradoxes*, Routledge, New York, 2017, pp. 146–7 and 'The OECD Teaching and Learning International Survey (TALIS) 2013 Results', Table 6.12.

26 'Reducing Class Size: Australasian Research Summary', *Evidence for Learning*, Melbourne Graduate School of Education, The University of Melbourne, 2019.

27 'Singapore: Teacher and Principal Quality', Center on International Education Benchmarking, Washington, DC, 2019.

28 Ng Pak Tee, *Learning from Singapore*, p. 10.

29 The average Singaporean salary is S$67,152 (US$49,631). Ming Feng, 'The Ultimate Salary Guide for Singaporeans', *Seedly*, 19 March 2019.

30 Ng Pak Tee, *Learning from Singapore*, pp. 150–1.

31 Vivien Stewart, 'How Singapore Developed a High-Quality Teacher Workforce', Center for Global Education, Asia Society, Hong Kong, New York and Texas, 2019.

32 ibid; 'Strong Performers and Successful Reformers in Education', p. 168; Bill Jackson, 'The Professional Lives of Teachers in Singapore', *The Daily Riff*, 10 September 2010.

33 'A High-Quality Teaching Force for the Future: Good Teachers, Capable Leaders, Dedicated Specialists', Press Release, Minister of Education and the Arts, Singapore Government, 14 April 2001.

34 See for further discussion 'Strong Performers and Successful Reformers in Education', p. 166.

35 Seng-Dao Keo, 'Shaping Strong Principals in Singapore: Success by Design', *Top of the Class Newsletter*, National Center for Education and the Economy, Washington, DC, 26 February 2019.

36 'International Migrant Stock (% of Population)', World Bank, Washington, DC, 2018.

37 Rebecca Bull et al., 'Evolving a Harmonised Hybrid System of ECEC: A Careful Balancing Act – A Case Study of the Singapore Early Childhood Education and Care System', Teachers College, National Center for Education and the Economy, 5 October 2018.

38 'Singapore', Center on International Education Benchmarking and 'Building Educational Bridges: Innovation for School Leaders', National Institute of Education, Nanyang Technological University, Singapore, 2019.

39 Office of Education Research – NIE, 'NIE Research in Practice Series: Building a Reading Culture Through School Libraries', YouTube, 23 March 2018 and 'Research in Action: Working With CHIJ St Nicholas (Secondary) on Six-Learnings Framework', National Institute of Education, 18 January 2016.

40 'Literacy Rate, Youth, Total (% of People Aged 15–24)' and 'Literacy Rate, Adult, Total (% of People Aged 15 and Above)', both World Bank, Washington, DC, 2019.

41 'Literacy', United Nations Educational, Scientific and Cultural Organization, Paris, 2019 and 'PISA 2015', pp. 18, 38, 72.

42 Ann Veneman, 'Education is Key to Reducing Child Mortality: The Link Between Maternal Health and Education', *UN Chronicle*, vol. XLIV, no. 4, December 2007 and Emmanuela Gakidou et al., 'Increased Educational Attainment and Its Effects on Child Mortality in 175 Countries Between 1975 and 2009: A Systemic Analysis', *The Lancet*, vol. 376, no. 9745, 18 September 2010, pp. 959–74.

43 Federico Cingano, 'Trends in Income Inequality and Its Impact on Economic Growth', OECD Social, Employment and Migration Working Papers No. 163, OECD, Paris, 2014, p. 6.

44 ibid., p. 22.

45 'Overview: Students' Well-Being' in 'PISA 2015 Results', vol. III, OECD, Paris, 2017, p. 11.

46 'Special Educational Needs', Ministry of Education, Singapore Government, 18 April 2019.

47 'Post-Secondary', Ministry of Education, Singapore Government, 9 October 2019 and Samantha Boh, 'Need for Greater Acceptance of Alternative Education Pathways', *The Straits Times*, 6 March 2016.

48 Amanda Wise, 'Behind the World's Best Students is a Soul-Crushing, Billion-Dollar Private Education Business', *Quartz*, 12 December 2016.

49 'You Know Anot? A Monthly Update on Singaporean Attitudes', *Private Tuition in Singapore: A Whitepaper Release*, Blackbox Research, July 2012, p. 4.

50 Janice Heng, 'Twelve Interesting Trends About Singapore Household Income and Spending', *The Straits Times*, 18 September 2014.

51 Figures refer to share of students achieving a result below level 2. 'PISA 2015', p. 373.

52 ibid., p. 222.

53 'Overview: Excellence and Equity in Education' in 'PISA 2015', p. 40; Stefanie Balogh, 'No Competition With Singapore Students', *The Australian*, 27 September 2017; 'PISA 2015', p. 228.

54 Deborah Lowe et al., 'Do Effects of Early Child Care Extend to Age 15 Years? Results from the NICHD Study of Early Childcare and Youth Development', *Child Development*, May–June 2010,

vol. 81, no. 3, pp. 737–56 and Kathy Sylva et al., 'Influences on Students' Development From Age 11–14, Final Report from Key Stage 3 Phase, EPPE', Faculty of Social Sciences, University of Wollongong, March 2012.

55 Kate Torii, Stacey Fox and Dan Cloney, 'Quality is Key in Early Childhood Education in Australia', Mitchell Institute Paper No. 1/2017, Mitchell Institute, Victoria University, Melbourne, October 2017, p. iv.

56 Sarah Wise et al., 'The Efficacy of Early Childhood Interventions', AIFS Research Report No. 14, Australian Institute of Family Studies, Department of Social Services, Government of Australia, Melbourne, 2005.

57 Lianne Chia, 'National Day Rally: 40,000 New Pre-School Places to be Added in Next Five Years', *Channel News Asia*, 20 August 2017 and Jolene Ang, '7 More MOE Kindergartens to be Set Up in 2021', *The Straits Times*, 7 August 2018.

58 'Education at a Glance 2014', p. 409 and 'Education at a Glance 2018', p. 277, both OECD, Paris.

59 'Private Schools: Who Benefits?', PISA in Focus 2011/7, OECD, Paris, 2011.

60 'Assessment for Learning: Formative Assessment' at 'Learning in the 21st Century: Research, Innovation and Policy', OECD/CERI International Conference, OECD Center for Educational Research and Innovation, Paris, 2008.

61 Jon Coles, 'Stability Will Raise Standards in Schools, Not Constant Reform', *The Guardian*, 13 February 2013.

62 'Parental Involvement', *Education GPS*, OECD, Paris, 25 October 2019.

63 ibid.

64 John Jerrim, 'Why Do East Asian Children Perform So Well in PISA? An Investigation of Western-born Children of East Asian Descent', *Oxford Review of Education*, vol. 41, no. 3, 2015, pp. 310–13.

65 Fayyadhah Zainalabiden, 'The Six Changes to Singapore's Education System MOE Announced Today', *Must Share News*, 28 September 2018.

66 Sean Lim, 'After 40 Years, Singapore is Ending the Streaming System That Divided Secondary Students Into Express and Normal Streams – Here's What You Need to Know', *Business Insider Singapore*, 5 March 2019.

67 'It Has the World's Best Schools But Singapore Wants Better', *The Economist*, 30 August 2018.

3: Partners in Crime

1 '1984: The Beginning of the End for British Coal', *BBC News*.

2 Mark Henderson, 'Professor Jonathan Shepherd Says Policy Should be Scientifically Researched', *The Times*, 20 July 2009.

3 Curtis Florence et al., 'Effectiveness of Anonymised Information Sharing and Use in Health Service, Police, and Local Government Partnership for Preventing Violence Related Injury: Experimental Study and Time Series Analysis', *British Medical Journal*, vol. 342, no. 7812, June 2011, p. 1405.

4 Jonathan Shepherd, Vivienne Avery and Saifur Rahman, 'Targeted Policing', *Police Professional*, 28 April 2016, p. 2.

5 Ruth Doherty, 'Jonathan Shepherd: "People Are Entitled to Their Own Opinions But Not Their Own Facts"', *British Dental Journal*, vol. 225, no. 10, 23 November 2018, p. 921.

6 'UK Economy Could Fall From Fifth to Seventh in Global Rankings in 2019', *PwC*, 19 December 2018.

7 Adam Winstock et al., 'Global Drug Survey 2019: Key Findings Report', Global Drug Survey, London, 2019, p. 31.

8 Peter Hayes, 'Riots in Thatcher's Britain' in Michael Davis (ed.), *Crowd Actions in Britain and France from the Middle Ages to the Modern World*, Palgrave Macmillan, London, 2015, pp. 256–69.

9 Because police-recorded crime data can vary across countries, this chapter – like the OECD, in its *Better Life Index* – mostly relies on the homicide rate calculated using medically certified 'deaths due to assault', recorded in country civil registration systems. The United Nations draws on police data to record a different measure of 'intentional homicide', or murders reported to police. On this measure, the UK also has a low rate of homicide, although not the lowest. Its rate is about 1.2 per

100,000 people, which is about the same as Australia. It compares with a rate of 1.7 in Canada and 5.4 in the United States. See 'Intentional Homicide (Per 100,000 People)', World Bank, Washington, DC, 2017. The World Health Organization defines death by assault as 'homicide; injuries inflicted by another person with intent to injure or kill, by any means'. See 'XX: External Causes of Morbidity and Mortality', *International Statistical Classification of Diseases and Related Health Problems (10th Revision)*, World Health Organization, 2016.

10   'Crime in England and Wales: Year Ending March 2019', Office for National Statistics, UK Statistics Authority, UK Government, London, 18 July 2019.

11   Pablo Fabjnzylber, Daniel Lederman and Norman Loayza, 'Inequality and Violent Crime', *Journal of Law and Economics*, vol. 45, no. 1, 2002, p. 8.

12   Vaseekaran Sivarajasingam et al., 'Violence in England and Wales in 2018: An Accident and Emergency Perspective', Crime and Security Research Institute, Cardiff University, April 2019, p. 5.

13   'Global Study on Homicide 2019: Executive Summary', United Nations Office on Drugs and Crime, Vienna, 2019, p. 12.

14   Manuel Eisner, 'Long-Term Historical Trends in Violent Crime', *Crime and Justice: Why Crime Rates Fall and Why They Don't*, University of Chicago Press, Chicago, 2003, p. 99.

15   Steven Pinker, *The Better Angels of Our Nature*, Penguin, London, 2011, p. xix.

16   Homicide rate for men (p. 19); effect on crime victims (p. 23); crime and economic growth (pp. 8–9), all in 'Global Study on Homicide 2019: Executive Summary', United Nations Office on Drugs and Crime.

17   'Homicide Data by Countries' in 'Global Study on Homicide 2019: Homicide, Development and the Sustainable Development Goals', United Nations Office on Drugs and Crime, Vienna, 2019.

18   ibid., p. 21.

19   Link between young people and violence (p. 10); between large cities and reduced crime (p. 34); differences between urban and rural homicide rates (p. 55), all in ibid.

20   Law-enforcement spending, income and gender inequity in ibid., p. 29. Pablo Fajnzylber, Daniel Lederman and Norman Loayza make a similar point about inequality in 'Inequality and Violent Crime', p. 8.

21   'Population, Data by Country (Recent Years) – Population Median Age (Years)', *Global Health Observatory Data Repository*, World Health Organization, Geneva, 15 June 2015.

22   'GDP Per Capita (Current US$)', World Bank, Washington, DC, 2018.

23   'Urban Population (Per Cent of Total Population)', World Bank, Washington, DC, 2018.

24   The UK has closed 77.4 per cent of the gender gap, making it the eleventh-best in the OECD; see Klaus Schwab et al., 'The Global Gender Gap Report 2018', World Economic Forum, Geneva, 2018. The UK has an income inequality gini score of 0.351. In the OECD, only Mexico, Chile, Turkey, the United States and South Korea are more unequal. 'Income Inequality, Gini Coefficient, 0=Complete Equality, 1=Complete Inequality, 2017 or Latest Available', OECD, Paris, 2017.

25   Philip Alpers et al., 'United Kingdom – Gun Facts, Figures and the Law', Sydney School of Public Health, University of Sydney, *GunPolicy.org*, 1 July 2019.

26   'Homicide', Harvard Injury Control Research Center, Harvard T.H. Chan School of Public Health, Harvard University, 2016.

27   Philip Alpers et al., 'United Kingdom – Gun Facts, Figures and the Law', 'Australia – Gun Facts, Figures and the Law' and 'United States – Gun Facts, Figures and the Law', Sydney School of Public Health, University of Sydney, *GunPolicy.org*, 1 July 2019.

28   'Global Study on Homicide 2019: Executive Summary', United Nations Office on Drugs and Crime, p. 38.

29   Emily Commander, 'Most UK Police Don't Carry Guns. What About Other Countries?', *Euro News*, 7 June 2018.

30· Keiligh Baker, 'Should All Frontline Police Officers Use Tasers?', *BBC News*, 24 August 2019.

31   Alexander Smith, 'The Vast Majority of UK Police Don't Carry Guns. Here's Why', *NBC News*, 24 March 2017.

32 Caroline Mortimer, 'M62 Shooting: Charts Show Difference Between Police Shootings in the US and the UK', *The Independent*, 3 January 2017.

33 There are approximately five police shootings per year in Australia, in a population of 25.5 million people. This equates to 0.2 police shootings per million people. See Lynne Peeples, 'What the Data Say About Police Shootings', *Nature*, 4 September 2019 and 'Population Clock', Australian Bureau of Statistics, Canberra, accessed 17 September 2019.

34 German Lopez, 'David Kennedy: If Cops Want the Public's Trust, They Must Admit to Centuries of Abuse', *Vox*, 16 September 2016.

35 Matthew Desmond, Andrew Papachristos and David Kirk, 'Police Violence and Citizen Crime Reporting in the Black Community', *American Sociological Review*, vol. 81, no. 5, 2016, pp. 1–20.

36 Calvin Beckford, 'The Peelian Principles', *The Crime Prevention Website*, 2016.

37 'Public Perceptions of Policing in England and Wales 2018, Prepared for Her Majesty's Inspectorate of Constabulary and Fire & Rescue Services', BMG Research, Birmingham, January 2019, p. 41.

38 Examples from Thames Valley in 'Using A&E Data to Prevent Violence in Communities', *Nursing Times*, 2 April 2011.

39 'Information Sharing to Tackle Violence: Guidance for Community Safety Partnerships on Engaging With the NHS', Department of Health and Social Care, UK Government, London, September 2012, pp. 4–5.

40 'Intimate Partner Violence and Alcohol' (fact sheet), World Health Organization and John Moores University Centre for Public Health, Geneva and Liverpool, 2006.

41 Melanie Pescud, 'Whether Teams Win or Lose, Sporting Events Lead to Spikes in Violence Against Women and Children', *The Conversation*, 13 July 2018.

42 Stuart Kirby, Brian Francis and Rosalie O'Flaherty, 'Can the FIFA World Cup Football (Soccer) Tournament Be Associated With an Increase in Domestic Abuse?', *Journal of Research in Crime and Delinquency*, vol. 51, no. 3, 2014, pp. 259–76.

43 Helen Pidd, 'Christmas Spike in Domestic Violence Keeps Courts Busy on New Year's Eve', *The Guardian*, 1 January 2014.

44 'Guidance Issued Under Section 182 of the *Licensing Act 2003*: Coming Into Force When Laid Before Parliament on 28 June 2007', Department for Culture, Media and Sport, UK Government, London, June 2007, p. 95.

45 Anthony Braga, Andrew Papachristos and David Hureau, 'Hot Spots Policing Effects on Crime', *Campbell Systematic Reviews*, Campbell Collaboration, Norway, 2012, p. 8.

46 Lizzie Dearden, 'How Technology is Allowing Police to Predict Where and When Crime Will Happen', *The Independent*, 7 October 2017.

47 Ronald Clarke and David Weisburd, 'Diffusion of Crime Control Benefits: Observations on the Reverse of Displacement', *Crime Prevention Studies*, vol. 2, 1994, pp. 165–84.

48 'Hot Spot Policing', *Crime Prevention Toolkit*, College of Policing, London and Anthony Braga et al., 'Hot Spots Policing Effects on Crime', p. 7.

49 'Understanding Problem-Oriented Policing', *Australian Institute of Criminology*, 13 January 2004.

50 Editorial, '*The Guardian* View on Stop and Search: Not a Solution', *The Guardian*, 12 August 2019.

51 'Hospital Admissions for Youths Assaulted with Sharp Objects Up Almost 60 Per Cent', NHS England, Department of Health and Social Care, UK Government, London, 9 February 2019.

52 Alastair Jamieson, 'Deadly Knife Crime: How Does London Compare to New York?', *Euronews*, 19 June 2019.

53 Lizzie Dearden, 'Knife Crime Rise "Linked to Youth Service Cuts", Parliamentary Report Finds', *The Independent*, 7 May 2019.

54 Rachel Schraer, 'Reality Check: What Has Happened to Police Numbers?', *BBC News*, 7 February 2018.

55 Grahame Allen and Yago Zayed, 'Police Service Strength', Briefing Paper No. 00634, House of Commons, UK Parliament, London, 31 July 2019, pp. 20–21.

56 'Crime Outcomes in England and Wales: Year Ending March 2018', Statistical Bulletin HOSB 10/18,

Home Office, UK Government, London, July 2018.

57 Thomas Mackintosh and Steve Swann, 'Domestic Violence Killings Reach Five-Year High', *BBC News*, 13 September 2019.

58 Sarah Marsh, 'Domestic Killings Will Not End if No Serious Action Taken: Refuge', *The Guardian*, 14 September 2019.

59 'Fact Check: Have Firearm Homicides and Suicides Dropped Since Port Arthur as a Result of John Howard's Reforms?', *ABC News*, 29 April 2016.

60 Matthew Schwartz, 'New Zealand Passes Law Banning Most Semi-Automatic Weapons', *National Public Radio*, 10 April 2019.

61 Jeremiah Mosteller, 'Militarisation of Police', Charles Kock Institute, Virginia, no date.

62 Jonathan Mummolo, 'Militarization Fails to Enhance Police Safety or Reduce Crime But May Harm Police Reputation', *Proceedings of the National Academy of Sciences of the United States of America*, vol. 115, no. 37, 2018, pp. 9181–6.

63 Laura Mercer Collar et al., 'Cardiff Model Toolkit: Community Guidance for Violence Prevention', Centers for Disease Control and Prevention, Atlanta, 2018.

64 'Cardiff Uni Anti-Crime Model Rolled Out in Australia', *BBC News*, 15 March 2016 and Peter Miller et al., 'Driving Change: A Partnership Study Protocol Using Shared Emergency Department Data to Reduce Alcohol-Related Harm', *Emergency Medicine Australasia*, 14 March 2019.

4: First Among Equals

1 'Maternity/Paternity Leave and Parental Leave', *Island.is*, no date.

2 'Gender Equality in Iceland', *The Official Gateway to Iceland*, Reykjavík, 2019 and Ingólfur V. Gíslason, 'Fathers on Leave Alone in Iceland: Normal Paternal Behaviour?' in Margaret O'Brien and Karen Wall (eds), *Comparative Perspectives on Work–Life Balance and Gender Equality: Fathers on Leave Alone*, Springer, New York, 2017, p. 149.

3 Klaus Schwab et al., 'The Global Gender Gap Report 2018', p. 18, and 'The Glass-Ceiling Index', *The Economist*, 8 March 2019.

4 History of Iceland and inheritance rights in Michael Chapman, 'Gender Equality in Iceland', *Guide to Iceland*, Reykjavík, 2017.

5 Nanna Gunnarsdóttir, '100 Years of Women Voting', *Guide to Iceland*.

6 Steven Johns, 'The Iceland Women's Strike, 1975', *LibCom.org*, 24 October 2016.

7 Kirstie Brewer, 'The Day Iceland's Women Went on Strike', *BBC News*, 23 October 2015.

8 'Icelandic Women Strike for Economic and Social Equality, 1975', *Global Nonviolent Action Database*, Swarthmore College, Pennsylvania, 2011.

9 Steven Johns, 'The Iceland Women's Strike, 1975'.

10 Annadis Rudolfsdottir, 'The Day the Women Went on Strike', *The Guardian*, 19 October 2005.

11 'The Best Place to Be a Woman', *Dateline*, SBS, Season 2019, episode 7, 23 April 2019.

12 'The 1975 Women's Strike: When 90 Per Cent of Icelandic Women Went on Strike to Protest Gender Inequality', *Iceland Magazine*, 24 October 2018.

13 There are multiple ways of measuring the gender pay gap, which are explored later in this chapter. This figure refers to the gap in average overall earnings, which is particularly large because women work in paid employment for fewer hours than men. The gap is smaller – though still significant – when considered on an hourly basis. For quotation, see 'Don't Change Women, Change the World!', *Kvennafrí 2018*, 21 October 2018.

14 'Global Gender Gap Report 2020', World Economic Forum, Geneva, 2020, p. 13.

15 Magnea Marinósdóttir and Rósa Erlingsdóttir, 'This Is Why Iceland Ranks First for Gender Equality', World Economic Forum, Geneva, 1 November 2017.

16 Klaus Schwab et al., 'The Global Gender Gap Report 2018', p. 121.

17 'Percentage of Women in National Parliaments, Ranking as of 1 September 2019', Inter-Parliamentary Union, Geneva, 2019 and Pamela Duncan and Mattha Busby, 'UK Elects Record Number of Female MPs', *The Guardian*, 13 December 2019.

18 Canada, the United Kingdom and Australia figures (p. 9), and the United States (p. 9 and p. 353), 'Global Gender Gap Report 2020'.

19 ibid., pp. 11–13.

20 ibid., p. 16.

21 'Gender Wage Gap, Employees, Percentage Points, 2017 or Latest Available', OECD, Paris, 2017.

22 'The Global Gender Gap Report 2020', pp. 5, 10.

23 DAC Network on Gender Equality, 'Women's Economic Empowerment: Issues Paper', OECD, Paris, 2011 and 'Gender Equality and the Environment: A Guide to UNEP's Work', United Nations Environment Programme, Nairobi, 2016, p. 4.

24 Joanna Barsh and Lareina Yee, 'Unlocking the Full Potential of Women in the US Economy', McKinsey & Company, 2011.

25 This point is also noted in 'Closing the Gender Gap – Act Now', OECD, Paris, 2012, p. 13.

26 Namita Datta, 'The Invisible Door: Three Barriers Limiting Women's Access to Work', World Bank Blogs, 8 March 2018.

27 Jonathan Woetzel et al., 'The Power of Parity: How Advancing Women's Equality Can Add $12 Trillion to Global Growth', McKinsey Global Institute, New York, September 2015.

28 Anna Aizer, 'The Gender Wage Gap and Domestic Violence', American Economic Review, vol. 100, no. 4, 2010, pp. 1847–59.

29 'Global Wage Report 2018/19: What Lies Behind Gender Pay Gaps', International Labour Organization, United Nations, Geneva, 2018, p. xv.

30 'The Pursuit of Gender Equality: An Uphill Battle', OECD, Paris, 2017, p. 17.

31 Twenty-six per cent from 'Don't Change Women, Change the World!', Kvennafrí 2018; 16 per cent from 'The Unadjusted Gender Pay Gap Around 16 Per Cent', Statistics Iceland, Reykjavík, 2016; median full-time earnings in 'Gender Wage Gap, Employees, Percentage Points, 2017 or Latest Available', OECD, Paris, 2017.

32 'The Gender Pay Gap Narrows', Statistics Iceland, Reykjavík, 7 March 2018, and Stefán Ólafsson, 'Iceland: Equal Pay Certification Legalised', ESPN Flash Report 2017/55, European Commission, Brussels, July 2017.

33 Jon Henley, '"Equality Won't Happen By Itself": How Iceland Got Tough on Gender Pay Gap', The Guardian, 20 February 2018.

34 Paul Fontaine, 'Poll: Most Icelanders Support Equal Pay Law', The Reykjavik Grapevine, 5 May 2017.

35 'The Best Place to Be a Woman', Dateline.

36 Women on government committees, councils and boards in 'Gender Equality in Iceland', Centre for Gender Equality, Reykjavík, 2012, p. 7; on private company boards in Thorgerdur Einarsdóttir, 'The Policy on Gender Equality in Iceland', European Parliament, Brussels, 2010, p. 7; on public company boards in Klaus Schwab et al., 'The Global Gender Gap Report 2018', p. 174; on boards of large companies in 'Proportion of Women as Board Members Unchanged Between Years', Statistics Iceland, Reykjavík, 9 May 2018.

37 ASX200 as at 2018 in 'Board Diversity Statistics', Australian Institute of Company Directors, 2018, and S&P 500 as at 2017 in '2017 Spencer Stuart US Board Index', Spencer Stuart, 2017, p. 3.

38 Vivian Hunt, Dennis Layton and Sara Prince, 'Diversity Matters', McKinsey and Company, 2015, p. 1.

39 'Maternity/Paternity Leave and Parental Leave', Island.is.

40 Ingólfur V. Gíslason, 'Fathers on Leave Alone in Iceland', p. 149.

41 Ásdís A. Arnalds et al., 'Equal Rights to Paid Parental Leave and Caring Fathers – The Case of Iceland', Icelandic Review of Politics and Administration, vol. 9, no. 2, 2013, pp. 323–44 and Noreena Hertz, 'Why Iceland is the Best Place in the World to Be A Woman', The Guardian, 25 October 2016.

42 See R. Kitterød, 'More Domestic Work and Less Paid Work Among Fathers of Young Children', in B. Brandth and E. Kvande (eds), Fedrekvoten og den farsvennlige velferdsstaten, Universitetsforlaget, Oslo, 2013, pp. 42–58; L. Nepomnyaschy and J. Waldfogel, 'Paternity Leave and Fathers' Involvement with Their Young Children', Community, Work & Family, vol. 10, no. 4, 2007, pp. 427–53;

M. Rege and I. Solli, *The Impact of Paternity Leave on Long-Term Father Involvement*, University of Stavanger, Stavanger, 2010; S. Tanaka and J. Waldfogel, 'Effects of Parental Leave and Work Hours on Fathers' Involvement With Their Babies: Evidence from the Millennium Cohort Study', *Community, Work & Family*, vol. 10, no. 4, 2007, pp. 409–26.

43   Leonid Bershidsky, 'No, Iceland Hasn't Solved the Gender Pay Gap', *Bloomberg*, 4 January 2018.

44   Andie Fontaine, 'Just in Time for the Holidays, Iceland Lengthens Parental Leave to 12 Months', *The Reykjavík Grapevine*, 18 December 2019.

45   Camilla Hedman, 'An Introduction to Icelandic Preschool Education', *Little Lives*, 18 September 2015, and 'Kindergarten Fees – Effective from January 1, 2019', City of Reykjavík, 2019.

46   'The Pursuit of Gender Equality: An Uphill Battle', OECD, pp. 33–4.

47   Workforce participation and STEM employment in Klaus Schwab et al., 'The Global Gender Gap Report 2018', p. 121.

48   Jóna G. Ingólfsdóttir et al, 'Family-Centered Services for Young Children with Intellectual Disabilities and Their Families: Theory, Policy and Practice', *Journal of Intellectual Disabilities*, vol. 22, no. 4, 2018, pp. 361–77.

49   Percentage of women who experience domestic violence at some point in their lives: Iceland, 22; Norway, 27; Sweden, 28; Finland and Denmark, 32. See 'Violence Against Women, Prevalence in the Lifetime, Percentage, 2014 or Latest Available', OECD, Paris, 2017. The 'Nordic paradox' is discussed in Anisha Chandar, 'A New Hope: Meet the Women Fighting Domestic Violence', *The Reykjavík Grapevine*, 14 July 2017.

50   'United Against Violence: Keeping the Window Open', Observatory of Public Sector Innovation, OECD, Paris.

51   Alda Hrönn Jóhannsdóttir, 'Domestic Violence Victims Need Help, Fast – In Iceland, They're Now Getting It', *Apolitical*, 22 September 2017.

52   'Gender Equality', OECD, Paris, 3 May 2018.

53   'The Pursuit of Gender Equality: An Uphill Battle', p. 28.

54   Andie Fontaine, 'Management Reluctantly Warming Up to Raising Minimum Wage in Iceland', *The Reykjavík Grapevine*, 11 October 2018.

55   Larissa Kyzer, 'Collective Agreement Opens Possibility for Shorter Work Week', *Iceland Review*, 5 April 2019.

56   Quoted in Jon Henley, '"Equality Won't Happen By Itself"'.

57   Magnea Marinósdóttir and Rósa Erlingsdóttir, 'This is Why Iceland Ranks First for Gender Equality'.

58   Quoted in Melissa Jun Rowley, 'What America Can Learn from Iceland About Gender Equality', *Forbes*, 8 March 2018.

59   Positive effects of highly involved fathers in Sarah Allen et al., 'The Effects of Father Involvement: An Updated Summary of the Research Evidence', Father Involvement Research Alliance, Centre for Families, Work & Well-Being, University of Guelph, Canada, 2007.

5: Multicultural Melting Pot

1   'Addressing Issues of Policing Refugee and Migrant Communities in Melbourne', Submission to Victoria Police, August 2013; 'Tackling Racism at a Broader Community Level', Submission to the Australian Human Rights Commission, May 2012; *Social Services Legislation Amendment (Encouraging Self-Sufficiency for Newly Arrived Migrants) Bill 2018*, Submission to the Senate Standing Committee on Community Affairs, 13 April 2018, all Brotherhood of St Laurence, Melbourne.

2   'Defining Moments: Evidence of First Peoples', National Museum of Australia, Canberra, 2019.

3   Henry Reynolds, *Forgotten War*, New South Books, Sydney, 2013.

4   'Australia's Immigration History', Australian National Maritime Museum, Sydney, 2019.

5   Australia's population: 'Table 1, Population by Sex, States and Territories, 1788 onwards', *3105.0.65.001 – Australian Historical Population Statistics*, Australian Bureau of Statistics, Canberra, 18 April 2019. Anti-Chinese sentiment: Tim Watts, *The Golden Country: Australia's Changing Identity*, Text Publishing, Melbourne, 2019, pp. 44–6.

6   Joanne Simon-Davies, 'Population and Migration Statistics in Australia', Australian Parliament House, Canberra, 7 December 2018.

7   Hansard, Parliament of Australia, Melbourne, 6 September 1901, pp. 4633–4.

8   ibid., 26 September 1901, p. 5223.

9   'Bulletin 4: Birthplace' in 'Census of Population and Housing, 30 June 1971', Commonwealth Bureau of Census and Statistics, Commonwealth of Australia, Canberra, p. 4.

10   Gough Whitlam quoted in Tim Watts, *The Golden Country*, p. 88.

11   'Fact Check: Does Australia Run the Most Generous Refugee Program Per Capita in the World?', *ABC News*, 23 February 2018.

12   These figures show the percentage of the population with a score of at least five on the International Standard Classification of Education (ISCED). People in this category have completed at least a short tertiary program. 'Settling In 2018: Main Indicators of Immigrant Integration', OECD and European Union, Brussels, 2018, p. 9.

13   George Megalogenis, 'The Rookie PMs: How Canberra's Leadership Circus is Damaging Ties with Asia', *Australian Foreign Affairs*, no. 5, February 2019, p. 74.

14   Joanne Simon-Davies, 'Population and Migration Statistics in Australia' and *3105.0.65.001 – Australian Historical Population Statistics*.

15   'Census 2016, Country of Birth of Person by Year of Arrival in Australia (Ranges)', Australian Bureau of Statistics, Canberra, 2017.

16   *3412.0 Migration, Australia 2017–18*, Australian Bureau of Statistics, Canberra, 3 April 2019 and 'Leading for Change: A Blueprint for Cultural Diversity', Australian Human Rights Commission, 2018, p. 7.

17   'Indicators of Immigrant Integration 2015: Settling In', OECD and European Union, Brussels, 2015, p. 41; James Button and Abul Rizvi, 'The Great Transformation: Hooked on Migration', *Griffith Review*, no. 61, 2018; 'Census 2016, Country of Birth of Person by Sex (LGA)', Australian Bureau of Statistics, Canberra, 2017.

18   George Megalogenis, 'The Rookie PMs', p. 74.

19   Andrew Markus, 'Mapping Social Cohesion: The Scanlon Foundation Surveys 2019', Scanlon Foundation, Melbourne, 2019, pp. 27, 31–2, 66–7 and Ana Gonzalez-Barrera and Phillip Connor, 'Around the World, More Say Immigrants Are a Strength Than a Burden', Pew Research Center, Washington, DC, March 2019, pp. 9, 17.

20   The mean PISA reading score for Australian-born students with Australian-born parents is 500, while the comparable score for Australian-born students with at least one foreign-born parent is 523. Thirty points equates to about one year of schooling. 'Settling In 2018', p. 27.

21   Tom Culley, 'Second-Generation Migrant Socio-Economic Outcomes Literature Review', Migrant Council Australia, Canberra, November 2015.

22   'Indicators of Immigrant Integration 2015', pp. 93, 115, 151 and 'Foreign-born Unemployment, Total, % of Foreign-born Labour Force, 2000–2017', OECD, Paris, 2018.

23   'Indicators of Immigrant Integration 2015', pp. 15, 17, 18.

24   Geoffrey Brahm Levey, 'National Identity and Diversity: Back to First Principles', *Griffith Review*, no. 61, July 2018.

25   Scott Morrison, 'Australia, The Land of Our Adoption', Address to the Menzies Centre for Australian Studies, King's College London, 24 January 2013.

26   'Language Spoken at Home – 2017 American Community Survey – 1 Year Estimates', United States Census Bureau, *American FactFinder*, 2018 and 'Migration und Integration', Statisches Bundesampt, 21 August 2019.

27   Percentages are calculated on the proportion of migrants in Australia from non-English-speaking countries. *3412.0 – Migration, Australia 2015–16*, 30 March 2017 and *2071.0 – Census of Population and Housing: Reflecting Australia – Stories from the Census, 2016*, 27 March 2018, both Australian Bureau of Statistics, Canberra.

28   'Dandenong North Primary School', Social Ventures Australia, 2019.

29 'Harmony Festival – Springvale Neighbourhood House', Cultural Diversity Week, Victorian Multicultural Commission, 2019 and 'Australia Day Festival Celebrates Community and Diversity', City of Greater Dandenong, Dandenong, 15 January 2019.

30 Harriet Spinks, 'Australia's Settlement Services for Migrants and Refugees', Research Paper No. 29 2008–09, Parliament of Australia, Canberra, 2009.

31 'Submission to the Joint Standing Committee on Migration', Australian Human Rights Commission, Sydney, 31 January 2017.

32 3222.0 – Population Projections, Australia, 2017 (base) – 2066, Australian Bureau of Statistics, Canberra, 22 November 2018 and 'Migrant Intake into Australia', Inquiry Report No. 77, Productivity Commission, Canberra, 2016, p. 2.

33 'Points Table for Skilled Independent Visa (Subclass 189)', Department of Home Affairs, Australian Government, Canberra, 2019.

34 Friedel Taube, 'Germany's New Immigration Laws Open Door for Skilled Labour', Deutsche Welle, 2 October 2018.

35 'Migrant Intake into Australia', pp. 13, 308–09.

36 'Export Income to Australia from International Education Activity in 2017', Research Snapshot, Department of Education and Training, Victorian Government, Melbourne, June 2018.

37 Philippa Stroud, Rhiannon Jones and Stephen Brien, Global People Movements, Legatum Institute, London, 2018, p. 7.

38 Michael Clemens, Claudio Montenegro and Lant Pritchett, The Place Premium: Wage Differences for Identical Workers Across the US Border, HKS Faculty Research Working Paper Series RWP09-04, John F. Kennedy School of Government, Harvard University, Cambridge, 2009 and 'Migration and Development: A Role for the World Bank', World Bank, Washington, DC, 2016, p. 9.

39 'World Migration Report 2018', International Organization for Migration, Geneva, 2018, p. 4.

40 Apple founder Steve Jobs was the son of a Syrian immigrant, Amazon CEO Jeff Bezos is a second-generation Cuban immigrant, Google founder Sergey Brin is a Russian immigrant and Facebook co-founder Eduardo Saverin is a Brazilian native. See Rani Molla, 'The Top US Tech Companies Founded by Immigrants Are Now Worth Nearly $4 Trillion', Vox, 12 January 2018 and Sara Salinas, 'More Than Half of the Top American Tech Companies Were Founded by Immigrants or the Children of Immigrants', CNBC, 30 May 2018.

41 'Immigrant Founders of the Fortune 500', Center for American Entrepreneurship, Washington, DC, 2017; 'Job Creators: The Immigrant Founders of Britain's Fastest Growing Businesses', The Entrepreneurs Network, London, 2019; Mariaclaudia Carella, 'Migrants and Startups: A Match Made in the EU', EU-Startups, 13 May 2019.

42 'World Migration Report 2018', Chapter 2.

43 Francesco Castelli, 'Drivers of Migration: Why Do People Move?', Journal of Travel Medicine, vol. 25, no. 1, 2018, pp. 1–7.

44 'World Migration Report 2020', p. 39.

45 Note that climate migration is mostly internal, with people not crossing borders. 'Groundswell: Preparing for Internal Climate Migration', World Bank, Washington, DC, 2018.

46 Andrew Markus, 'Mapping Social Cohesion', p. 2.

47 Rebecca Huntley, Australia Fair: Listening to the Nation, Quarterly Essay, no. 73, 2019, pp. 43, 45.

48 Sarah Martin, '$600bn of Spending Needed Over Next 15 Years, Infrastructure Australia Says', The Guardian, 13 August 2019 and 'An Assessment of Australia's Future Infrastructure Needs: The Australian Infrastructure Audit 2019', Infrastructure Australia, Sydney, June 2019, p. 7.

49 'Government at a Glance 2017', OECD, Paris, 2017, p. 215.

50 Rebecca Huntley, Still Lucky, Penguin Books, Melbourne, 2017, p. 100.

51 Rebecca Huntley, Still Lucky, p. 76 and Andrew Markus, 'Mapping Social Cohesion', p. 3.

52 Paul Keating, After Words: Post–Prime Ministerial Speeches, Allen & Unwin, Sydney, 2012.

53 Tim Watts, The Golden Country, pp. 184, 186.

54 Nick Baker, 'A History of Australia's Offshore Detention Policy', SBS, 20 February 2019 and Damien

Cave, 'A Timeline of Despair in Australia's Offshore Detention Centers', *The New York Times*, 26 June 2019.

55   John Howard, Address at the Federal Liberal Party Campaign Launch, Sydney, 28 October 2001.

56   Sara Dehm and Max Walden, 'Refugee Policy: A Cruel Bipartisanship' in Anika Gauja et al. (eds), *Double Disillusion: The 2016 Australian Federal Election*, ANU Press, Canberra, 2018.

57   Damien Cave, 'In Proudly Diverse Australia, White People Still Run Almost Everything', *The New York Times*, 10 April 2018.

58   Jarni Blakkarly, 'Australia's New Parliament Is No More Multicultural Than the Last One', *SBS News*, 21 May 2019 and The Data Journalism Team, 'Election 2019: Britain's Most Diverse Parliament', *BBC News*, 17 December 2019.

59   Dimitria Groutsis, Rae Cooper and Greg Whitwell, 'Beyond the Pale: Cultural Diversity on ASX100 Boards', University of Sydney, Sydney, 2018 and 'Capitalising on Culture and Gender in ASX Leadership', Diversity Council Australia, Sydney, 2019.

60   'Settling Better: Reforming Refugee Employment and Settlement Services', Centre for Policy Development, Sydney, 2017, pp. 5, 23.

61   James Button and Abul Rizvi, 'The Great Transformation'.

62   Charles Foran, 'The Canada Experiment: Is This the World's First "Postnational" Country?', *The Guardian*, 4 January 2017.

63   'Engaging the Public Productively: Strategies to Advance the Conversation about Comprehensive Immigration Reform' in *Building Public Understanding of Comprehensive Immigration Reform: A Communications Toolkit*, Frameworks Institute, Washington, DC, 2019.

64   'Settling In 2018', p. 21.

65   Andrew Markus, 'Mapping Social Cohesion', p. 66.

66   Geoffrey Brahm Levey, 'National Identity and Diversity' and Siew-Ean Khoo, Bob Birrell and Genevieve Heard, 'Intermarriage by Birthplace and Ancestry in Australia', *People and Place*, vol. 17, no. 1, 2009, pp. 15–28.

67   Siew-Ean Khoo, 'Intermarriage, Integration and Multiculturalism: A Demographic Perspective' in Michael Clyne and James Jupp (eds), *Multiculturalism and Integration: A Harmonious Relationship*, ANU Press, Canberra, 2011.

68   Valentina Romei, 'How Japan's Ageing Population is Shrinking GDP', *Financial Times*, 16 May 2018.

6:   Paradise in the Snow

1   Gunnar Garfors, *198: How I Ran Out of Countries*, Garfors Media, 2015 and *Ingenstad: On Tour to the World's Least Visited Countries*, Skald, 2019.

2   'The Inclusive Development Index 2018: Summary and Data Highlights', World Economic Forum, Geneva, 2018, pp. 18–22.

3   'Poverty Rate, Total, Ratio, 2017 or Latest Available', OECD, Paris, 2018.

4   'Gross Domestic Product (GDP), Total, US Dollars/Capita, 2018', OECD, Paris, 2018.

5   'The Inclusive Development Index 2018', pp. 18–22, '2019 Social Progress Initiative: Executive Summary', Social Progress Imperative, Washington, DC, 2019, p. 7; 'Human Development Indices and Indicators: 2018 Statistical Update', United Nations Development Programme, New York, 2018, p. 2; 'The Legatum Prosperity Index 2019', Legatum Institute, London, 2019, p. 14; 'Global Gender Gap Report 2020', World Economic Forum, Geneva, 2019, p. 9; John Hudson and Stefan Kühner, 'Fairness for Children: A League Table of Inequality in Child Well-being in Rich Countries', UNICEF Office of Research, Florence, 2016.

6   Fahmida Rahman and Daniel Tomlinson, 'Cross Countries: International Comparisons of Intergenerational Trends', Resolution Foundation, London, 2018, p. 41.

7   'Democracy Index 2018: Me Too? Political Participation, Protest and Democracy', Economist Intelligence Unit, London, 2019, pp. 36, 51–60 and 'Freedom in the World 2019', Freedom House, Washington, DC, 2019.

8   'Subjective wellbeing ranking': Finland has a happiness score of 7.769, Denmark 7.6 and Norway

7.554; see John Helliwell, Richard Layard and Jeffrey Sachs, 'World Happiness Report 2019', Sustainable Development Solutions Network, New York, 2019. 'General satisfaction rate': 'Life Satisfaction', Better Life Index, OECD, Paris, 2018.

9   'Average and Minimum Salary in Oslo, Norway', *Check in Price: News and Articles for Expats and Travelers*, 10 July 2019.

10   Anders Melin and Wei Lu, 'CEOs in US, India Earn the Most Compared with Average Workers', *The Economic Times*, 28 December 2018 and Ryan Derousseau, 'Why Do American CEOs Make Twice as Much as German CEOs?', *Fortune*, 4 November 2014.

11   'Trade Union', OECD, Paris, 2018.

12   Kristin Alsos, 'Norway: Quick Settlement in the 2017 Bargaining Round', European Foundation for the Improvement of Living and Working Conditions, Loughlinstown, 15 May 2017.

13   'Temporary Employment, Total, % of Dependent Employment, 2017 or Latest Available', OECD, Paris, 2018.

14   Johan Røed Steen, 'Norway: Provisions of Working Environment Act Come Into Effect', European Foundation for the Improvement of Living and Working Conditions, Loughlinstown, 23 September 2015.

15   Erik Engeland, 'Be Aware of the Strict Rules for Termination of Employment in Norway', *Magnus Legal*, 19 February 2019.

16   'Hours Worked, Total, Hours/Worker, 2018 or Latest Available', OECD, Paris, 2018.

17   Working hours in Norway and most OECD countries: 'LMF2.1: Usual Working Hours Per Week by Gender', 17 July 2018 and 'Incidence of Employment by Usual Weekly Hours Worked', 2018, both OECD, Paris. Overtime provisions: 'Working Time Regulations According to the Norwegian Labour Act', Tekna (Norwegian Society of Graduate Technical and Scientific Professionals), Oslo, 16 March 2015.

18   Figures represent GDP per hour worked. 'GDP Per Hour Worked, Total US Dollars, 2017 or Latest Available', OECD, Paris, 2018.

19   Eric Roberts, 'The Relationship Between Hours Worked and Productivity' and 'Factors Contributing to Decreased Productivity', *Crunch Mode: Programming to the Extreme*, no date and Marion Collewet and Jan Sauermann, 'Working Hours and Productivity', Discussion Paper Series, IZA DP No. 10722, IZA Institute of Labour Economics, Bonn, 2017.

20   Eleanor Ainge Roy, '"No Downside": New Zealand Firm Adopts Four-Day Week After Successful Trial', *The Guardian*, 2 October 2018 and James Purtill, 'Switching to a Four Day Working Week Could Make Us Happier and More Productive', *Hack*, Triple J, 21 February 2019.

21   'Unemployment Benefits', Norwegian Labour and Welfare Administration, 27 June 2019 and 21 February 2019.

22   Thomas Lorentzen and Espen Dahl, 'Active Labour Market Programs in Norway: Are They Helpful for Social Assistance Recipients?', *Journal of European Social Policy*, vol. 15, no. 1, 2005, pp. 27–45.

23   'Long Term Unemployment Rate, Total, % of Unemployed, 2018 or Latest Available', OECD, Paris, 2018.

24   Maddison Stoff, 'Dole-Bludgers, Leaners and Other Neoliberal Fantasies', *Overland*, 19 January 2017 and Florence Sutcliffe-Braithwaite, 'Margaret Thatcher, Individualism and the Welfare State', *History & Policy*, 15 April 2013.

25   'Employment Rate, Total, % of Working Age Population, Q2 2019 or latest available' and 'Unemployment Rate, Total, % of Labour Force, Q4 2018 or Latest Available', both OECD, Paris, 2018.

26   Schwab et al., 'The Global Gender Gap Report 2018', p. 211 and 'Gender Wage Gap, Employees, Percentage Points, 2017 or Latest Available', OECD, Paris, 2018.

27   'Norway – Overview of the Education System (EAG 2018)', Education GPS, OECD, Paris, 2018, and 'Norway', Better Life Index.

28   Gemma Corrigan, 'Lessons from Norway, the World's Most Inclusive Economy', World Economic Forum, Geneva, 12 April 2017 and Elin Kvande and Berit Brandth, 'Fathers on Leave Alone in Norway: Changes and Continuities' in Margaret O'Brien and Karin Wall (eds), *Contemporary*

Perspectives on Work–Life Balance and Gender Equality, Springer, New York, 2017, pp. 29–44.

29   'Early Childhood Education and Care', Ministry of Education and Research, Government of Norway, 25 November 2014.

30   98.5 per cent of all expenditure on education is public. For student–teacher ratio, see 'Norway – Overview of the Education System (EAG 2018)', OECD Education GPS, OECD, Paris, 2018. For educational outcomes, see 'PISA 2018 Results (Volume I): What Students Know and Can Do', OECD, Paris, 2019, p. 17.

31   Lina Gjerde quoted in George Lorenzo, 'How Post-Collegiate Life in Scandinavia Compares to the US', *Fast Company*, 30 July 2015.

32   Population living on less than US$1.90 per day (figures from 2011 and in US dollars, adjusted for purchasing power parity, p. 23) and decline in extreme poverty (p. 1) in 'Poverty and Shared Prosperity 2018: Piecing Together the Poverty Puzzle', World Bank, Washington, DC, 2018.

33   'Five Shocking Facts About Extreme Global Inequality and How to Even it Up', Oxfam, Nairobi, 2019.

34   Facundo Alvaredo et al. (eds), 'World Inequality Report 2018', World Inequality Lab, Paris School of Economics, Paris, 2018 and 'Humanity Divided: Confronting Inequality in Developing Countries', United Nations Development Programme, New York, 2013, p. 64.

35   'Does Economic Inequality Hurt Economic Growth?', OECD, Paris, December 2014.

36   Ben Geier, 'Even the IMF Now Admits Neoliberalism Has Failed', *Fortune*, 3 June 2016.

37   David Vandivier, 'What is the Great Gatsby Curve?', The White House, Washington, DC, 11 June 2013.

38   Orsetta Causa and Mikkel Hermansen, 'Income Redistribution Through Taxes and Transfers Across OECD Countries', OECD Economics Department Working Papers, Working Paper No. 1453, 22 July 2019, pp. 30–1.

39   This after-tax figure might seem low to some, but it's important to consider that it is the average of everyone in the country regardless of whether they work – from babies through to the very elderly. It is an after-tax figure that also includes benefits paid by government, and it's adjusted for 'purchasing power parity' to make sure there's a fair comparison across countries.

40   'IMF Fiscal Monitor: Tackling Inequality, October 2017', International Monetary Fund, Washington, DC, October 2017, p. 13 and 'Higher Taxes Can Lower Inequality Without Denting Economic Growth', *The Economist*, 19 October 2017. For support among economists, see Peter Diamond and Emmanuel Saez, *The Case for a Progressive Tax: From Basic Research to Policy Recommendations*, CESifo Working Paper No. 3548, CESifo, Munich, August 2011.

41   Peter Diamond and Emmanuel Saez, 'The Case for a Progressive Tax: From Basic Research to Policy Recommendations', CESifo Working Paper No. 3548, CESifo, 2011.

42   Dan Ariely, 'Americans Want to Live in a Much More Equal Country (They Just Don't Realise It)', *The Atlantic*, 2 August 2012 and Michael Norton and Dan Ariely, 'Building a Better America – One Wealth Quintile at a Time', *Perspectives on Psychological Science*, vol. 6, no. 1, 2011, pp. 9–12. See also Questions 25–29 in 'Fox News Poll Document 1/30/19', Fox News, New York, 1 January 2019.

43   Ida Irene Bergstrøm, 'The History of Norwegian Equality', *Kilden*, 27 September 2013.

44   'Society at a Glance 2016', OECD, Paris, 2016, p. 129.

45   Ricardo Perez-Truglia, 'The Effects of Income Transparency on Well-being: Evidence from a Natural Experiment', Social Science Resource Network, New York, 23 February 2019.

46   'Tax Revenue, % of GDP, 2017 or Latest Available', OECD, Paris, 2017.

47   'All-in Average Personal Income Tax Rates at Average Wage by Family Type', OECD, Paris, 2017.

48   'General Government Spending, % of GDP, 2018 or Latest Available', OECD, Paris, 2018.

49   'Production of Crude Oil Including Lease Condensate', International Energy Statistics, United States Energy Information Administration, Washington, DC, no date.

50   Paul Cleary, *Trillion Dollar Baby: How Norway Beat the Oil Giants and Won a Lasting Fortune*, Black Inc., Melbourne, 2016 and Mikael Holter, 'Oil Tax on the Table in Norway's Government Coalition Talks', *Bloomberg*, 6 November 2018.

51   'The Government's Revenues', Norwegian Petroleum Directorate, Storting, 3 October 2019.

52 'General Government Deficit, Total, % of GDP, 1970–2018', OECD, Paris, 2018.

53 Eshe Nelson, 'How Norway's Sovereign Wealth Fund Made $130 Billion in One Year', World Economic Forum, Geneva, 5 March 2018.

54 Natural resources as a curse, see Peter Hartcher, 'Heed the Curse of a Lucky Country', *The Sydney Morning Herald*, 9 May 2008; economic growth in Jeffrey Sachs and Andrew Warner, 'Natural Resource Abundance and Economic Growth', National Bureau of Economic Research, Working Paper 5398, December 1995; researchers' observations in Richard Auty, *Sustaining Development in Mineral Economies: The Resource Curse Thesis*, Routledge, London, 1993.

55 Joseph Stiglitz, 'Making Natural Resources Into a Blessing Rather Than a Curse' in Svetlana Tsalik and Anya Schiffrin (eds), *Covering Oil: A Reporter's Guide to Energy and Development*, The Open Society Institute, New York, 2005, pp. 13–20.

56 Jim Minifie, 'How We Spent the Mining Bounty We Should Have Saved', *The Australian Financial Review*, 29 July 2013.

57 Paul Leo Eckbo, 'Regulatory Intentions and Realities: The Case of the Norwegian Oil Industry' in Terry Barker and Vladamir Brailovsky (eds), *Oil or Industry? Energy, Industrialisation and Economic Policy in Canada, Mexico, the Netherlands, Norway and the United Kingdom*, Academic Press, London, 1981, p. 280.

58 'Foreign-Born Population, Total, % of the Population', OECD, Paris, 2018.

59 'Immigrants and Norwegian-born to Immigrant Parents, 1 January 2017', *Statistics Norway*, 11 September 2017.

60 Rise in anti-immigration sentiment: Thomas Hylland Eriksen, 'Immigration and National Identity in Norway', Migration Policy Institute, Washington, DC, March 2013. The 2017 election results: Johan Bjerkem, 'The Norwegian Progress Party: An Established Populist Party', *European View*, vol. 15, no. 2, 1 December 2016.

61 'Immigration Tests the Welfare State', *News in English: Views and News from Norway*, 2 February 2017 and David Nikel, 'Asylum Applications Lowest in 22 Years', *Life in Norway*, 18 July 2019.

62 Maddy Savage, 'Unlike Most Millennials, Norway's Are Rich', *BBC*, 10 July 2018.

63 Gunn Elisabeth Berkelund, Kristian Heggebø and Jon Rogstad, 'Additive or Multiplicative Disadvantage? The Scarring Effects of Unemployment for Ethnic Minorities', *European Sociological Review*, vol. 33, no. 1, 2017, pp. 17–29.

64 Hannah McKinnon et al., 'The Sky's Limit Norway: Why Norway Should Lead the Way in a Managed Decline of Oil and Gas Extraction', Oil Change International, Washington, DC, 2017.

65 Damian Carrington, '"Historic Breakthough": Norway's Giant Oil Fund Dives Into Renewables', *The Guardian*, 6 April 2019 and Senay Boztas, 'A Future After Oil and Gas? Norway's Fossil-Free Energy Startups', *The Guardian*, 28 March 2017.

66 Mikael Holter, 'Norway is Walking Away From Billions of Barrels of Oil', *Bloomberg*, 8 April 2019.

67 'The Global Fleet Revealed', *The Maritime Executive*, 5 November 2017.

68 'Equity in Education: Breaking Down Barriers to Social Mobility', OECD, Paris, 2018, p. 27 and Sarah Butrymowicz, 'Is Estonia the New Finland?', *The Atlantic*, 23 June 2016.

69 Klaus Schwab, 'The Global Competitiveness Report 2019', World Economic Forum, Geneva, 2019, pp. xi, xiii.

70 'Petroleum Fund Annual Report: Financial Year 2017', Ministry of Finance, Democratic Republic of Timor-Leste, 2018.

7: From Dictatorship to Democracy

1 Indonesia's uprising: 'The May Riots', *Inside Indonesia*, Digest no. 61, 29 May 1998; Nurfika Osman and Ulma Haryanto, 'Still No Answers, or Peace, For Many Rape Victims', *Jakarta Globe*, 14 May 2010; 'Indonesia: Five Years After May 1998 Riots, Those Responsible for the Atrocities Remain at Large', Asian Human Rights Commission, Hong Kong, 7 April 2003.

2 '1997–98 Asian Financial Crisis in Indonesia', *Facts and Details*, 2019 and 'Asian Financial Crisis in Indonesia', *Indonesia Investments*, 2019.

3 William Liddle, *The 1977 Indonesian and New Order Legitimacy*, South East Asian Affairs, Jakarta, 1978 and Adrian Vickers, *A History of Modern Indonesia*, Cambridge University Press, Cambridge, 2005.

4 Thushara Dibley, 'Orphans No More', *Inside Indonesia*, no. 56, October–December 1998.

5 'Indonesia' in 'Freedom in the World 2019', Freedom House, Washington, DC, 2019.

6 Ben Bland and Stephen Hutchings, 'Indonesia's Incredible Elections', The Lowy Institute, Sydney, 2019.

7 Rosamond Hutt, 'These Are the Countries with the Highest Voter Turnout', World Economic Forum, Geneva, 7 November 2018 and 'Election Results 2019: Analysis in Maps and Charts', *BBC News*, 13 December 2019.

8 Between 1974 and 1999, there were 102,800 conflict-related deaths in East Timor, including 18,600 killings and 84,200 deaths due to hunger and illness. See 'Timor Leste: Executive Summary' in 'Chega! The Report of the Commission for Reception, Truth and Reconciliation', The Commission for Reception, Truth and Reconciliation Timor-Leste, Dili, 2005, p. 44.

9 John Gittings, 'Suharto', *The Guardian*, 28 January 2008.

10 Edward Aspinall and Mark Berger, 'The Break-Up of Indonesia? Nationalisms After Decolonisation and the Limits of the Nation-State in Post–Cold War Southeast Asia', *Third World Quarterly*, vol. 22, no. 6, 2001, pp. 1003–24.

11 Dan Slater, 'Party Cartelization, Indonesia Style: Presidential Power-Sharing and the Contingency of Democratic Opposition', *Journal of East Asian Studies*, vol. 18, no. 1, 2018, pp. 23–46.

12 The exception is the province of Aceh, in which local parties are allowed. See Ben Hillman, 'Ethnic Politics and Local Political Parties in Indonesia', *Asian Ethnicity*, vol. 13, no. 4, 2012, pp. 419–40.

13 Simon Butt and Tim Lindsey, *Indonesian Law*, Oxford University Press, Oxford, 2018, p. 104.

14 'New Zealand Best, Indonesia Worst in World Poll of International Corruption', Transparency International, Berlin, 15 July 1995.

15 Jonah Blank, 'How the (Once) Most Corrupt Country in the World Got Clean(er)', *The Atlantic*, 2 May 2019.

16 'Corruption Perceptions Index 2018', Transparency International, Berlin, 2019.

17 Isobel Coleman and Terra Lawson-Remer, 'A Users' Guide to Democratic Transitions: A How-To Guide for Reformers Around the World', *Foreign Policy*, 18 June 2013.

18 Edward Aspinall, 'Indonesia: The Irony of Success', *Journal of Democracy*, vol. 21, no. 2, 2010, pp. 27, 28–29.

19 ibid., p. 24.

20 'Indonesia 2017/18', Amnesty International, London, 2019 and 'Indonesia: Police and Military Unlawfully Kill Almost 100 People in Papua in Eight Years with Near-total Impunity,' *Amnesty International*, 2 July 2018.

21 Edward Aspinall, 'Indonesia', p. 24.

22 'Methodology 2019' in 'Freedom in the World 2019'.

23 'Indonesia', *The World Fact Book*, Central Intelligence Agency, 2019.

24 Edward Aspinall, 'Indonesia', p. 30.

25 Farabi Fakih, 'Indonesia Elections: What Does Jokowi's Re-Election Mean for the Rise of Political Islam?', *Economic and Political Weekly*, vol. 54, no. 26–27, 29 June 2019. See also Rizky Alif Alvian, 'Political Islam Navigates and Changes Indonesia's Democratic Landscape', *The Conversation*, 18 October 2018.

26 'Indonesia's Social Media Landscape: An Overview', *Greenhouse*, 15 May 2019.

27 'Percentage of Women in National Parliaments – Ranking as of 1 September 2019', Inter-Parliamentary Union, Geneva, 2019.

28 Matt Cole, 'Britain's Road to Democracy: Slow and Not Always Steady', *History Extra*, 7 June 2017.

29 'Democracy Index 2018: Me Too? Political Participation, Protest and Democracy', The Economist Intelligence Unit, London, 2019, p. 2.

30 Larry Diamond, 'The Democratic Rollback: The Resurgence of the Predatory State', *Foreign Affairs*, vol. 87, no. 2, 2008, pp. 36–48.

31 'Democracy Index 2017: Free Speech Under Attack', The Economist Intelligence Unit, London, 2018 and 'Freedom in the World 2018', Freedom House, Washington, DC, 2018.

32 Edward Luce, *The Retreat of Western Liberalism*, Little, Brown, London, 2017.

33 Michiko Kakutani, 'In *The Retreat of Western Liberalism*, How Democracy is Defeating Itself', *The New York Times*, 19 June 2017.

34 Democracies less likely to go to war: Dan Reiter, 'Democratic Peace Theory', *Oxford Bibliographies*, 25 October 2012. Average annual income: Max Roser, 'Democracy', *Our World in Data*, 2018.

35 Daron Acemoglu et al., 'Does Democracy Cause Growth?', *Journal of Political Economy*, vol. 127, no. 1, 2019, pp. 47–100.

36 Carl Henrik Knutsen, 'Democracy and Economic Growth: A Survey of Arguments and Results', *International Area Studies Review*, vol. 15, no. 4, 2012 and Joseph Siegle et al., 'Why Democracies Excel', *Foreign Affairs*, 1 September 2004.

37 Michael Ross, 'Does Oil Hinder Democracy?', *World Politics*, vol. 53, no. 3, 2001, pp. 325–61.

38 Charles Rowley and Nathanael Smith, 'Islam's Democracy Paradox: Muslims Claim to Like Democracy, So Why Do They Have So Little?', *Public Choice*, vol. 193, no. 3/4, 2009, pp. 273–99.

39 Barbara Geddes, 'What Causes Democratisation?', *The Oxford Handbook of Political Science*, July 2011; Eduardo Aleman and Yeaji Kim, 'The Democratizing Effect of Education', *Research and Politics*, October–December 2015, pp. 1–7; Edward Glaeser et al., 'Why Does Democracy Need Education?', *Journal of Economic Growth*, no. 12, 2007, pp. 77–99.

40 Study of forty democracies: Jonathan Krieckhaus et al., 'Economic Inequality and Democratic Support', *The Journal of Politics*, vol. 76, no. 1, 2013, pp. 139–51. Implications of excessive financial inequality: Robert Anderson, 'Inequality, Democracy and Redistribution', Paper Presented to Expert Group Meeting on Inequality and Its Impacts, United Nations, New York, 2018. 'Flawed democracies': 'Democracy Index 2018'.

41 Ina Kubbe and Annika Engelbert, 'Corruption and the Impact of Democracy', *Crime, Law and Social Change*, vol. 70, no. 2, 2018, pp. 175–8.

42 UK: Matthew Flinders, 'MPs' Expenses: The Legacy of a Scandal', *BBC News*, 7 May 2019. US: Alex Schultz and Jay Willis, 'How Trump Corrupted the American Presidency in Every Imaginable Way', *GQ*, 1 November 2019. Australia: Eddie Obeid was convicted for misconduct in public office; see Lucy Carter and Kathleen Calderwood, 'Eddie Obeid Sentenced to Five Years' Jail for Misconduct in Public Office', *ABC News*, 16 December 2016. Damien Mantach was sentenced to five years' jail for taking more than $1.5 million from the party's finances; see Sarah Farnsworth, 'Damien Mantach: Victorian Liberal Party Ex-Director Jailed for Stealing $1.5m from Party Coffers', *ABC News*, 19 July 2016.

43 Sean Lynn-Jones, 'Why the United States Should Spread Democracy', Discussion Paper, Belfer Center for Science and International Affairs, Harvard Kennedy School, Harvard University, Cambridge, March 1998.

44 Max Walden, 'Indonesian Election Likely to be Plagued by Vote Buying, Marginalised Voters and Accusations of Electoral Fraud', *ABC News*, 24 April 2019.

45 Emma Connors, 'Indonesia Guts Corruption Watchdog with "Dirty" New Law', *Australian Financial Review*, 1 November 2019.

46 'Indonesia' in 'Freedom in the World 2019' and Alan Weedon, 'West Papua's in the Grip of an "Unprecedented Crisis" – Is Australia Turning a Blind Eye?', *ABC News*, 6 October 2019.

47 Stephan Haggard, *The Political Economy of Democratic Transitions*, Princeton University Press, Princeton, 1995.

48 Isobel Coleman and Terra Lawson-Remer, 'A User's Guide to Democratic Transitions'.

49 Milan Svolik, 'Authoritarian Reversals and Democratic Consolidation', *American Political Science Review*, vol. 102, no. 20, May 2008, pp. 153–68.

8: Winning from Globalisation

1 '"Baywatch Bobbies"' on Beach Patrol off the Dorset Coast', *Daily Mail*, 4 August 2012, and 'Dorset Police Case Study', 'Uvex Solves Boot Problem for Hochtief Murphy on Crossrail Project', 'Uvex Removes Denby Pottery's PPE Concerns', all Uvex, Bonn, no date.

2 'Air and Greenhouse Gas Emissions, Carbon Dioxide (CO_2), Million Tonnes, 1990–2001', OECD, Paris, 2018 and Ralph Bueller et al., 'How Germany Became Europe's Green Leader: A Look at Four Decades of Sustainable Policymaking', *Solutions*, vol. 2, no. 5, 2011, pp. 51–63.

3 'Uvex Is Again One of Germany's Best Employers', Uvex, Bonn, no date.

4 Evert-jan Quak, 'The Race to the Bottom Explained', *The Broker*, 18 December 2015.

5 See David Autor et al., 'The China Syndrome: Local Labor Market Effects of Import Competition in the United States', *American Economic Review*, vol. 103, no. 6, 2013, pp. 2121–68 and Mariya Mileva et al., 'The Effects of Globalisation on Wage Inequality: New Insights from a Dynamic Trade Model with Heterogeneous Firms', Working Paper No. 49, WWW for Europe, December 2013.

6 'Value Added by Activity, Manufacturing, % of Value Added, 1992–2018', OECD, Paris, 2018 and Susan Helper et al., 'Why Does Manufacturing Matter? Which Manufacturing Matters?: A Policy Framework', Brookings Institution, February 2012.

7 Max Opray, 'Holden On: Can Adelaide Shift Gears After the Loss of its Car Industry?', *The Guardian*, 11 April 2018 and Josh Boak, 'For Many Factory Towns Such as Erie, White Collar Job Loss Hurts the Most', *The Morning Call*, 12 March 2018.

8 See Robert Reich, 'Manufacturing Jobs Are Never Coming Back', *Forbes*, 28 May 2009 and Jagdish Bhagwati, 'The Manufacturing Fallacy', *Project Syndicate*, 27 August 2010.

9 Susan Helper et al., 'Why Does Manufacturing Matter?', pp. 1, 14.

10 'World Economic Outlook, April 2018: Cyclical Upswing, Structural Change', International Monetary Fund, Washington, DC, 2018.

11 'Value Added by Activity, Manufacturing, % of Value Added, 2017 or Latest Available', OECD, Paris, 2018.

12 Quoted in Stephen Dubner, 'What Are the Secrets of the German Economy – and Should We Steal Them?', *Freakonomics Radio*, Episode 304, 11 October 2017.

13 'Tax Revenue, Total, % of GDP, 2018 or Latest Available' and 'Tax on Corporate Profits, Total, % of Taxation, 2018 or Latest Available', OECD, Paris, 2019.

14 'Effective Tax Rates', OECD, Paris, 2018.

15 Wolfgang Dauth et al., 'The Rise of the East and the Far East: German Labor Markets and Trade Integration', IAB Discussion Paper 16/2012, Institute for Employment Research, Nuremberg, 2012, p. 8.

16 Export rate and Zettelmeyer's comments in Stephen Dubner, 'What Are the Secrets of the German Economy – and Should We Steal Them?'.

17 'Current Account Balance (BOP, Current US$)', World Bank, Washington, DC, 2018.

18 Jared Bernstein and Dean Baker, 'Why Trade Deficits Matter', *The Atlantic*, 8 December 2016.

19 'International Investment Position', US Bureau of Economic Analysis, Maryland, 30 September 2019.

20 Joseph Gagnon, 'The Unsustainable Trajectory of US International Debt', Petersen Institute for International Economics, 29 March 2017.

21 Catherin Schaer, 'Secrets of German SME Success Revealed', *Handelsblatt Today*, 2 March 2018.

22 'Labour Cost Comparison Across EU Countries (Annual Estimate of Labour Costs)', Federal Statistical Office of Germany, Wiesbaden, 7 May 2019.

23 Quoted in Stephen Dubner, 'What Are the Secrets of the German Economy – and Should We Steal Them?'

24 'German Corporate Governance Code 2019', Government Commission, Frankfurt, 9 May 2019, p. 1.

25 David Block and Anne-Marie Gerstner, 'One-Tier vs. Two-Tier Board Structure: A Comparison Between the United States and Germany', Comparative Corporate Governance and Financial Regulation, Select Seminar Papers, Spring 2016.

26 David Block and Anne-Marie Gerstner, 'One-Tier vs. Two-Tier Board Structure'.

27 Dalia Marin, *Germany is Not Volkswagen*, Bruegel, Brussels, 12 October 2015 and Esteban

Ortiz-Ospina and Max Roser, 'Trust', *Our World in Data*, Oxford, 2018.

28 David Block and Anne-Marie Gerstner, 'One-Tier vs. Two-Tier Board Structure', p. 39 and 'Why Germany's Current Account Surplus is Bad for the World Economy', *The Economist*, 8 July 2017.

29 Anders Melin and Wei Lu, 'CEOs in US, India Earn the Most Compared with Average Workers', *The Economic Times*, 28 December 2018 and Ryan Derousseau, 'Why Do American CEOs Make Twice as Much as German CEOs?', *Fortune*, 4 November 2014.

30 Zettelmeyer quotations in this and previous paragraph in Stephen Dubner, 'What Are the Secrets of the German Economy – and Should We Steal Them?'

31 Josie Misko, 'Vocational Education and Training in Australia, the United Kingdom and Germany', National Centre for Vocational Education Research, Adelaide, 2006, p. 22.

32 'What is Kurzarbeit?', *eZonomics*, ING Think Tank, online, 24 November 2009.

33 'Employment Outlook 2009 – How Does Germany Compare?', OECD, Paris, 2018.

34 Jack Ewing, 'In Germany, A Broad Recovery is Under Way', *The New York Times*, 3 August 2010.

35 'Employment Outlook 2009 – How Does Germany Compare?' and 'Unemployment Rate, Total, % of Labour Force, Q1 2006 – Q1 2011', OECD, Paris, 2012.

36 See Charles Wessner, 'How Does Germany Do It?', The American Society of Mechanical Engineers, New York, 13 November 2013.

37 'Facts and Figures', Fraunhofer Society, Munich, 31 March 2019 and Charles Wessner, 'How Does Germany Do It?'

38 Charles Wessner, 'How Does Germany Do It?'

39 'Gross Domestic Spending on R&D, Total, % of GDP, 2018 or Latest Available', OECD, Paris, 2019.

40 'Innovation Policy', Federal Ministry for Economic Affairs and Energy, Government of Germany, Berlin, 2019 and Neil Savage, 'How Germany Is Winning at Turning Its Research to Commercialisation', *Nature Career Guide*, Germany, 27 March 2019.

41 Charles Wessner, 'How Does Germany Do It?'

42 Neil Savage, 'How Germany Is Winning at Turning Its Research to Commercialisation'.

43 Olaf Storbeck, 'German Mittelstand Faces Battle to Overcome Skills Shortages', *Financial Times*, 7 January 2019.

44 'Population Ages 65 and Above (% of Total Population) – Germany', World Bank, Washington, DC, 2019 and Jeff Desjardins, 'Germany Will Hit a Significant Demographic Milestone Over the Next Year', World Economic Forum, Geneva, 18 January 2018.

45 'Study: Germany Needs 260,000 Immigrants a Year to Meet Labour Demand', 12 February 2019 and Friedel Taube, 'Germany's New Immigration Laws Open Door for Skilled Labour', 2 October 2018, both *Deutsche Welle*.

46 Astrid Krenz, Klaus Prettner and Holger Strulik, 'Robots, Reshoring and the Lot of Low-Skilled Workers', Centre for European Governance and Economic Development Research, Discussion Paper No. 351, July 2018.

47 James Shotter and Lindsay Whipp, 'Robot Revolution Helps Adidas Bring Shoemaking Back to Germany', *Financial Times*, 8 June 2016.

48 Jesus Felipe, Aashish Mehta and Changyong Rhee, 'The Manufacturing Conundrum', *World Bank Blogs*, 18 February 2015.

49 Kira Schacht and Olaya Argüeso, 'Germany's Minimum Wage is Barely Above the Poverty Line', *Deutsche Welle*, 1 January 2019.

50 'Digital Personal Protective Equipment: Uvex Techware', Uvex, Fürth, 17 October 2017.

9: Urban Revival

1 Mark Muro and Sifan Liu, 'Tech in Metros: The Strong Are Getting Stronger', Brookings Institution, Washington, DC, 8 March 2017.

2 Startup hub rankings, venture capital and angel investment in Richard Florida and Ian Hathaway, *Rise of the Global Startup City: The New Map of Entrepreneurship and Venture Capital*, Center for American Entrepreneurship, October 2018, pp. 40, 49, 55.

3   Gross household disposable income in the United States was US$50,203 in 2017, ahead of the next highest in the OECD, Luxembourg, which has household disposable income of US$44,446. 'Household Disposable Income, Gross Adjusted, US Dollars/Capita, 2018 or Latest Available', OECD, Paris, 2018.

4   See also Bruce Katz and Julie Wagner, 'The Rise of Innovation Districts: A New Geography of Innovation in America', Brookings Institution, Washington, DC, May 2014, p. 1.

5   History of innovation based on Heather Whipps, 'A Brief History of US Innovation', *Live Science*, 4 August 2009; Ufuk Akcigit, John Grigsby and Tom Nicholas, 'When America Was Most Innovative, and Why', *Harvard Business Review*, 6 March 2017; Kirk Long, '20 Immigrants and Refugee Scientists Who Made America Greater (Part 1)', *StarTalk*, 26 February 2017; Corey Protin, Matthew Stuart and Matt Weinberger, 'Animated Timeline Shows How Silicon Valley Became a $2.8 Trillion Neighbourhood', *Business Insider Australia*, 30 May 2017; Stuart Leslie, 'The Biggest "Angel" of Them All: The Military and the Making of Silicon Valley' in Martin Kenney (ed.), *Understanding Silicon Valley: The Anatomy of an Entrepreneurial Region*, Stanford University Press, Palo Alto, 2000, p. 49; 'Bristol-Myers Squibb Breaks Ground on New Biologics Manufacturing Facility in Massachusetts', Bristol-Myers Squibb, New York, 2 May 2007; Priyanka Dayal McCluskey, 'Mass. Leads Nation in Life Sciences Jobs, Says Report', *The Boston Globe*, 18 June 2014.

6   Shawna Vogel, 'An MIT Inventor's Guide to Startups: For Faculty and Students', MIT Technology Licensing Office, Massachusetts Institute of Technology, 2010, p. 23.

7   Benjamin Swasey, Daigo Fujiwara and Ally Jarmanning, 'The Biotech Boom: By the Numbers', *WBUR*, 4 June 2018.

8   '68% of the World Population Projected to Live in Urban Areas by 2050, says UN', United Nations Department of Economic and Social Affairs, New York, 16 May 2018.

9   'Nations Are No Longer Driving Globalisation – Cities Are', *QZ*, 3 May 2013.

10 'Executing an Open Innovation Model: Cooperation is Key to Competition for Biopharmaceutical Companies', Deloitte, New York, 2015.

11 Luke Hendrickson et al., 'The Employment Dynamics of Australian Entrepreneurship', Research Paper 4/25, Office of the Chief Economist, Department of Industry, Innovation and Science, Canberra, 2015, and 'Small Business Administration and Job Creation', Congressional Research Service, Washington, DC, 20 December 2018, p. 11.

12 'Global Startup Ecosystem Report 2019', Startup Genome, San Francisco, 2019, p. 12.

13 Klaus Schwab, 'The Global Competitiveness Report 2019', World Economic Forum, Switzerland, 2018, p. 585.

14 'Tech Cities in Motion', Savills World Research, London, 2019 and 'Global Startup Ecosystem Report 2019', p. 12.

15 Venture capital investment patterns and figures in Richard Florida and Ian Hathaway, *Rise of the Global Startup City*, pp. 8, 10, 11, 44.

16 'Cream City Labs – Inspiring Innovation', Northwestern Mutual, Milwaukee, 2018 and Alan Lally, 'Philanthropy's Role in Detroit's Revitalisation', *Learning to Give*, no date.

17 Klaus Schwab, 'The Global Competitiveness Report 2018', p. 11.

18 Mariana Mazzucato, *The Entrepreneurial State: Debunking Public vs. Private Sector Myths* (revised edition), Public Affairs, New York, 2013, p. 6.

19 'About DARPA', Defense Advanced Research Projects Agency, Arlington, no date.

20 Mariana Mazzucato, *The Entrepreneurial State*, p. 6.

21 'About SBIR', SBIR-STTR: America's Seed Fund, Alexandria, no date.

22 Philip Auerswald and Lewis Branscomb, 'Valleys of Death and Darwinian Seas: Financing the Invention to Innovation Transition in the United States', *The Journal of Technology Transfer*, vol. 28, no. 3–4, 2003, pp. 227–39.

23 'About SBIR' and Sarah Russell and Tim Finerty, 'Money on the Table: Taking Advantage of the R&E Tax Credit', *Control Design*, 6 March 2017.

24 'Loans Program Office', Department of Energy, Government of the United States, no date and

Mark Harris, 'The Loan Program That Buoyed Tesla, Stalled Out, and Landed on Trump's Cut List', *Ars Technica*, 14 March 2018.

25 Accelerate New York Seed Fund, http://www.anyseedfund.com/ and 'The Seed Fund', Massachusetts Life Sciences Center, Boston, 2019.

26 'Developing Products for Rare Diseases and Conditions', US Food & Drug Administration, Maryland, 20 December 2018.

27 'AbbVie Buys Special Review Voucher for $350 Million', *Reuters*, 20 August 2015.

28 Bruce Katz and Julie Wagner, 'The Rise of Innovation Districts'.

29 Andrew Levine, 'It's the Talent, Stupid: Cities Build Marketing Campaigns to Attract Skilled Workers', *Forbes*, 5 February 2015.

30 Bruce Katz and Julie Wagner, 'The Rise of Innovation Districts'.

31 Emily Badger, 'The Real Reason Cities Are Centers of Innovation', *CityLab*, 7 June 2013 and Wei Pan et al., 'Urban Characteristics Attributable to Density-Driven Tie Formation', *Nature Communications*, vol. 4, no. 1961, 2013.

32 ibid.

33 Richard Florida, 'Richard Florida's 10 Rules For a City's "Quality of Place"', *The Globe and Mail*, 5 June 2017.

34 Richard Florida, 'Why America's Richest Cities Keep Getting Richer', *The Atlantic*, 12 April 2017.

35 Frances Cairncross, 'The Death of Distance: How the Communications Revolution Will Change Our Lives', Harvard Business School, Harvard University, Cambridge, 1997.

36 Shirin Ghaffary, 'Even Tech Workers Can't Afford to Buy Homes in San Francisco', *Vox*, 19 March 2019 and Alistair Barr, 'An RV Camp Sprang Up Outside Google's Headquarters. Now Mountain View Wants to Ban It', *Bloomberg*, 21 May 2019.

37 The 2018 median house price in San Jose was US$1.1 million, while the median house price in Phoenix was US$252,000. 'Home Prices in the 100 Largest Metro Areas', *Kiplinger*, January 2019.

38 'About WPSI', West Philadelphia Skills Initiative, University City District, no date.

39 Klaus Schwab et al., 'The Global Competitiveness Report 2018', p. 8.

40 Kenan Fikri, 'Towards a More Socially and Spatially Inclusive Innovation Economy', Brookfield Institute, Toronto, 22 April 2019.

41 Richard Florida, *The New Urban Crisis: How Our Cities are Increasing Inequality, Deepening Segregation, and Failing the Middle Class – and What We Can Do About It*, Basic Books, New York, 2017.

42 Simona Iammarino, Andres Rodriguez-Pose and Michael Storper, 'Regional Inequality in Europe: Evidence, Theory and Policy Implications', *Journal of Economic Geography*, vol. 19, no. 2, 2019, pp. 273–98.

43 Klaus Schwab et al., 'The Global Competitiveness Report 2018', p. 9 and 'Main Science and Technology Indicators', vol. 2018, no. 1, OECD, Paris, 2018, p. 31.

44 Irena Szarowská, 'Does Public R&D Expenditure Matter for Economic Growth? GMM Approach', *Journal of International Studies*, vol. 10, no. 2, 2017, pp. 90–103, and Dominique Guellec and Bruno Van Pottelsberghe, 'The Impact of Public R&D Expenditure on Business R&D', OECD Science, Technology and Industry Working Papers, No. 2000/04, OECD, Paris, 2000.

45 Julie Wagner, Bruce Katz and Thomas Osha, 'The Evolution of Innovation Districts: The New Geography of Global Innovation', Global Institute on Innovation Districts, online, June 2019.

46 'Strategies for the New Economy: Skills as the Currency of the Labour Market', World Economic Forum, Geneva, 2019, pp. 1, 8–9.

10: From Warzone to World's Healthiest Nation

1 Werner Gruhl, *Imperial Japan's World War Two: 1939–1945*, Transaction Publishers, New Brunswick, 2007, p. 111 and Yoshiaki Yoshimi (trans. Suzanne O'Brien), *Comfort Women: Sexual Slavery in the Japanese Military During World War II*, Columbia University Press, New York, 2001.

2 Bethany Lacina and Nils Petter Gleditsch, 'Monitoring Trends in Global Combat: A New Dataset of Battle Deaths', *European Journal of Population,* vol. 21, 2005, pp. 145–166, 154.

3 Kongdan Oh, 'Korea's Path from Poverty to Philanthropy', Brookings Institution, 14 June 2010.

4   'Freedom in the World 2019', Freedom House, Washington, DC, 2019, p. 15 and 'Country Comparison: GDP – Per Capita (PPP)', *The World Factbook,* Central Intelligence Agency, 2019.

5   Twelfth-largest economy: 'GDP (Current US$)', World Bank, Washington, DC, 2019. Global Competitive Index statistics: Klaus Schwab, 'Global Competitiveness Report 2018', World Economic Forum, Switzerland, 2018, pp. viii, xi.

6   Italy and Japan: 'The Inclusive Development Index 2018: Summary and Data Highlights', World Economic Forum, 2018, p. 18. The 2016 gross national income per capita among European member countries of the OECD was US$39,585: 'Gross National Income, Total, US Dollars/Capita, 1960–2018', OECD, Paris, 2018.

7   'Life Expectancy at Birth, Total (Years)', World Bank, Washington, DC, 2019. See also Seungmi Yang et al., 'Understanding the Rapid Increase in Life Expectancy in Korea', *American Journal of Public Health,* vol. 100, no. 5, 2010, pp. 896–903.

8   Charlotte Edmond, 'South Korean Women Will Soon Outlive Us All. What's Their Secret?', World Economic Forum, 27 July 2017 and Meera Senthilingam, 'South Korea Will Lead in Life Expectancy by 2030, Study Predicts', *CNN,* 23 February 2017.

9   'Life Expectancy at Birth, Female (Years)' and 'Life Expectancy at Birth, Male (Years)', World Bank, Washington, DC, 2017.

10   Vasilis Kontis et al., 'Future Life Expectancy in 35 Industrialised Countries: Projections with a Bayesian Model Ensemble', *The Lancet,* 21 February 2017, vol. 389, p. 1323.

11   'Healthy Life Expectancy (HALE) Data by Country', Global Health Observatory Data Repository, World Health Organization, Geneva, 6 April 2018.

12   'Society at a Glance 2009: OECD Social Indicators', OECD, Paris, 2009, p. 110. Note that the study specifically states that immigration of comparatively short people in recent times cannot explain height stagnation in the United States.

13   'A Century of Trends in Adult Human Height', NCD Risk Factor Collaboration, *eLife,* no. 5, 2016, p. 2 and 'Average Height by Country 2019', *World Population Review,* 10 September 2019.

14   'Life Expectancy at Birth, Total (Years)'.

15   Young-Ho Khang, 'Two Koreas, War and Health', *International Journal of Epidemiology,* vol. 42, no. 4, 2013, pp. 925–29 and Young-Ho Khang, 'Author's Response to Two Koreas and Public Health: "First, Do No Harm"', *International Journal of Epidemiology,* vol. 43, no. 4, 2014, pp. 1341–2.

16   Seungmi Yang et al., 'Understanding the Rapid Increase in Life Expectancy in Korea', vol. 100, no. 5, 2010, pp. 896–903.

17   Ji-Young Chang et al., 'Decreasing Trends of Neonatal and Infant Mortality Rates in Korea: Compared with Japan, USA and OECD Nations', *Journal of Korean Medical Science,* vol. 26 (9), 2011, pp. 1115–23 and 'Mortality Rate, Infant (Per 1000 Live Births)', World Bank, Washington, DC, 2019.

18   'Fertility Rate, Total (Births Per Woman)', World Bank, Washington, DC, 2019.

19   Ji-Young Chang et al., 'Decreasing Trends of Neonatal and Infant Mortality Rates in Korea'.

20   Seungmi Yang et al., 'Understanding the Rapid Increase in Life Expectancy in Korea'.

21   'Road Accidents, Deaths Per 100,000,000 Inhabitants, 1996–2017' and 'Health Status: Causes of Mortality', both OECD, Paris, 2018.

22   'Potential Years of Life Lost, Total, Per 100,000 Inhabitants Aged 0–69, 2016 or Latest Available', OECD, Paris, 2017.

23   Seungmi Yang et al., 'Understanding the Rapid Increase in Life Expectancy in Korea' and 'Health Status: Causes of Mortality'.

24   Risk factors in Anthony Axon, '*Helicobacter Pylori* and Public Health', *Helicobacter,* vol. 19 (s1), 2014, pp. 68–73.

25   Ji Han Kim and Jae-Joon Yim, 'Achievements In and Challenges of Tuberculosis Control in South Korea', *Emerging Infectious Diseases,* vol. 21, no. 11, 2015, pp. 1913–20.

26   NCD Risk Factor Collaboration, 'Worldwide Trends in Blood Pressure from 1975 to 2015: A Pooled Analysis of 1479 Population-Based Measurement Studies with 19.1 Million Participants', *The Lancet,* no. 389, 2017, pp. 37–55.

27 'The Curious Case of High Blood Pressure Around the World', *The Economist,* 13 January 2017.

28 Alexander Danilenko and Aroha Bahuguna, 'Korea: A Model for Development of the Water and Sanitation Sector', *World Bank Blog,* 26 October 2016.

29 Lee Jong-Chan et al., 'The Institutionalisation of Public Hygiene in Korea, 1876–1910', *Korean Journal of Medicine,* no. 4, 1995, pp. 51–60.

30 Annual economic output: 'GDP Per Capita (Current US$)', World Bank, Washington, DC, 2019. Average income: '20 June 2018 Economic Survey of Korea', *Korea Economic Snapshot,* OECD, Paris, 2019. Income and life expectancy: 'Health at a Glance 2017: OECD Indicators', OECD, Paris, 2017, p. 31.

31 'Urban Population (% of Total)', World Bank, Washington, DC, 2019 and Seungmi Yang et al., 'Understanding the Rapid Increase in Life Expectancy in Korea', p. 901.

32 Jong-Hun Kim, Hae-Kwan Cheong and Byoung-Hak Jeon, 'Burden of Disease Attributable to Inadequate Drinking Water, Sanitation and Hygiene in Korea', *Journal of Korean Medical Science,* vol. 33, no. 46, p. 288.

33 Noriyo Isozaki, 'Education, Development and Politics in South Korea' in Keiichi Tsunekawa and Yasuyuki Todo (eds), *Emerging States at Crossroads: Emerging-Economy State and International Policy Studies,* Springer, Singapore, 2019 and 'School Enrolment, Secondary (% Gross)', World Bank, Washington, DC, 2019.

34 'Health at a Glance 2017', pp. 9, 40.

35 ibid., p. 25.

36 Chhabi Ranabhat et al., 'The Influence of Universal Health Coverage on Life Expectancy at Birth (LEAB) and Healthy Life Expectancy (HALE): A Multi-Country Cross-Sectional Study', *Frontiers in Pharmacology,* vol. 960, no. 9, 2018.

37 'Health Spending, Total, % of GDP, 2018 or Latest Available', OECD, Paris, 2019.

38 'Health at a Glance 2017', p. 48.

39 Marian Chu, 'Medical Screening Often Ends Up Representing Status Symbols Here', *Korea Biomedical Review,* 13 March 2017.

40 Hyuncheol Bryant Kim, Suejin Lee and Wilfredo Lim, 'Knowing Is Not Half the Battle: Impacts of the National Health Screening Program in Korea', *IZA Institute of Labor Economics,* Discussion Paper Series, March 2017.

41 'Health at a Glance 2017', p. 169.

42 'World's Best Hospitals 2019', *Newsweek,* 25 October 2019.

43 'Health at a Glance 2017', p. 125 (cancer survival rates) and p. 109 (stroke survival rates).

44 'Life Expectancy at Birth, Total (Years)' and Ajay Tandon et al., 'Measuring Overall Health System Performance for 191 Countries', GPE Discussion Paper Series, no. 30, World Health Organization, Geneva, 2000.

45 MRI and CT scanners: 'Health at a Glance 2017', p. 171. Mammograph machines: 'Mammography Machines, Total, Per 1,000,000 Inhabitants, 2017 or Latest Available', OECD, Paris, 2019.

46 Kwak Sun-Sung, 'Korea to Allow Fast-Track Review For Innovative Medical Technologies', *Korea Biomedical Review,* 13 December 2018.

47 Oliver Pickup, 'Reducing Heart Disease: Defying the Odds as a "Heart-Healthy" Country', *Raconteur,* 29 September 2017.

48 'Health at a Glance 2019', OECD, Paris, pp. 95, 97.

49 Taejung Woo, 'The School Meal System and School-Based Nutrition Education in Korea', *Journal of Nutritional Science and Vitaminology,* vol. 61, 2015, pp. S23–S24.

50 'Life Expectancy at Birth, Total (Years)'.

51 Hannah Ritchie and Max Roser, 'Causes of Death', *Our World in Data,* April 2019 and 'Health at a Glance 2017', p. 80.

52 Kate Pickett and Richard Wilkinson, 'Income Inequality and Health: A Causal Review', *Social Science & Medicine,* vol. 128, 2015, pp. 316–26.

53 'Suicide Rates, Total, Per 100,000 Persons, 2017 or Latest Available', OECD, Paris, 2018 and Yonhap, 'Suicide No. 1 Cause of Death for S. Korean Teens, Youths', *The Korea Herald,* 1 May 2019.

54 'Hours Worked, Total, Hours/Worker, 2018 or Latest Available', OECD, Paris, 2018.

55 Ana Singh, 'The "Scourge of South Korea": Stress and Suicide in Korean Society', *Berkeley Review,* 31 October 2017.

56 Steve Miller, 'South Korea Takes Aim at High Suicide Rate', *Voice of America,* 14 November 2018.

57 'Poverty Rate, 66-Year-Olds or More, Ratio, 2017 or Latest Available', OECD, Paris, 2018.

58 'Pension Spending, Public, % of GDP, 2017 or Latest Available', OECD, Paris, 2018 and Justin McCurry, 'South Korea's Inequality Paradox: Long Life, Good Health and Poverty', *The Guardian,* 2 August 2017.

59 Sungyeon Kim, 'Spotlight on Retirement: South Korea', Society of Actuaries, Chicago, 2018.

60 Justin McCurry, 'South Korea's Inequality Paradox: Long Life, Good Health and Poverty'.

61 'Daily Smokers, Men/Women, % of Population Aged 15+, 2017 or Latest Available', OECD, Paris, 2018 and Min Kyung Lim and Hong-Jun Cho, 'Current Status of Tobacco Control Policies in Korea Compared with International Treaty and Its Implementation', *Journal of the Korean Medical Association,* vol. 61, no. 3, 2018, pp. 148–56.

62 Kelly Kasulis, 'The South Korean Government Tried to Scare Smokers Into Quitting – but a Fashion Trend Erupted', *Mic,* 16 March 2018.

63 'Health at a Glance 2017', p. 84.

64 ibid., p. 85 and India State-Level Disease Burden Initiative Air Pollution Collaborators, 'The Impact of Air Pollution on Deaths, Disease Burden and Life Expectancy Across the States of India: The Global Burden of Disease Study 2017', *The Lancet Planetary Health,* vol. 3, no. 1, 2019, PE26-E39.

65 Justin McCurry, '"Social Disaster": South Korea Brings in Emergency Laws to Tackle Dust Pollution', *The Guardian,* 13 March 2019.

66 'Health at a Glance 2017', pp. 48–9.

67 ibid., pp. 40–1.

68 ibid., p. 91.

69 'Health Spending, Government/Compulsory, US Dollars/Capita, 2018 or Latest Available', OECD, Paris, 2018.

11: Achieving World-Best Outcomes

1 Johan Norberg, *Progress: Ten Reasons to Look Forward to the Future,* Oneworld, London, 2016, p. 3.

2 Max Roser, 'Life Expectancy', *Our World in Data,* Oxford, 2017.

3 Peter Diamandis and Steven Kotler, *Abundance: The Future is Better Than You Think,* Free Press, New York, 2012.

4 Robert Gordon, 'Is U.S. Economic Growth Over? Faltering Innovation Confronts the Six Headwinds', National Bureau of Economic Research Working Paper No. 18315, August 2012.

5 'Health at a Glance 2017: OECD Indicators', OECD, Paris, 2017, p. 48.

6 'New ILO Figures Show 164 Million People are Migrant Workers', International Labour Organization, United Nations, Geneva, 5 December 2018.

7 Klaus Schwab, 'Global Competitiveness Report 2018', World Economic Forum, Switzerland, 2018, p. vii.

8 Saul Eslake, 'Population, Participation and Productivity: How to Think About Long-Run Economic Growth', presentation to International Conference of Commercial Bank Economists, Paris, 4–6 July 2017.

9 'China's Ageing Population, Low Birth Rate to Cause "Unstoppable" Population Decline, Experts Say', *ABC News,* 6 January 2019 and 'Fertility Rates, Total, Children/Women, 2017 or Latest Available', OECD, Paris, 2018.

10 'Population Ages 65 and Above (% of Total Population)', World Bank, Washington, DC, 2018.

11 'Population and Poverty', United Nations Population Fund, New York, 2014.

12 'Labor Force Participation Rate, Female (% of Female Population Ages 15+) (Modelled ILO estimate)', World Bank, Washington, DC, 2019.

13 'Employment Schemes', Norwegian Welfare and Labour Administration, Oslo, 2019.

14   Maximiliano Dvorkin and Hannah Shell, 'The Growing Skill Divide in the US Labor Market', *On the Economy*, Federal Reserve Bank of St Louis, Missouri, 18 May 2017.

15   'Net Childcare Cost for Parents Using Childcare', OECD, Paris, 2019.

16   'Social Spending, Public, % of GDP, 2018 or Latest Available', OECD, Paris, 2019.

17   Orsetta Causa and Mikkel Hermansen, 'Income Redistribution Through Taxes and Transfers Across OECD Countries', OECD Economics Department Working Papers No. 1453, OECD, Paris, 22 July 2019, pp. 30–1.

18   'IMF Fiscal Monitor: Tackling Inequality, October 2017', International Monetary Fund, Washington, DC, October 2017, p. 13 and 'Higher Taxes Can Lower Inequality Without Denting Economic Growth', *The Economist*, 19 October 2017.

19   'Health at a Glance 2017', p. 31 and 'Tax Policies for Inclusive Growth in a Changing World', OECD Report to the G-20 Finance Ministers and Central Bank Governors, July 2018, pp. 7–9.

20   'Tax Policies for Inclusive Growth in a Changing World', pp. 16–20.

21   'Tax on Personal Income, Total, % of Taxation, 2017 or Latest Available'.

22   Eduardo Aleman and Yeaji Kim, 'The Democratizing Effect of Education', *Research and Politics*, October–December 2015.

23   'PISA 2018 Results: Where All Students Can Succeed', vol. II, OECD, Paris, 2019, p. 60.

24   Colleen Ricci, 'Looking to the Swedish Model of Childcare and Education', *The Sydney Morning Herald*, 18 May 2015.

25   Study of forty democracies: Jonathan Krieckhaus et al., 'Economic Inequality and Democratic Support', *The Journal of Politics*, vol. 76, no. 1, 2013, pp. 139–51. Implications of excessive financial inequality: Robert Anderson, 'Inequality, Democracy and Redistribution', Paper Presented to Expert Group Meeting on Inequality and Its Impacts, United Nations, New York, 2018.

26   'What Makes Urban Schools Different?', PISA in Focus, OECD, Paris, May 2013; 'Global Study on Homicide: Homicide, Development and the Sustainable Development Goals', United Nations Office on Drugs and Crime, Vienna, 2019, p. 10; see for example Gopal Singh and Mohammad Siahpush, 'Widening Rural–Urban Disparities in All-Cause Mortality from Major Causes of Death in the USA, 1969–2009', *Journal of Urban Health*, vol. 91, no. 2, 2014, pp. 272–92.

27   Data for all three tables is drawn from the following sources. Economic growth: 'GDP Per Capita (Current US$)' and 'GDP Per Capita, PPP (Current International $)'*, World Bank, Washington, DC, 2019. Income: 'Adjusted Net National Income Per Capita (Current US$)', World Bank, 2019 (East Asia data available only for South Korea and Singapore). Global competition: Klaus Schwab, 'Global Competitiveness Report 2019', World Economic Forum, Switzerland, 2019 and Soumitra Dutta, Bruno Lanvin and Sacha Wunsch-Vincent (eds), 'Global Innovation Index 2019: Creating Healthy Lives – The Future of Medical Innovation', INSEAD and WIPO, Fontaineblue and Geneva, 2019. Immigration: 'International Migrant Stock (Per Cent of Population)', World Bank, 2019.* Current account balance: 'Current Account Balance (Per Cent of GDP)', World Bank, 2019.* Government deficit: 'General Government Deficit, Total, Per Cent of GDP, 2018 or Latest Available', OECD, Paris, 2018.† Education outcomes: 'PISA 2018 Results, Volume I'. Inequality: 'The Inclusive Development Index 2018: Summary and Data Highlights', World Economic Forum, Geneva, 2018, p. 18.** Poverty: 'Poverty Rate, Total, Ratio, 2017 or Latest Available', OECD, 2018.† Gender gap: Schwab et al., 'The Global Gender Gap Report 2018', World Economic Forum, 2018, pp. 10–11. Longevity: 'Life Expectancy at Birth, Total (Years)'* and 'Mortality Rate, Infant (Per 1000 Live Births)'**, World Bank, 2019. Murder rates: 'Intentional Homicides (Per 100,000 people)', World Bank, 2019.* Carbon emissions: 'Air and GHG Emissions, Carbon Dioxide (CO_2), Tonnes/Capita, 2016 or Latest Available', OECD, 2017.* Democracy: 'Democracy Index 2018: Me Too? Political Participation, Protest and Democracy', The Economist Intelligence Unit, London, 2019 and 'Freedom in the World 2019', Freedom House, Washington, DC, 2019. Corruption: 'Corruption Perceptions Index 2018', Transparency International, Berlin, 2018. Productivity: 'GDP Per Hour Worked, Total, US Dollars, 2018 or Latest Available', OECD, 2019.† Working hours: 'Hours Worked, Total, Hours/Worker, 2018 or Latest Available', OECD, 2019.† Research and development:

'Research and Development Expenditure (Per Cent of GDP)', World Bank, 2019.* Happiness: John Helliwell, Richard Layard and Jeffrey Sachs, 'World Happiness Report 2019', Sustainable Development Solutions Network, New York, 2019.

* Data not available for Taiwan.

** Data not available for Hong Kong or Taiwan.

† Insufficient data available to calculate a figure for East Asia.

28 'GDP Per Capita, PPP (Current International $)'.

29 'General Government Debt, Total, % of GDP, 2018 or Latest Available'.

30 'Government at a Glance 2017', p. 63.

31 The gini coefficient for net income (after taxes and transfers) is 0.362 in the English-speaking countries and 0.284 in Northern Europe. It is 0.307 in South Korea and 0.398 in Singapore. 'The Inclusive Development Index 2018', p. 18. Data not available for Hong Kong and Taiwan.

32 'Health Status, Causes of Mortality, Assault, Deaths Per 100,000 Population (Standardised Rate)', OECD, Paris, 2019.

33 'Air and Greenhouse Gas Emissions, Carbon Dioxide (CO_2), Tonnes/Capita, 2016 or Latest Available'.

34 John Helliwell, Richard Layard and Jeffrey Sachs, 'World Happiness Report 2019'.

35 'GDP Per Capita (Current US$)'.

36 John Helliwell, Richard Layard and Jeffrey Sachs, 'World Happiness Report 2019'.

37 Overseas-born populations: in Singapore, the share of the population born overseas is 45.4 per cent, while the share in Hong Kong is 38.9 per cent. However, in South Korea only 2.6% of the population was born overseas. See 'International Migrant Stock (% of Population)'. Workforce participation: in East Asia, the ratio of female to male workforce participation is 0.76. The comparable figure in the English-speaking countries is 0.86, and in Northern Europe and Scandinavia it is 0.9. See Schwab et al., 'The Global Gender Gap Report 2018', pp. 53–298. Gender breakdown of domestic labour in South Korea: ibid., p. 9.

12: Tools for the Future

1 'Health at a Glance 2017: OECD Indicators', OECD, Paris, 2017, p. 88.

2 'Ageing Singapore to Raise Key Tax for First Time in Years', The Star, 20 February 2018.

3 See John Power, 'Why South Korea and Japan are Slowly Learning to Accept Foreign Workers', The Week in Asia, 11 May 2019.

4 Richard Rose, 'Ten Steps in Learning Lessons from Abroad', EIU Working Papers, RSC No 2002/5.

5 Rachel Flottman, 'Getting Early Childhood onto the Reform Agenda: An Australian Case Study', International Journal of Child Care and Education Policy, vol. 6, no. 1, 2012, pp. 17–33.

6 Ron Elving, 'The Florida Recount of 2000: A Nightmare That Goes on Haunting', NPR, 12 November 2018.

7 Hannah Gobbett, 'Composition of the 45th Parliament: A Quick Guide', Parliament of Australia, Canberra, 29 August 2016. The Queensland seat of Forde was won by Liberal–National Party representative Bert van Manen by 1062 votes. See Australian Electoral Commission, 'Forde, QLD: AEC Tally Room, 2016 Federal Election', Australian Electoral Commission, Canberra, 2016.

8 Joseph de Maistre quoted in Alexander Boot, 'Do We Really Deserve a Better Government?', Daily Mail, 28 January 2012.

Get in touch

If you enjoyed this book, or know of other success stories you think should be told, I would love to hear from you. Follow me on Twitter (@andrewwear) or Facebook (@andrewwearauthor) and visit my website at www.andrewwear.com.